KNOWLEDGE ENCYCLOPEDIA

OUR PLANET EARTH

Wonder House

(An imprint of Prakash Books)

contact@wonderhousebooks.com

Disclaimer: The information contained in this encyclopedia has been collated with inputs from subject experts. All information contained herein is true to the best of the Publisher's knowledge.

ISBN : 9789354404276

Table of Contents

Mountains & Forests

Amazing Earth	7
Majestic Mountains	8–9
Types of Mountains	10–11
The Magnificent Mountains	12
Famous Mountain Ranges	13
Other Landforms On Earth	14
Plateaus: Elevated Plains	15
Deep in the Valleys	16–17
Strolling the Plains	18–19
Our Ecosystem	20
Forests: Not Just a Collection of Trees	21
Temperate Forests	22–23
Evergreen Forests	24
Deciduous Forests	25
Taiga	26–27
Vegetation in Antarctica	28
Grassy Grasslands	29
Temperate Grasslands	30
Rolling in the Deserts	31
Desert Survivors	32
The Treeless Tundra	33
Deforestation and Conservation	34–35

Natural Wonders

What Are Natural Wonders?	37
The Grand Canyon	38–39
The Great Barrier Reef	40–41
The Amazon Rainforest	42–43
The Iguazu Falls	44–45
The Mount Everest	46–47
Auroras or Polar Lights	48–49

The Dead Sea 50–51

The Victoria Falls 52–53

Mount Kilimanjaro 54–55

The Sundarbans 56–57

The Giant Crystal Cave 58–59

The Galápagos Islands 60–61

The Great Blue Hole 62–63

The HaLong Bay 64–65

Oceans & Waterbodies

The Great Ocean 67

What is an Ocean? 68–69

Peeling Back Layers 70–71

The Five Major Oceans 72–73

Life in the Ocean 74–75

The Ocean in Motion 76–77

Importance of Oceans 78

Sources of Water 79

The Splendid Seas 80–81

Home to History 82–83

The Grand Rivers 84–85

Famous Rivers 86–87

Cascading Waters 88

Small Waterbodies 89

Natural Lakes 90–91

Artificial Lakes 92–93

Global Warming 94–95

Rocks & Minerals

A Rocky Planet 97

What Are Rocks? 98–99

Igneous Rocks 100–101

Examples of Igneous Rocks 102–103

Sedimentary Rocks 104–105

Examples of Sedimentary Rocks 106–107

Metamorphic Rocks	108–109
Quartzite	110
Marble	111
Crystals and Gemstones	112–113
Soil	114–115
Weathering, Erosion, and Conservation	116–117
Minerals	118
Grouping Minerals	119
Native Elements	120–121
Sulphides	122
Sulphates	123
Other Mineral Groups	124–125

Volcanoes and Earthquakes

Deadly Disasters	127
What Is a Volcano?	128
How Are Volcanoes Formed?	129
Parts of a Volcano	130–131
Categories & Types of Volcanoes	132–133
Cinder Cone Volcanoes	134
Composite Volcanoes	135
Shield Volcanoes	136
Calderas	137
Lava Domes	138
The Great Eruption	139
History's Deadliest Eruptions	140–141
The Ring of Fire	142–143
Tremors and Terrors	144–145
Studying Earthquakes	146–147
The Aftermath	148
Famous Earthquakes	149
Earthquakes: A Case Study	150–151
Devastating Waves	152–153
Safety Measures	154–155

Weather and Climate

Nice Weather, Isn't It?	157
What Is Weather?	158–159
Atmosphere: The Air Up There	160
The Current Affair	161
What Is Climate?	162–163
Types of Climates	164–165
Climatic Zones	166–167
Seasons	168–169
Oceans and Continents	170
The Water Cycle	171
Shaping Clouds	172–173
Precipitating Weather	174–175
Fog and Mist	176–177
Extreme Weather	178
Typhoons and Tornadoes	179
Hurricanes and Cyclones	180–181
Predicting Weather	182–183
Changing Climate	184–185
Word Check	186–190
Image Credits	191–192

MOUNTAINS, FORESTS, & OTHER ECOSYSTEMS

AMAZING EARTH

The Earth is a unique and splendid planet. It is the only planet we know that supports life with its diverse **landforms** and oceans. Deserts, glaciers, plains, mountains, valleys, and plateaus are examples of Earth's landforms. There are also other rare landforms like **buttes** and **canyons** that are spread across our planet.

The varieties of landforms are all a gift of nature, each of which have their very own characteristics and functions that impact the environment and affect life on Earth.

Any region where the **biotic** components—plants and animals—and the **abiotic** components—landforms and climate—depend on each other to support life is called an **ecosystem**. Rainforests, tundras, grasslands, and deserts are examples of major ecosystems, while coral reefs and ponds are minor ecosystems.

In this book, you will read about the different landforms and vegetation found on Earth. Landforms like mountains are not unique to Earth; they can be found on other planets as well. Forests are home to a variety of plants, animals, and bird species unique to Earth.

▼ *The elegant snow-capped mountains and the green forest covering are two examples of Earth's diverse ecosystems*

Majestic Mountains

Mountains proudly rise above the Earth's crust, both on land and water. They have steep sloping sides, rounded ridges, and a **summit**. Mountains should not be confused with hills. Mountains are steeper, larger, and taller than hills and rise at least 1,000 metres above the surrounding landforms. Mountains rarely occur individually. They rise next to each other forming a chain that is called a mountain range.

Making Mountains

The Earth's crust is made up of large slabs of rocks called tectonic plates. These plates fit into each other like the pieces of a jigsaw puzzle.

They move constantly, but slowly. Mountains are formed along the boundaries of these tectonic plates when they move towards each other.

While moving, they collide with each other, causing a kind of deformity in the crust. This leads to a crustal uplift and formation of a mountain. This process happens horizontally, causing the crust to fold into several layers and form wrinkles along the convergent plate boundaries. These wrinkles eventually become mountains. This process, however, is not simple, and it takes millions of years for a mountain to be formed.

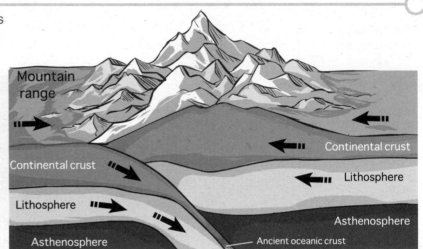

▲ The diagram shows the tectonic plates converging and forming a mountain

▼ A view of the Mount Everest, the highest summit in the world, with its peak rising 8,848 metres above sea level

Convergent Plate Boundaries

Tectonic plates form convergent plate boundaries when they move towards each other. They can form a continental-oceanic convergence, oceanic-oceanic convergence, or continental-continental convergence.

- **Continental-oceanic convergence:** The oceanic plate being heavier moves underneath the continental plate. This process is called **subduction**. Volcanoes and earthquakes are formed through this process.

- **Continental-continental convergence:** When two continental plates converge, neither of them moves beneath the other because of their thickness. So, this collision leads to the formation of big mountains with particles of oceanic sediments within them, even in the highest peaks. This type of convergence formed the Himalayan mountain range.

- **Oceanic-oceanic convergence:** When two oceanic plates converge, the older, denser plate sinks below the other. This creates a subduction zone, forming a chain of curved volcanic mountains called island arcs.

▲ *The Aleutian mountain range in Alaska was formed by oceanic-oceanic convergence*

Fault Lines

Mountains are also formed along natural fault lines. These mountains form when faults or cracks in Earth's crust force some materials or blocks of rock upwards. In this case, instead of the crust folding over, it fractures and pulls apart. Due to this immense force, blocks of rock along the sides of these faults are lifted up and tilted sideways.

On the opposite sides of the faults, the ground tilts downwards forming a depression. With the slow **erosion** of the mountains above, this depression gets filled in and levelled over time.

The Vosges Mountains in France and the Black Forest mountain range in Germany are fault mountains separated by the Rhine Valley.

Volcanic Eruptions

Mountains are also formed due to volcanic eruptions. During an eruption, molten rock, or magma, comes out as lava through a vent in the mountain, on the Earth's surface. After a while, the lava cools down and forms hard rock. The softer rocks erode away to reveal a dome-shaped mountain. The Hawaiian Islands were formed by the eruption of undersea volcanoes. The islands are actually the tops of the remaining volcanoes. At times, volcanic eruptions break down mountains instead of building them up, like the 1980 eruption that blew off the top of Mount St. Helens.

▶ *Volcanic eruption of Anak Krakatau, Indonesia in 2018*

Types of Mountains

Mountains differ in their appearance and formation. They can be classified based on the types of rocks, shape and placement on land. From the perspective of formation, they can be divided into these types: fold mountains, fault-block mountains, volcanic mountains, dome mountains, and plateau mountains.

 Fold Mountains

Fold mountains are formed when two tectonic plates collide with each other. This **compression** forces one tectonic plate to crumple and buckle under another. Slowly, the fold that forms from this movement takes the shape of a mountain. The process through which fold mountains are created is known as **orogeny**.

Fold mountains are most common on Earth. The vast mountain ranges that stretch for thousands of kilometres are fold mountains. Many of the world's great mountain ranges like the Himalayas in Asia, the Andes in South America, the Rocky Mountains in North America, the Alps in Europe, and the Ural Mountains in Russia fall under this category. Fold mountains are the youngest mountains formed on Earth.

▼ *Mount Kangchenjunga, the third highest peak in the Himalayan mountain range at 8,586 metres, is a fold mountain*

◄ *Another name for volcanic mountains is mountains of accumulation. Mauna Kea and Mount Fuji are volcanic mountains*

 Incredible Individuals

People once dreamed of reaching the summit of Mount Everest. After years of dreaming, Edmund Hillary of New Zealand and Tenzing Norgay of Nepal reached the peak of Mount Everest. It took them seven weeks of climbing to achieve this feat. Against all odds, they became the first to reach Mount Everest's peak on 29 May 1953 at 11:30 AM.

 Volcanic Mountains

Volcanic mountains are formed when magma comes out onto Earth's surface. At the surface, the magma erupts as lava, ash, rocks, and volcanic gases. They fall around the vent in successive layers, like a volcanic cone, that pile up and form a mountain. The best examples of volcanic mountains are Mauna Loa and Mount Kea on the Big Island of Hawaii. Volcanic mountains are also common in the Circum-Pacific belt. Volcanic peaks such as Mount Fuji in Japan, Mount Mayon in Philippines, and Mount Merapi in Sumatra are great examples of volcanic mountains.

Dome Mountains

Dome mountains are formed when a large amount of magma pushes its way upwards from beneath Earth's crust. The magma never reaches the top surface of the crust and never breaks out of the crust. Even before it can erupt, the source of magma goes away, leaving the pushed-up rocks as they were. These rocks then cool and form a mountain. With time, it takes the shape of a dome and gets warped due to erosion. Gradually, circular mountain ranges are created. The Black Hills and the Adirondack Mountains in the USA are examples of dome mountains.

Isn't It Amazing!

The Himalayan Mountains are actually just 50 million years old. This is young in mountain years. Other mountains on Earth are much, much older by millions of years. Older mountains are shrinking, but the young Mount Everest grows in size every year despite being the tallest mountain in the world. As the Indian tectonic plate pushes into Asia constantly, Mount Everest grows by 4 millimetres every year.

▼ Dome mountains are not found in mountain belts; instead they are isolated and individual structures

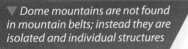

▼ Block mountains are surrounded by faults on either side of rift valleys or grabens

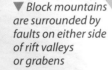

Fault-block Mountains

Fault-block mountains are formed along faults where some large blocks of rock are forced upwards, while others are pushed downwards. As a result, instead of folding, they break up into chunks. Large areas or blocks of Earth's crust are broken and displaced vertically by divergent plates. Fault-block mountains often have a steep slope on one side and a gentle slope on the other. The area of land lifted up near the divergent plate is called a **horst**, and the dropped area of land near the divergent plate is called a **graben**. The Sierra Nevada Mountains in the USA and the Harz Mountains in Germany are examples of fault-block mountains.

▼ Plateau mountains can rise more than 600 metres above the sea level

Plateau Mountains

Plateau mountains are generally formed by erosion and not because of the activities taking place beneath Earth's crust. Over billions of years, rivers and streams cut deep into a plateau creating mountains. These mountains are found near fold mountains. North Island Volcanic Plateau in New Zealand and the Catskill Mountains of the USA are examples of plateau mountains. These are also classified as plateaus as there isn't much difference to set them apart.

The Magnificent Mountains

Mountains have impressed man since time immemorial. Millions of people around the globe visit these natural features and are left in awe at their elegance and grandeur. Owing to their remote locations, there are some mountains still protected from being exploited by human activities. However, that is not the case everywhere. Deforestation has destroyed the natural habitats of plants and animals of many mountainous regions.

 ## Impact of Mountains

Mountains have always had a great impact on Earth's environment and life. They define natural borders between countries and at the same time protect countries from external disturbances. They are the major source of freshwater on Earth and influence the climate in a big way. Mountains also provide people with food, energy, biodiversity, and medicinal products.

 ## Sources of Freshwater

Most of the mighty rivers have their sources in mountains. They provide us with water that is required for the survival of all living beings, from human beings to animals and plants. Mountains preserve the snow in winter and release it during the dry seasons. In many parts of the world, irrigation depends on the water from melting snow. Mountains covered with forests help 'absorb' the rain water and allow it to flow gently to the rivers, avoiding potential floods.

 ## Effect on Climate

Mountains have a great impact on the climate across the globe. One such effect is the orographic effect. Mountains can block the wind and as a result receive more rainfall than the surrounding lower areas.

Winds carrying moist air are forced upwards when their flow is blocked by a mountain. This leads to condensation of water vapour at high altitudes and cloud formation, followed by precipitation (rain). More rain falls on the **windward** side (the side that faces the wind) of a mountain. The **leeward** side gets the warmer air and no rainfall, and it experiences the rain shadow effect. This is why mountains have two completely different landscapes on either side. One side may receive a lot of rain, while the other side could even be a desert.

Due to the high altitudes, the summit of a tall mountain is usually covered with snow. Snow has significant **reflectivity**; therefore, it can increase the amount of reflected sunlight. This, in turn, reduces the overall amount of energy absorbed at the Earth's surface.

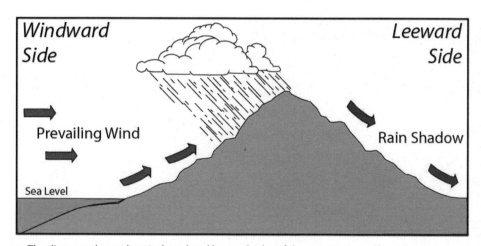

▲ The diagram shows the windward and leeward sides of the mountain and how they are impacted by rainfall

In Real Life

Mountains are rich in flora and fauna. Until recently, these were untouched and were home to a variety of species of plants and animals. Several food crops come from wild plants that grow in the mountains. However, these flora and fauna are now threatened by increased human activity in these regions, resulting in these species losing their habitats and becoming endangered.

Famous Mountain Ranges

People love and admire the mountains. They try to climb them, trek them, explore them, draw them and even write poems about them. Let us take a look at some of the most impressive and famous mountain ranges from around the world.

◀ *The Andean mountain cat is a threatened member of the cat family. Fewer than 2,500 of these animals exist today*

Andes, South America

The Andes Mountains run parallel to the Pacific Coast to the west of South America. The highest peak in the Andes, as well as the Western Hemisphere, is Aconcagua, with an elevation of 6,961 metres. It lies along the border of Argentina and Chile; both countries benefit from abundant forests. The Andes stretch for 8,900 kilometres. Most other mountains in the Andes have an elevation above 4,000 metres. There are many plants and animals that are spread across different altitudes of the mountains. Animals of the cat family live above 4,000 metres, while the llamas and alpacas live lower, near the 3,400 metres mark.

▲ *Outside Asia, the Andes are the highest mountain range in the world*

Alps, Europe

The Alps run across several European countries like Italy, France, Switzerland, Slovenia, Germany, Austria, and Liechtenstein. This mountain range is 1,200 kilometres long and 201 kilometres wide. Mount Blanc is the highest peak in the Alps, with a height of 4,809 metres.

◀ *As the human population in the Alpine Mountains have increased, the wildlife population has decreased*

Rocky Mountains, USA

The Rocky Mountains are made up of over 100 individual mountains that extend from Alberta in Canada to New Mexico in the USA. These mountains span over 4,828 kilometres. The highest peak in the Rocky Mountains is Mount Elbert, with a height of 4,399 metres. They are home to the ferocious black bear, grizzly bear, wolverines, and mountain lions. They also have various species of deer, sheep, and bison. Pine trees, spruce, and fir grow in the forests and are spread across the lower regions of the mountains. Human activities such as hunting, camping, hiking, and trekking are very popular here.

▼ *Mount Elbert is the tallest peak in the Rocky Mountains range with a height of 4,399 metres*

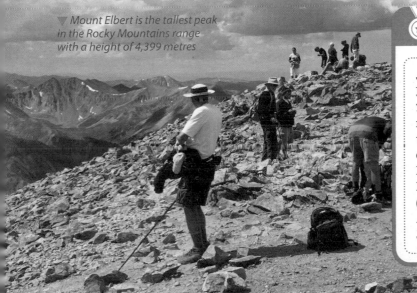

⍟ Incredible Individuals

Junko Tabei was the first woman to reach the summit of Mount Everest. She completed this achievement on 16 May 1975. She also became the first woman to reach the summit of the tallest mountain in each of the seven continents. Collectively, these peaks are called the Seven Summits. She climbed Tanzania's Mount Kilimanjaro (5,895 metres), Argentina's Mount Aconcagua (6,961 metres), Alaska's Mount Denali (6,190 metres), Russia's Mount Elbrus (5,462 metres), Antarctica's Vinson Massif (4,892 metres), and Puncak Jaya (4,884 metres) in Indonesia.

Other Landforms On Earth

Landforms occur naturally on Earth's crust. The regal mountains are one such landform. Other landforms like hills, plateaus, plains, glaciers, valleys, and deserts add to the natural beauty of our planet and make it a marvellous place to live in. All these landforms have their own special characteristics and have a great impact on the environment and life on Earth.

Landforms are created due to the movement of tectonic plates inside Earth's crust. Some are formed by erosion—the movement of water and wind. They wear down the land and create landforms like valleys and canyons. Both processes happen over a long period of time, sometimes taking millions of years.

 ## Hills

A hill is a part of land that is elevated above everything that surrounds it. It is shorter than a mountain and less steep. However, like a mountain, a hill has an obvious summit, which is its highest point.

▲ *Hills are also formed by erosion and deposition by wind and water*

 ## Formation of Hills

Natural hills are formed in the same way as mountains, through different **geological** activities. The rocks underneath the Earth's surface are constantly moving and forming different landscapes. Hills are formed by the movement of tectonic plates and faulting and can continue to grow due to activity below the Earth's surface. Some other examples of hills include the Britton Hill, Florida, USA (approximately 105 metres), the Pen Hill, Somerset, England (approximately 305 metres), and the Sparrow Hill, Moscow, Russia (79 metres).

Erosion is another way in which hills are formed. They are formed when pieces of rock, soil, and sediment wash away and accumulate somewhere else. Hills are sometimes destroyed by wind and water. On the other hand, a mountain can become a hill with constant erosion.

Types of Hills

Like mountains, there are different types of hills. A drumlin is a type of hill that is long and formed due to the movement of glaciers. These types of hills are mostly found in broad lowland areas. The glacier side is steep, whereas the leeward side is smoother. They are seen in Canada and in some other parts of North America.

Butte is another type of hill. These are hills that usually stand alone in a flat area. They have steep sides and a flat top. The rest of the hill has been eroded away. A tor is a rock formation on top of a hill.

▼ *A puy is the local name for cone-shaped volcanic hills in the Auvergne region of France*

👤 In Real Life

Earlier, hills that were 300 metres or higher were considered to be mountains. However, geologists who study landforms have now put forth a ruling that hills only above 1,000 metres will be considered as mountains.

Plateaus: Elevated Plains

A plateau is an elevated, flat-topped landform that rises sharply above the surrounding area. The word 'plateau' is derived from the French word '*platel*', which means flat or plate. It is usually bounded by steep slopes on all sides and is sometimes enclosed by mountains. They are different from mountains as they have a totally flat top. These landforms are found in all the continents.

 ## Types of Plateaus

Dissected plateaus are formed due to the upward movement of Earth's crust. This upward movement is caused by the collision of tectonic plates. The best examples of dissected plateaus are the Allegheny Plateau, the Cumberland Plateau, and the Ozark Plateau. Volcanic plateaus are formed by a number of small volcanic eruptions, and the accompanying lava flows. The North Island Volcanic Plateau in New Zealand is a great example of this type. The three active volcanoes here are Mount Tongariro, Mount Ngauruhoe, and Mount Ruapehu. Another plateau formed by volcanic eruption is the Deccan Plateau in India.

▲ The Deccan Plateau was formed due to volcanic activity over thousands of years. The volcanoes became extinct but left a region of highlands with vast stretches of flat areas on top like a table

 ## Shape of a Plateau

The shape of a plateau can be influenced by erosion. Soft rocks get eroded away, making the top of the plateau hard. This hard and durable surface is called the **caprock**. The caprock prevents the erosion of the soil underneath. Sometimes, the action of erosion is so intense that the plateau breaks up into smaller raised sections called outliers. These outlier plateaus are made up of very old and dense rock formations. Iron ore and coal are found in plateau outliers. Valleys are also formed when a river cuts through a plateau.

▼ Plateaus are formed in the same way as mountains and hills, that is, by the movement of tectonic plates or by volcanic activity

 ## World's Largest Plateau

The Tibetan Plateau is the largest plateau in the world. It is located in Central Asia and stretches through the countries of Tibet, China, and India. The plateau occupies an area of 2.5 million square kilometres. This is a region of mountains and uplands that are 13,000–15,000 feet above sea level. The plateau lies between the Kunlun Mountains to the north, and the Himalayas and Karakoram ranges to the south. The plateau is called 'the roof of the world'.

▲ The Qinghai–Tibet railway line is the world's highest railway line as it passes across the Tibetan Plateau

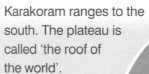 ## Isn't It Amazing!

The Colorado Plateau is a dissected plateau that lies in the western part of the USA. It has been rising by .03 centimetres every year, for more than 10 million years.

Deep in the Valleys

A valley is a depression in the Earth's surface, between hills or mountains. Valleys are formed due to erosion caused by rivers. This process takes millions of years. Valleys are also formed by shifts in tectonic plates, or by the movement of glaciers. They all take the form of a 'U' or a 'V'. The kind of valley formed is defined by the type of geological process it has gone through. There are three main types of valleys—river valleys, glacier valleys, and rift valleys.

Glacier Valley

A glacier valley, as the name suggests, is created by glaciers. A glacier is a huge mass of ice that is slowly moving. At one time, Earth's surface was covered with ice and snow. While moving, the glaciers flow downwards, due to gravity, carving a valley. This forms a U-shaped valley where the valley walls curve more at the bottom. The floor of the valley is broader and flat. As the glaciers move along, they scrape the land and carry away giant boulders and huge amounts of soil. Consequently, they leave behind valleys. The Yosemite Falls in California is an example of glacier valleys.

▲ Glaciers sometimes follow a river valley and change its shape from 'V' to 'U'

▼ The walls of the 'Iao Valley are covered with forests. The gorge is 8 kilometres long

River Valley

A valley created by the erosive movement of a river or stream is called a river valley. The river erodes the land through which it flows, and in the process, carves the valley. This happens over a period of thousands of years. A river valley takes the shape of the letter 'V'. All landforms on the Earth change with time, and river valleys are no exception. Rivers continuously erode the land they flow through and make the valleys deeper. Simultaneously, other factors such as rain, frost, and wind loosen materials on the walls of the valleys. These materials fall into the river, and get carried away. The 'Iao Valley in Hawaii is a V-shaped river valley.

In Real Life

There are valleys that have sunk below the sea level and are called sunken valleys. Their shape makes a good harbour, like the sunken valley in Sydney Harbour, Australia.

Rift Valley

Rift valleys differ from river valleys and glacier valleys as they are not formed due to erosion. Rift valleys are formed when the tectonic plates move apart or away from each other creating depressions. These types of valleys are found on land as well as at the bottom of the ocean. Many rift valleys are found in the ocean dividing long mountain ranges called mid-ocean ridges. The Albertine Rift Valley, located in Africa, is an example of a rift valley.

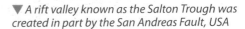
▼ A rift valley known as the Salton Trough was created in part by the San Andreas Fault, USA

💡 Isn't It Amazing!

There is another kind of 'valley' called a dell, which is a small, wooded or partially-wooded hollow. Dells that are covered with ravines or trees are called dingles. In Scotland, a dell is called a glen.

Some Spectacular Valleys

Barun Valley: This is a valley at the foothills of Makalu (the fifth-highest mountain in the world), in Nepal. Its stunning natural beauty can be experienced in green forests, snow-capped peaks, and splendid waterfalls. It is known for its diversity of wildlife, flowers such as orchids and rhododendrons, and snow leopards prowling along the clifftops.

Valley of Ten Peaks: This valley is enclosed in an arch of ten peaks in Canada. It is a beautiful valley covered with dense forests of pine trees and hanging glaciers. There are many species of animals that hide in the shadows of thick branches. The Moraine Lake is the main attraction here.

Nubra Valley: Originally known as 'Ldumra', which means, 'valley of flowers', this valley is located to the northeast of the Ladakh Valley, in India. It was formed by the Shyok River and the Nubra or Siachen River. It separates Ladakh and the Karakoram range. The famous Siachen glacier lies north of the valley. Known for its scenic beauty, the valley is home to many species of birds.

▲ Trekking in the Barun Valley is tough along the valley, but the scenic beauty of the Himalayas makes it worth it. Tourists like to explore caves like the Shiva Dhara

▲ The Moraine Lake is unique due to its blue colour and stunning reflections of snow-capped mountain

▲ People riding the double-humped camel found in this part of India. They are natives of Mongolia in central Asia and were brought to Nubra Valley during the golden era of trade on the Silk Route

Strolling the Plains

Plains are broad areas of flat land. They cover one-third of the world's area and are present on all continents on Earth. Entire civilisations were built on plains because early hunters and gatherers found fertile land for agricultural purposes, giving them a chance to settle down.

Formation of Plains

Plains are formed in various ways. Some were formed when ice and water eroded the rocks on higher lands. **Sediments** that were carried by the water and ice got deposited in layers to form a plain.

Volcanic activity is also responsible for the formation of plains. Lava that bursts out during an eruption flows across the land, forming lava plains. Plains are also formed by the movement of fast-flowing rivers. When a river flows through a valley, it takes a winding course or **meanders**. In the process, the land gets eroded by the action of the water. This leads to the formation of plains.

Major Plains of the World

Great Plains: Amongst the major plains of the world are the Great Plains of USA. These plains have large agricultural lands and are popularly called the 'Food Basket' of the region. Wheat is the main crop grown here. These plains also have natural reserves of oil and gas.

Indus Valley Plain: The Indus River Plain runs along the River Indus and its tributaries. This is also a fertile plain and is a great source of food in India.

Indo-Gangetic Plain: One-seventh of the world's population lives in this region. These plains are rich, fertile, and intensely cultivated. The main crops of the Indo-Gangetic Plains are rice, wheat, sugarcane, and cotton.

▲ *Much of the Great Plains are covered in prairies, steppes, and grasslands*

North China Plain: This plain is the most densely populated region in the world. It covers a land of 409,500 square kilometres. Crops like maize, millets, cotton, peanuts, and wheat are grown here.

◀ *The North China Plain is surrounded by the lower Yellow River and its tributaries. It has an empty steppe to its north*

▼ *Plains are suitable for agriculture*

Types of Plains

There are many types of plains. These are the flood plains, alluvial plains, coastal plains, and abyssal plains. Plains do not show much elevation. They occur alongside of rivers, coastlines, bottoms of valleys, and next to plateaus.

Flood Plains

Rivers flood and consequently overflow their banks. The flood leaves behind lots of mud and sand, which remain on the land for a long time after the water recedes. This sediment builds up plains which are called flood plains. They are rich in nutrients and create fertile land for cultivation. The fertile flood plain surrounding the Nile River is what helped the Egyptian Civilisation to flourish.

▶ Flood plains remain dry when there is less water in the river, but if there is a lot of water, the excess water floods the area

Alluvial Plains

Alluvial plains are formed at the foot of a mountain. A river flows downhill carrying with it sediments and hits the immediate flat land. It then deposits the sediments which create alluvial plains. The Hwang Ho River in China has created an alluvial plain that covers an area of about 409,500 square kilometres.

Coastal Plains

There are rivers that deposit their sediments in the ocean. This sediment builds up to form what are commonly known as the coastal plains along oceans and seas. The best example of a coastal plain is the Atlantic Coastal Plain. It stretches along much of the eastern coast of North America.

▼ Coastal plains are near an ocean, river, or lake and are separated from the inland by a mountain or hilly range

Abyssal Plains

Abyssal plains are found at the bottom of the ocean. They lie 5,000–7,000 metres below sea level. Abyssal plains have not been explored fully as scientists have had a hard time studying them. However, according to scientists, abyssal plains are among the flattest and smoothest places on the Earth.

Our Ecosystem

What is an ecosystem? It includes all the living things (biotic)—such as plants, animals, and other organisms—interacting with each other, and with the non-living things (abiotic)—such as the weather, the Sun, soil, water, and air—in a particular region.

Influencing Factors

Every single factor in an ecosystem is dependent on every other factor, either directly or indirectly. If there is a change in the temperature of an ecosystem, all the plants and animals in it will be affected. An increase or decrease in temperature might harm the plants and, in turn, have an effect on the animals that feed on those plants. They either have to adapt to these changes, move to another ecosystem, or perish.

For example, a pond has different types of living things like insects, plants, fish, and other aquatic animals. They require favourable abiotic factors like the Sun, water, air, soil, and temperature to survive. Therefore, if any abnormal changes occur, for example in the level of water, there might be an imbalance in the pond ecosystem that could harm the organisms living there.

SOLAR ENERGY

PHOTOSYNTHESIS PHOTOSYNTHESIS PHOTOSYNTHESIS

NUTRIENTS PHYTO - PLANKTON ZOO - PLANKTON MACROPHYTE NUTRIENTS

PHYTO-PLANKTON EATER

ZOO-PLANKTON EATER HERBI-VOROUS

OMNIVOROUS ANIMAL

PREDATOR

ORGANIC MATTER MINERALIZATION OR SEDIMENTATION

BENTHOS

▲ *In an ecosystem each organism has its own role to play*

Biomes

The whole surface of Earth is a series of connected ecosystems which are again connected in a larger biome. A biome is a large region of Earth that has a particular type of climate and living organisms. The major biomes of Earth include forests, grasslands, and deserts, and each one has many ecosystems. The animals and plants within have particular characteristics that help them survive in that biome.

For example, it can be said that the biome of the Sahara Desert has different kinds of ecosystems. The climate is hot and dry, but there are also **oases** with date palm trees, freshwater, and animals such as crocodiles. The Sahara also

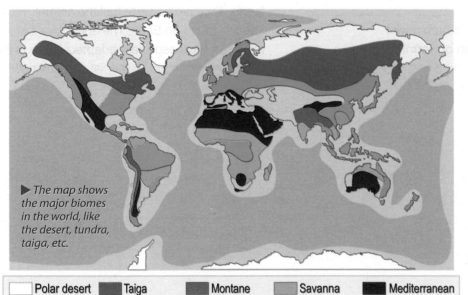

▶ *The map shows the major biomes in the world, like the desert, tundra, taiga, etc.*

has **dune** ecosystems with animals such as snakes or scorpions, which have the ability to survive in sand dunes for long periods of time. However, similar sounding biomes can have very different ecosystems. For instance, the biome of the Gobi Desert, which is a cold desert, experiences snowfall and freezing temperatures. Here there are grasses that are able to grow in the cold, dry climate and consequently have grazing animals such as gazelles and even takhi, an endangered species of wild horse.

◀ *The map shows the major biomes in the world, such as the desert, tundra, taiga, etc.*

☐ Polar desert	■ Taiga	■ Montane	■ Savanna	■ Mediterranean
☐ Tundra	■ Mixed forest	■ Steppe	■ Tropics	■ Desert

Forests: Not Just a Collection of Trees

A forest is a complex ecosystem that consists of many different types of trees, plants, and animals. The trees help sustain life on Earth as they give out oxygen that human beings and animals need to survive. They are an important component of the environment as they have the ability to clean the air, cool it on hot days, conserve heat at night, and act as excellent sound absorbers. Forests can be divided into three types—tropical forests, temperate forests, and **boreal** forests, which are also known as 'taiga.'

Tropical Rainforests

Tropical rainforests are found in areas that receive a considerable amount of rainfall, mostly in wet tropical uplands and lowlands around the Equator. These areas have tall, evergreen trees and are incredibly dense with flora and fauna. Tropical rainforests are very important for this planet as they supply a significant amount of oxygen to the atmosphere. Rainforests are believed to be the oldest ecosystem on Earth, perhaps as old as 100 million years, having the greatest variety of plants and animals.

Location

Tropical rainforests are mostly found in South and Central America, West and Central Africa, Eastern Madagascar and the Zaire basin, Indonesia, parts of Southeast Asia, and tropical Australia. Some of the largest rainforests in the world are the Amazon Rainforest spread over South America, the Congo Rainforest in Central Africa, and the Sundaland in South East Asia.

Climate

The climate in the tropical rainforest regions is humid with very little seasonal variation. The combination of warmth and rainfall creates this humid environment. Temperatures remain high, usually about 30° C during the day and 20° C during the night. The environment in the rainforest is humid and humidity can be around 77–88 per cent, the whole year. Rainfall measures between 200–1,000 centimetres and can be as high as 5 centimetres in an hour.

Isn't It Amazing!

80 per cent of the flowers that are found in the Australian rainforests are unique and cannot be found anywhere else in the world.

Flora and Fauna

The tropical rainforests contain more than two thirds of the world's flora species. The plants provide food and shelter to the animals of these regions. Due to the dense vegetation, very little sunlight can penetrate the cover of trees (canopy). Therefore, plants at the ground level receive less sunlight. Some even grow on the branches of other trees. The roots of these rainforest trees do not grow deep into the ground but spread out, as the soil decreases in fertility as you go deeper. Their biodiversity is also shown by their fauna. They are home to half the animal species found on Earth. The animals of the rainforest have especially adapted to live in this unique environment. A special characteristic of animals like mammals, reptiles, and amphibians is their ability to live in trees. Many large invertebrates like giant snails and butterflies are common here. Birds like toucans and parrots are also common in rainforests. Different animals live in different parts of the rainforest. For example, large animals live on the forest floor, birds live in tree canopies or at the tops of taller trees, arboreal animals live on trees, and insects are found everywhere.

Temperate Forests

Temperate forests are found between the tropics and the polar regions, within the temperate zone. Temperate means neither too cold nor too hot, and so these forests are found in those regions of the world where the climate is moderate, approximately between 25° and 50° latitude in both the hemispheres. They are also called the four-season forests, as the mid-latitude climate harbouring them tends to experience four distinct seasons. Temperate forests are primarily deciduous, with tall, broad-leafed hardwood trees that shed their leaves and change colour during autumn. There are also **coniferous** trees in these regions such as cypress, cedar, redwood, fir, juniper, and pine trees. These trees have needle-like leaves and cones.

Location

Temperate forests are dominant in large areas of North America and Eurasia and in smaller portions of the Southern Hemisphere. Temperate deciduous forests are found in eastern USA, Canada, Europe, China, Japan, and western Russia.

Climate

As read earlier, temperate forests exist in regions having moderate climate. They are not too hot like the tropical rainforests, or too cold like the boreal forests. They experiences the four seasons—summer, autumn, winter, and spring. Seasons occur due to the Earth's tilted axis. As the axis is tilted, the Sun's rays hit some parts of the world more directly than others, causing variations in temperature, which lead to different seasons. After the rainforests, temperate forests receive the highest rainfall. It measures between 30 and 60 inches throughout the year. However, in winter, precipitation is in the form of snow. Summers here are mild, and the average temperature is about 21° C, and in winter it is mostly below freezing point. Soil here is also very fertile due to adequate rainfall and decaying matter that helps trees establish strong roots.

▲ *Leaves change colour because the chlorophyll is consumed by the trees as the climate changes*

▲ *Coniferous trees have long trunks that make them look like tall buildings*

Flora

Temperate forests have a great variety of plant species. Small plants like lichen, moss, ferns, and wildflowers are found on the forest floor. Shrubs fill in the middle level. Temperate forests are dominated by deciduous trees such as oak, maple, and beech. Beech and basswood are rare, but oaks and maples are more widespread. Conifer and evergreen trees have needle-like leaves. Other hardwood trees are birch, magnolia, and sweet gum. Conifers like cedar, spruce, fir, and pine trees can also be found mixed in with the hardwood trees in this biome. Sometimes the taiga and the temperate deciduous forests overlap. Parts of the Japanese islands have temperate forests with trees like oak, ash, and conifers.

▲ *Deodar, a kind of cedar, is mostly found in the western Himalayas of India*

▼ *The mona monkey is found in lowland forests of eastern Ghana, Togo, Benin, Nigeria, and western Cameroon*

Fauna

The temperate forests have great diversity of life. Animals need to adapt to these changes. Wildlife in these forests either endures the winter or migrates to warmer climates. However, the advent of spring brings some relief. As the days become shorter and temperatures drop during fall, the leaves of deciduous trees change their colours and begin shedding.

At this point, animals also begin to store food for the winter as some hibernate during winter. Some even get ready to migrate. Animals such as slugs, frogs, turtles, and salamanders are common in temperate forests. Birds such as broad-winged hawks, snowy owls, and pileated woodpeckers are also found here. Apart from these animals, mammals such as the white-tailed deer, raccoons, opossums, porcupines, and red foxes are quite common in temperate forests.

Evergreen Forests

Temperate forests can be broadly divided into evergreen and deciduous forests. Evergreen forests are made up of evergreen trees. The word 'evergreen' means trees that do not shed their leaves completely. Different trees shed their leaves at different times of the year, thus such forests always appear to be green. They are found in all the continents, except Antarctica. Tropical evergreen forests are found in the regions where there is ample rainfall and the temperature is 15–30°C.

Some trees are deciduous, and lose their leaves seasonally. They have broad, flat leaves that enable them to receive plenty of sunlight. They also require an ample amount of water. Before shedding their leaves, these trees reabsorb essential nutrients and store them in other parts like the roots. Deciduous trees are found in almost all parts of the world. Some examples of deciduous trees are oak, maple, etc.

 ## Location

Evergreen trees are found all over the world, especially in the cold regions of the Northern Hemisphere. Coniferous forests cover approximately 15 per cent of the land on Earth and have evergreen trees like cedars, junipers, pines, Douglas firs, and hemlocks. Tropical rainforests, the largest of which are found in South America, sub-Saharan Africa, and East Asia, also have evergreen trees. This is due to the warm, humid climate and few seasonal changes.

 ## Soil and Sunlight

Evergreen trees usually require a lot of sunlight, but there are exceptions. Though they need an excess of rainfall to grow, some evergreen trees can thrive in conditions of draught. Coniferous evergreen trees require dry and well-drained soil, whereas rainforests can adapt to moist and soggy soil. Coniferous evergreens have the potential to thrive in cold climates, but rainforest evergreens need consistent and warm temperatures to survive.

▲ Evergreen trees can grow almost anywhere, but some types cannot thrive in cooler climates

Types of Evergreen Forests

The northern Eurasian coniferous forests and the equatorial rainforests are the most sizeable evergreen forests on Earth. The equatorial rainforests are dense, with rainfall measuring approximately upto 200 centimetres. There is a wide variety of flora and fauna in these forests. The plants found in these regions are tall hardwood trees with broad leaves for transpiration of excess water. The diversity of this region is such that it can accommodate various species of terrestrial animals and birds. Some of the common rainforest trees are eucalyptus, fern ally, cycad, and even palm. The evergreen forests also include trees like conifers, live oak, and holly in cold climates.

The height of the evergreen trees and the **foliage** colour differ from each other. Trees in the coniferous forest have leaves that are needle-like, while in the Mediterranean type they have waxy and leathery leaves. There are some species with foliage in red, yellow, brown, or other colours. Evergreen trees provide human beings with everything, from lumber to firewood and medicine.

👤 In Real Life

Leaves that fall during the autumn season in temperate forests litter the forest floor. These leaves decay and decompose to form a rich and moist soil. Mushrooms and other fungi can grow in this soil.

Deciduous Forests

Deciduous is a word derived from the Latin word 'decidere', which means 'tending to fall off.' Therefore, deciduous forests have trees and plants that shed their leaves most often in autumn and regain them in spring.

▲ *Autumn in a deciduous forest*

Location

Deciduous forests are found almost all over the planet in both the hemispheres. However, the world's largest deciduous forests are seen in the Northern Hemisphere, in North America, Europe, parts of Russia, China, and Japan. In the Southern Hemisphere, deciduous forests are found in some parts of Australia, southern Asia, and South America. However, these are smaller than those in the Northern Hemisphere. Deciduous forests tend to thrive in areas that have mountains, and particularly in places that have a range of different types of soil.

Temperature and Precipitation

Deciduous forests are found practically all over the world, but the temperature of each region varies, depending on its location. The average temperature of a deciduous forest is usually around 10° C, with winters being much colder. Trees in these forests lose their leaves once a year. Deciduous forests require ample rain to promote new leaf growth on trees. However, the amount also varies. Rainfall gives enough moisture to the lower plants despite the canopy cover. In some areas, snowfall is common in the winter.

Types of Deciduous Forests

Deciduous forests can be divided into two types:

Temperate Deciduous Forests

Temperate deciduous forest biomes are found in North and South America, Asia, the southern slopes of the Himalayas, and Europe. Here, the temperature is variable, trees grow during the summers, and they shed their leaves during autumn. These regions have diverse life forms that are influenced by the different seasons and climate.

Tropical and Subtropical Deciduous Forests

Tropical and subtropical deciduous forests have developed not due to the different temperatures in different seasons, but due to the seasonal rainfall patterns. In these regions, during the dry periods, the foliage drops to conserve water. It also prevents death from drought. Shedding of leaves can occur at any time of the year unlike temperate forests. The timing of leaf drop varies from region to region.

▼ *Siberian tigers are also found in the deciduous forests*

Flora and Fauna of Deciduous Forests

Deciduous forests are home to many different species of plants. There are times when the overhead canopy changes due to the fall, affecting the kind of plant life that can survive these tough times. Some common plants of deciduous forests are oak, maple, spruce, pine, birch, and beech etc. Some unique inhabitants are the orchids and rhododendrons. Shrubs such as lichen and moss are quite common in these forests.

The change in canopy cover also affects the animal life here. There are a variety of animals in this biome. However, human activities have, as usual, disturbed the animal life. Common animals in the deciduous forests are red pandas, black bears, otters, leopards, Siberian tigers, and smaller animals such as squirrels. Deciduous forests are also home to various birds such as owls, hawks, and woodpeckers. Insects like bees, butterflies, and moths help in **pollination**.

Taiga

Taiga forests are located to the south of the tundra and north of the temperate forests. It is in the subarctic region, lying to the south of the Arctic Circle. It is also known as the boreal forest with cone-bearing, needle-shaped leaves on the evergreen trees. The word taiga is Russian for 'land of little sticks'.

 ## Location

The regions in the world that have taiga forests are Alaska, Canada, Scandinavia, and Siberia. Russia has the largest stretch of taiga forests from the Pacific Ocean to the Ural Mountains. It covers around 5,800 kilometres. Taiga forests occupy 27 per cent of Earth's surface. They are located above the Tropic of Cancer.

▲ The map marks the taiga regions

 ## Climate

The taiga biome is very close to the Arctic Circle and is extremely cold with temperatures mostly below 0° C. Throughout the year, the area experiences freezing cold weather. Due to the tilt of Earth's axis, the Sun's rays fall slanting on the surface, making it cooler than the areas where they fall vertically. Therefore, the place is naturally colder than the temperate zone. The region does not receive enough heat from the Sun. Precipitation is mostly in the form of snow. In the winter, temperatures drop below -54° C and go as high as -1° C. As a result, during winter, there is a lot of snow fall, and the land is frozen with ice. Summers are only present for three months. Autumn and spring are just as insignificant. However, during the short stay of spring, animals come out from their hibernation.

 ## Flora

Due to the cold climate, there is less diversity in the type of vegetation here. The trees here are conifers like spruce, pine, fir, cedar, hemlock, and larches and the boreal forest is a wooded biome. These trees have needle-like leaves, and their seeds grow inside protective woody cones. The needles contain very little **sap** that prevents the leaves from freezing. The dark colour and triangle-shaped sides help them absorb as much sunlight as possible. The taiga is a thick forest with **muskegs** and lakes formed by glaciers.

Unlike the shrubs and flowers seen in the temperate forests, the taiga is covered with mosses, lichens, and mushrooms. The plants in this region have developed special key features to adapt to the varying climate of the taiga biome. They can grow directly on the ground and have very shallow roots. They can survive in the cold with little water and sunlight.

▲ The Bald Eagle is an iconic bird of North America, but did you know that its calls are dubbed in most programs? Editors feel that its actual calls are like a "high-pitched giggle or weak scream"

💡 Isn't It Amazing!

Canada's boreal forest is home to 300 bird species during the summer. Of them, only 30 species stay back during the winter. The other species migrate to places with warmer climates.

Fauna

Due to the freezing cold of the taiga region, the number of animals found here is also low. The animals, like the plants, need to adapt to these tough conditions to survive. Animals found here are mammals such as bears, deer, moose, elk, caribou, ermines, moles, squirrels, chipmunks, and bobcats. Herbivorous animals are seen in areas that have a greater number of trees. Many species of birds such as sparrows, finches, woodpeckers, crows, and eagles are also seen here, along with a variety of species of insects.

Ponds and lakes are formed as some snow melts during spring and summer. This becomes the breeding ground for insects. Animals and birds migrate to warmer places during winter. Some animals hibernate. Bears can store food in their dens, and have the ability to survive off body fat for six months till they next see daylight.

In Real Life

The soils of the boreal forest are often acidic, due to falling pine needles. They are also low on nutrients since the cold temperatures do not allow much foliage to rot and turn into dirt.

▼ *Crows and ravens are among the smartest creatures on Earth, with some of them having a bigger brain-to-body ratios than even humans. But being smart, that also means they will remember faces, and can hold a grudge*

◄ *The Siberian tiger weighing around 300 kilograms is the largest cat in the world. They live in a small part of eastern Siberia. They hunt moose and wild boars*

◄ *Animals like bears are fairly common in this biome*

Vegetation in Antarctica

The continent of Antarctica is permanently covered with snow. A mere 1 per cent is left for plants to grow. Only along the Antarctic Peninsula (and its associated islands in the coastal regions), will you see some land without the snow cover.

 ## Climate

The climate of Antarctica is extremely cold and dry. The temperature in winter, along the coast, ranges from -10 to -30° C. However, in the mountainous regions, the temperature drops below -60° C. Precipitation is only in the form of snow, and the desert in the Antarctica is the driest on Earth.

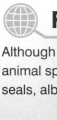 ## Fauna

Although Antarctica is covered in snow, it is home to numerous animal species. The most familiar animals are penguins, whales, seals, albatrosses, and a variety of marine life in the ocean.

▶ *Only 5 out of 18 species of penguins live in Antarctica*

 ### ⊕ Incredible Individuals

Erik Gulbranson and John Isbell, who are paleoecologists, discovered fossil fragments of trees. Both these geologists climbed the McIntyre Promontory's frozen slopes in the Transantarctic Mountains from November 2016 through January 2017. By the end of the expedition, they uncovered 13 fossil fragments from trees dating back to more than 260 million years. This proves that forests existed on Earth even more than 47 million years ago.

 ## Flora

There are very few species of plants in the Antarctica. It is hard to find trees or shrubs. Only two species of flowering plants are found, the Antarctic hair grass and Antarctica pearlwort in the South Orkney Islands, the South Shetland Islands, and along the western Antarctic Peninsula, where the climate is warmer and wetter than in other places in the continent. Vegetation here consists of mosses, liverworts, lichens, and fungi which has adapted to the conditions, especially the dryness. Algae, fungi, and lichens are found in the dry valley of Victoria Land. The climate in the subantarctic is wetter, so there are some flowering plant species and ferns here.

◀ *The tussock grass grows really tall, upto 2 metres in the subantarctic region*

Grassy Grasslands

Grasslands are areas where different species of grasses dominate the vegetation. They are the most agriculturally useful habitats on Earth. Grasslands are found in regions where the rainfall received is not enough to support the growth of forests. However, the rainfall is not so scarce that the region turns into a desert. Grasslands are usually located in an open and fairly flat terrain, mostly in the drier portions of the interiors of different continents.

Tropical Grasslands

Tropical grasslands are found mainly near the Equator, between the Tropic of Cancer and the Tropic of Capricorn. They are present in Africa, as well as in large areas of Australia, South America, and India. These grasslands are warm and have a dry and a rainy season. One such tropical grassland is the African Savanna. This is home to some of the world's most recognisable species like elephants, giraffes, rhinoceroses, zebras, lions, hyenas, and warthogs. Apart from the Savanna, there are other grasslands such as the Veldts in South Africa, and Campos and Llanos in South America. In this region rainfall measures about 50–130 centimetres per year.

▲ *Grasses that dominate this ecosystem with a lot of widely spaced trees are termed as savannas*

Characteristics

Grasses in the tropical regions are 91–180 centimetres tall. The tropical grasslands have more woody shrubs than the temperate ones. During the rainy season, flowers bloom, and some survive till the winter as they have thick stems to store water. The grasslands have an open shrub layer that is dark and gloomy with very little vegetation between the trees. This area gets flooded during heavy rainfalls. Saplings await for larger plants and trees to die, leaving a gap in the canopy which they can grow into.

Animals of the Grasslands

There are many animals native to the tropical grasslands. They include giraffes, zebras, buffaloes, kangaroos, mice, moles, gophers, ground squirrels, snakes, worms, termites, beetles, lions, leopards, hyenas, and elephants. However, it is not necessary that all these animals are found in all the tropical grasslands. Some are native and unique to certain regions, while others may appear across different regions as different sub-species.

▼ *Animals such as buffaloes, elephants, giraffes, and zebras are commonly found in the savannas*

👤 In Real Life

▲ *Sometimes, the burning of sawdust and dry leaves due to friction results in spontaneous fires in the grasslands*

Periodic fires occur in the grasslands and are quite common. This is required to destroy unwanted plants that tend to encroach into the grassland. Fires can be induced by human beings or they may start spontaneously. Forest fires do not burn down the grassland plants as their buds are below the ground. Animals are also protected by fire as many live underground. Other animals and birds are mobile enough to cope with the problem.

Temperate Grasslands

Also called the prairies, temperate grasslands are mainly found in the belt between the forests and deserts on the Great Plains of North America. Similar to the savannas, temperate grasslands are areas of open grasslands with very few trees. However, they are located in colder regions and receive little precipitation. These are located to the north of the Tropic of Cancer and south of the Tropic of Capricorn.

The climate of the temperate grasslands includes warm summers and cold winters. Temperatures vary with changing seasons in this region. In the summer, the temperature can be well over 32°C. In winter, temperatures can drop down to below -17°C in some areas.

Temperate grasslands have short grasses, and sometimes they do not grow due to excessive cold in winters. Plants either die, or hibernate until the weather changes and spring comes. They receive about 25–88 centimetres of precipitation a year. In the temperate grasslands of the Northern Hemisphere, most of the precipitation is in the form of snow. Temperate grasslands are important for our survival. They also play a pivotal role in helping manage climate change.

 ## Rainfall in Temperate Grasslands

Temperate grasslands receive low to moderate precipitation. This is the reason tall trees and large shrubs are not found here. Droughts and fires restrict trees from growing. However, grasses have adapted to cold temperatures, droughts, and occasional fires because they have deep-rooted systems that can hold in the soil.

The vegetation in these grasslands depends on the amount of precipitation. The areas that are warmer and receive a little bit more rainfall have taller grasses. Grasses remain close to the ground where precipitation is less. Some examples found in these grasslands are buffalo grass, cacti, sagebrush, perennial grasses, sunflowers, clovers, and wild indigos. There are some 100 species of flowers that grow among the grasses.

▲ The various species of grasses found in these regions include purple needle grass, blue grama, sorghum, and galleta

Wildlife in Temperate Grasslands

Wildlife is abundant in temperate grasslands. They are home to many large herbivores such as bisons, gazelles, zebras, rhinoceroses, and wild horses. There are also carnivores such as lions and wolves in the temperate grasslands. Some smaller animals are also found here, such as deer, prairie dogs, mice, jackrabbits, skunks, coyotes, snakes, foxes, badgers, and grasshoppers. Sparrows, blackbirds, quails, meadow larks, owls, and hawks are among the birds found in the temperate grasslands.

▼ Grasslands are also called pampas in South America and steppes in Eurasia. They have tough plants that can tolerate freezing temperatures, droughts, fires, and grazing animals

Rolling in the Deserts

A desert is dry land with sparse vegetation. Deserts cover around 20 per cent of Earth's surface. They are found in all the continents. A desert is a place that receives less than 25 centimetres of rainfall per year. There is a definite deficit of moisture in these regions as they lose more moisture than they receive from precipitation. It is an ecosystem that supports plants and animals with special characteristics required to survive in a tough environment. Deserts are usually only thought to be sandy, hot and dry, but surprisingly, there are cold deserts as well.

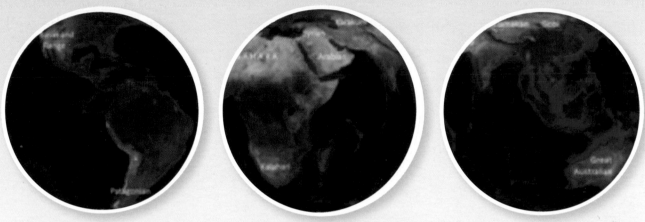

▲ The different deserts of the world, located within each continent

Location

Deserts are generally found around the Tropics of Cancer and Capricorn. They are located between 15° and 30° latitudes North and South of the Equator. Deserts are mainly located towards the west of different continents. This is mainly due to the easterly winds of the tropics, which are also known as the trade winds. They prevail in the lower portion of Earth's atmosphere, rather in the lower part of the troposphere. By the time these winds reach the western sides of the continents they become dry, and do not bring rain with them. Therefore, these regions become devoid of moisture, forming deserts. There are four types of deserts based upon their geographic situation—polar deserts, subtropical deserts, cold winter deserts, and cool coastal deserts.

The world's largest desert is the Sahara Desert in the Northern Hemisphere. Other large deserts are the Arabian Peninsula in West Asia, and the Thar Desert in India and Pakistan. There is a cold desert in Central Asia known as the Gobi Desert. Some deserts of the Southern Hemisphere are Atacama and Patagonia in South America, Namib and Kalahari in Africa, and the Great Sandy Desert in Australia.

Desert Landforms

Deserts have different landforms like mountains, hills, valleys, and canyons. Plains, sand dunes, and oases are also found here. These landforms have been created by windblown sand, water, and the heat of the Sun that affects the same area over thousands of years.

▼ The driest deserts get less than 1 centimetre of precipitation each year from condensed fog, not rain

Climate

The climate of deserts is usually hot and dry as there is very little precipitation. In the hot deserts, the day temperatures are often above 38° C in summer. However, there is a drastic fall in the temperature at night. The climate of the Gobi Desert and the deserts on the continent of Antarctica is always cold. Cold deserts are found in the mountainous regions. Here the days are warm, but the nights are very cold. There are even deserts on the coastal regions where the land and oceans meet. Winds that blow over the deserts do not bring rain but fog. The Namib Desert is a coastal desert. To sum up, the fluctuations in the temperature and scarcity of water make the deserts a harsh place to live.

Desert Survivors

The plants and animals in desert regions have special features that help them survive the dry climate. They try to adapt themselves to the prevailing conditions of the region. However, both the plants and animals face quite a few challenges here. They not only require food and water but also a suitable temperature for their body.

 ## Desert Flora

In deserts, plants do not get water for a long period of time. Therefore, there are certain plants with special roots that help them absorb the small amount of water that is available. On the other hand, some have long roots to tap water from under the ground. Some of the plants that are found in deserts are cacti and Yuccas. They have a unique way of storing water in their stems. Some cacti can live up to 100 years.

▲ *Different types of cacti found in the desert region*

▲ *Camels are smarter than horses, and they pee on their back legs to help cool them down*

 ## Desert Fauna

Animals have also adapted themselves to the harsh conditions of deserts. Camels can go for days without food and water, and their nostrils and eyelashes protect them from the sand. There are animals that come out in the night when the temperature falls. Animals like the desert tortoise in south-western USA spend much of their time underground. Birds in the desert region are nomadic. They fly across the sky for food. Apart from camels, other animals common in desert areas are gazelles, snakes, lizards, and small rodents.

 ## Land Use and Climate Change in the Deserts

There are some semi-arid regions that are fast becoming deserts. This is happening through a process called 'desertification'. It occurs due to deforestation and the utilisation of resources by people who have settled in these places. Other major causes of desertification are overgrazing, urbanization, climate change, overuse of groundwater, and natural disasters. Another reason is tillage practices in agriculture which make soils more vulnerable to wind. Increase in temperature results in wildfires that alter desert landscapes by eliminating slow-growing trees and shrubs, and replacing them with fast-growing grasses. All these changes harm the habitats of the animals here.

 ## Effects of Climate Change

While there are many aspects to climate change, the one that poses most threat to us is global warming. It is destroying the foundations of many ecosystems, eliminating many species of crucial components—such as plants and insects—which is going to make it very difficult for the rest of the living species to flourish.

To illustrate this, let us look at the Mojave Desert in the United States. A local type of flora, the Joshua tree is facing challenges because of the hotter climate. It is a type of plant that stores water in its trunk. They usually have a single trunk and grow three to nine feet tall before branching, and can further grow to 6–22 metres in height over 150 years. If these trees do not survive, then neither will species like the Yucca moth, as they lay their eggs in these trees. And these would be the first steps of chain reaction where we won't like the eventual outcome.

▼ *The iconic Joshua tree in California*

The Treeless Tundra

Tundra is a vast, flat, treeless Arctic region spanning across Europe, Asia, and North America. In the tundra, the subsoil is permanently frozen. It is listed among Earth's coldest and harshest biomes. There is little rainfall, but the ground is covered with snow, almost throughout the year, until summer brings a burst of wildflowers.

Other areas described as part of the tundra biome are Antarctica (Antarctic tundra) and the tops of high mountains (Alpine tundra).

Climate

The temperature in the Arctic tundra is -12°–-6° C. This biome has long, cold winters with the temperature being -34° C. The summers are cool and short with the average temperature being 3°–12° C. The summer temperature enables this biome to sustain life. Rainfall is scanty and varies from region to region in the Arctic. Annual precipitation is 15–25 centimetres. The winds blowing here are dry, making the tundra like a desert. The ground in the Arctic tundra is permanently frozen which distinguishes it from other biomes.

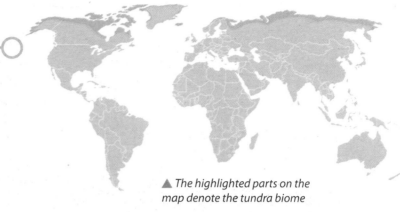
▲ *The highlighted parts on the map denote the tundra biome*

Flora

The climate in the tundra region is not conducive to a variety of flora and fauna. Therefore, the flowers found within the biome are very few. Majority of the plants are mosses, grasses, lichens, sedges, and shrubs. They are also known as alpine plants. Cotton grass is very common in this region. This vegetation has been able to adapt to its environment. Most plants are threatened by environmental phenomena like global warming. Within the Antarctic Peninsula, plants are aquatic and terrestrial, such as algae, liverworts, reindeer mosses, sedges, shrubs, and pearlwort.

Fauna

The Arctic tundra supports a variety of species of animals including Arctic foxes, polar bears, grey wolves, caribou, snow geese, and musk-oxen. There are some migrating birds and rabbits. In the Alpine tundra, animals such as goats, caribou, marmots, elk, and pikas are common. In the Antarctic tundra, penguins are found, along with a variety of fish species. There is a bird called the Arctic tern which travels a distance of about 35,000 kilometres every year.

▼ *The tundra is a very fragile biome that is shrinking as the permafrost melts*

Isn't It Amazing!

The Arctic willow is one of the smallest trees in the world with a height of a mere 20 centimetres. It has the strength to bear the frigid dry climate of the tundra. Its branches look like they are hugging the ground.

Deforestation and Conservation

Forests cover 30 per cent of Earth's surface. But the rapid felling of trees, known as deforestation, is causing the forest cover to reduce drastically. Deforestation takes place to use forest land for other purposes such as agricultural cropland, urbanisation, or mining operations around the world. It is important to practice afforestation instead, that is, planting trees on open land with the aim of creating a forest.

▲ *Wood being cut down for commercial use*

 ## Causes of Deforestation

Deforestation is caused both naturally and due to human activities. Natural causes include fire, floods, and hurricanes. Human activities include agricultural expansion, livestock grazing, timber extraction, mining, and oil extraction. As the population is increasing, the demand for food is also rising. To meet this challenge, farmers are using these lands for cultivation and animal grazing. Forests are being cut down to develop dwellings in this age of urbanisation. Old trees are cut down to make furniture and paper. Dam construction and industrial exploitation of mines contribute to massive deforestation.

Effects of Deforestation

Deforestation has an adverse effect on the environment. Due to the felling of trees, plants and animals lose their natural habitat. The animals not only lose their homes, but in the process, become endangered, and many are even on the verge of extinction.

Deforestation also affects the climate in a big way. The unprotected soil exposed to sunlight dries faster. Trees help in the water cycle by returning water vapour to the atmosphere. Without trees to fill these roles, many former forest lands could quickly become barren deserts.

If big trees are cut down, forests are deprived of their canopies, which can block sunlight during the day and hold the heat at night. All of these lead to drastic changes in the temperature and harm the ecosystem.

Trees produce oxygen that is necessary for living things to breathe. They take in carbon dioxide and keep pollution under check. However, deforestation reduces forest cover and increases the greenhouse gases in the atmosphere. This too aggravates the issue of global warming.

To fight the effects of deforestation, it is mandatory to balance it by planting enough trees and creating awareness. Deforestation needs to be managed properly, mainly through the conservation of forests.

◀ *Deforestation might also be caused naturally by wildfires and overgrazing*

Conservation of Forests

Conservation is a way to prevent any loss of the natural resources on Earth and take care of them with a focus on sustainability. Forests are natural resources that are being destroyed due to deforestation. Therefore, steps should be taken to conserve them.

Steps for Conservation

The following are some steps that we can take to conserve forests:

Trees are used for many purposes, and sometimes felling is required. However, anything in excess is not good. Therefore, the cutting down of trees must be regulated and planned.

Destruction of forests due to forest fires is common. Fire can start by natural processes like lightning, friction between the trees due to winds, or by human activities. Hence, it is important to control these fires.

Whenever trees are cut down, whether in a planned way or not, the number of trees cut should be reforested or planted. This is called afforestation. The trees to be planted should be selected according to the geology of a region and taken care of in the initial stages.

In the past, forests were cleared for agriculture. However, excessive clearing is dangerous for the ecosystem. Therefore, shifting agriculture should be practiced the way it is done in some parts of Asia, Africa, and South America.

Forests should be protected from diseases resulting from fungi, viruses, rusts, etc.

Trees can also be conserved through recycling. This is possible by reusing wastepaper. If half the world's paper was recycled, much of the worldwide demand for new paper would be fulfilled, saving many of Earth's trees. The key to conservation of forests is through forest management. Governments around the world are trying to work towards conserving forests to the best of their abilities.

⭐ Incredible Individuals

▲ *Sunderlal Bahuguna*

Sunderlal Bahuguna was a noted environmentalist who initiated the Chipko Movement in India. The name of the movement comes from the Hindi word meaning 'to cling to'. This movement was to protect the trees from being cut down. The villagers hugged the trees and prevented the contractors from felling them. Bahuguna is also known for coining the Chipko slogan— 'ecology is permanent economy'.

▼ *It is in our hands to adopt sustainable practices and save the environment*

◀ *Environmental activists from all over the world are fighting to save Earth for the future generations*

NATURAL WONDERS

WHAT ARE NATURAL WONDERS?

Earth is an amazing planet. It has some spectacular and diverse physical features, for example, beautiful waterfalls, tall mountains, blazing volcanoes, dense forests, and sandy deserts. All these physical landscapes and structures were formed naturally. Mother Nature has provided us with these breathtaking physical formations.

Natural wonders are the greatest landscapes on our planet Earth. They are awe-inspiring, and as human beings we can only study their origins, not recreate them. Some striking natural wonders on Earth are the Victoria Falls, Mount Everest, the Grand Canyon, the Great Barrier Reef, and some more. However, that is not the only reason they are valued. These also provide us with resources and are homes to our animals. That is why various governments across the globe have taken initiatives to protect these natural features.

▼ Stunning and beautiful natural geysers at the Yellowstone National Park, USA

The Grand Canyon

A canyon is an interesting landform found in many places on Earth. It is a steep-walled, deep, V-shaped valley cut by a river through resistant rocks. These kinds of valleys are usually formed in the upper courses of rivers where there are swift currents that help dig valleys at a rapid pace. Canyons are formed over millions of years, by erosion. This happens when land is worn away over time by the force of the moving water of a river. One such canyon is the Grand Canyon, Arizona, USA. It is known for its multitude of geological features and rich archeological history. While it was already known to the native Americans, the first European to spot the site was Spain's Gracia Lopez de Cardenas in 1540.

Location

Grand means large and canyon refers to a big crack in the ground. The Grand Canyon is located in the southwestern part of the Colorado Plateau. It is a canyon that has steep sides carved by the Colorado River. It is 446 kilometres long, 29 kilometres wide, and boasts a depth of over 1,857 metres. This canyon is the result of constant erosion by the Colorado River, however its formation took millions of years. The Grand Canyon is famous for its splendid shape and colour. The colour of the rocks is mostly red. However, some are buff, grey, green, pink, and violet in colour. There are peaks, **buttes**, **gorges**, and **ravines** between its outer walls. It comprises horizontal layered rocks and lava flows.

Formation

▼ *Bald eagles or American eagles are common in the Grand Canyon*

Millions of years ago, the area where the canyon exists presently was a giant, flat slab of layered rock called the Colorado Plateau. The Colorado River—formed by rain and snow—had been flowing over the plateau for millions of years. In this way, it cut into the rock surface, and the Grand Canyon was formed. A recent study has revealed that this process might have begun 70 million years ago. The erosion was caused mainly due to wind and rain. The cutting action of the river determined its depth. However, rain, wind, temperature, and chemical erosion have steadily widened the canyon.

The weather at the Grand Canyon varies drastically. Its elevation ranges from 2,000 feet to over 8,000 feet, and this effects both solar heating and air circulation. The temperature can change by 3° C every 304.8 metres. This allows tourists to witness a host of weather conditions.

Plant Life

The natural vegetation of the Grand Canyon includes trees like willow, cottonwoods, pine, fir, spruce, and aspen. Bush vegetation consists mainly of scrub oak and mountain mahogany found in the drier regions.

▲ *Horseshoe Mesa, the main stopping point, as viewed from Grandview trail, located approximately 140 miles from both the South Rim and the North Rim of the Grand Canyon*

Animal Life

As the canyon is very old, it is quite natural for palaeontologists to want to look for dinosaur bones here, but surprisingly, nothing was found at the site. Scientists are unsure about the age of the canyon. While one theory for the absence of dinosaur remains is that the rocks that make up the canyon are much older than the dinosaurs. On the other hand, possibly, the canyon was formed long after the dinosaurs were gone. However, today, animal life is quite abundant and varied in the Grand Canyon. Great varieties of animals are found here, including coyotes, foxes, deer, badgers, rabbits, squirrels, and chipmunks. The Grand Canyon is also home to many species of birds and fish.

Incredible Individuals

▲ A portrait of John Wesley Powell

John Wesley Powell (1834–1902) was an American geologist, and the first person to lead an expedition to the Grand Canyon in 1869. He was also the first to use the name 'Grand Canyon', as previously it was known as the 'Big Canyon' or 'Great Canyon'. He also organised expeditions to the Colorado River. He wrote about Native Americans, the Colorado Plateau and its surrounding regions, as well as the Rocky Mountains.

Special Status

Some area of the canyon was set aside as the Grand Canyon Forest Reserve by US President Benjamin Harrison in 1893. Later, in 1903, US President Roosevelt designated it as a game preserve, and in 1908, it was declared as a national monument. A national park was also made there, which was declared as a UNESCO World Heritage Site in 1979. Today, it is a popular tourist destination with several million visitors per year.

The Grandview Trail, a unique tourist attraction, offers a splendid view of an old miner's cave called the 'Cave of the Domes'. Before it became a national park, tourists were able to take mule rides down an old mining route to this limestone cave which was the only cave open to them. This trail has green conifers and red ridged slopes. The main stopping point is the Horseshoe Mesa.

▼ In 1919, the Grand Canyon National Park was established by the US Congress

The Great Barrier Reef

There are two types of corals, the first being hard corals or reef building corals, such as brain corals and elkhorn corals. Soft corals, such as sea fans and sea whips, do not produce reefs. Soft corals do not have rocky skeletons, and zooxanthellae—symbiotic algae that live with corals and help them with photosynthesis—are not usually present. They live in tropical areas as well as cooler, darker parts of the ocean. While coral polyps are among the smaller creatures, their physical homes and colonies—the reefs—are the largest living structures on the Earth, and the only homes visible from space. They are home to other species as well.

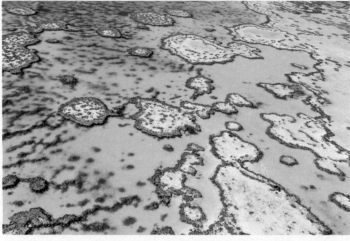
▲ The Great Barrier Reef is a living and magnificent natural wonder on Earth

▼ The photo shows tiny polyps growing in a coral structure inside an aquarium

Formation of Coral Reefs

They are formed by free-swimming coral polyp larvae that attach themselves to rocks or other hard surfaces along the edges of islands or continents. As they mature and secrete calcium carbonate, the reefs start to grow and expand. They can become one of four types: barrier, fringing, patch, or atolls. With a growth rate of 0.3–2 centimetres per year for large corals, and up to 10 centimetre for branching corals, it can take anywhere from 10,000-30,000,000 years to develop.

Reef-building corals cannot tolerate water temperatures below 18° C, so most coral reefs are found in waters that are 23°–29° C. They also require water with high salt content, and a lot of light. The majority of them are found in subtropical and tropical waters.

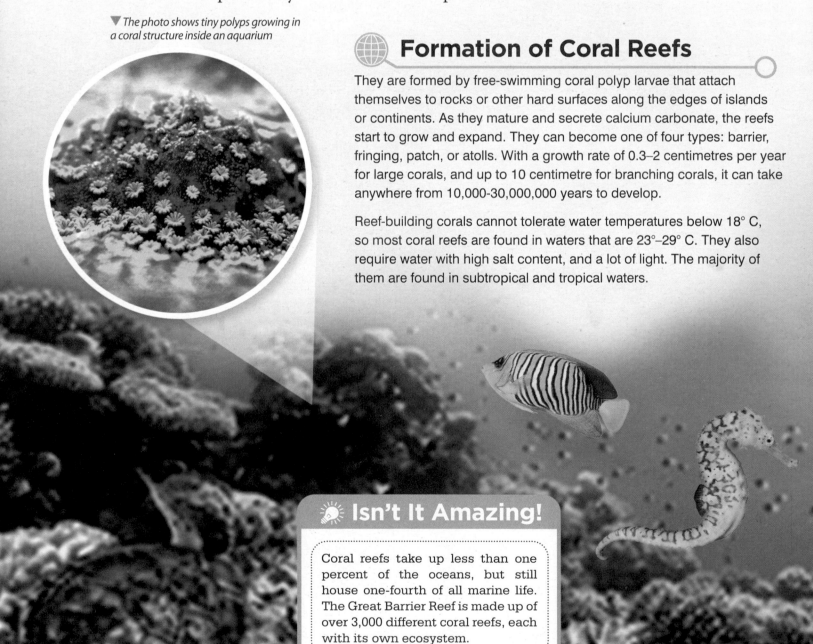

Isn't It Amazing!

Coral reefs take up less than one percent of the oceans, but still house one-fourth of all marine life. The Great Barrier Reef is made up of over 3,000 different coral reefs, each with its own ecosystem.

Geology

Coral reefs had been growing for millions of years when the coral sea basin was formed. When the continent of Australia moved to its present location, sea levels changed, and the coral reefs grew rapidly. According to modern scientists, the complete structure of the Great Barrier Reef was formed approximately 600,000 years back. However, most of it died due to climate changes. The structure that is visible today was formed 20,000 years ago. Coral reefs grew as the sea level rose, at the end of the last **glaciations**. They grew on the flooded plains and over the submerged islands around 13,000 years back. Thus, it can be deduced that the current, living Great Barrier Reef may be only 6,000 to 8,000 years old.

Location

The Great Barrier Reef is located in the Coral Sea, off the coast of Queensland, Australia. It extends for more than 2,000 kilometres at an offshore distance and covers an area of 349,648 square kilometres, ranging from 16–160 kilometres.

It stretches from the low-water mark along the coast up to 250 kilometres offshore, giving it a wide depth range which includes vast, shallow inshore areas, mid-shelf and outer reefs, and beyond the continental shelf to ocean waters over 2,000 metres deep.

It comprises of around 2,500 individual reefs of different shapes and sizes, over 900 islands-ranging from small sandy cays and larger vegetated cays, to large islands that are over 1,100 metres above sea level.

▲ The Great Barrier Reef , by latitude, extends from 10° S to 24° S

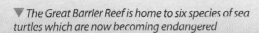

▼ The Great Barrier Reef is home to six species of sea turtles which are now becoming endangered

Ecology

The Great Barrier Reef has a wide variety of sea life such as fish, sea turtles, giant clams, seahorses, sea snakes, sharks, and many more. It contains about 1,500 species of fish. Whales, dolphins and dugong can also be seen here. There are many species of birds that come to the reef, like the white-bellied sea eagle and the roseate tern.

There are about 2,195 species of plants, and about 400 species of coral, in the islands of the Great Barrier Reef. The plant species in the northern islands are woody, but in the southern islands, the plants are **herbaceous**. The Whitsunday region of the Great Barrier Reef has 1,141 plant species.

This natural wonder is facing the biggest threat due to climate change. Pollutants like sediments and agricultural pesticides are also harming the Great Barrier Reef. In 2015, the Australian government formed a plan named the 'Reef 2050 Plan' to protect and preserve the reef's universal heritage until 2050. Another effort is the Great Barrier Reef Marine Park, formed in 1975, meant to preserve the reef and the species within it.

Every year around two million tourists visit this reef. It is a UNESCO World Heritage Site. The Great Barrier Reef is a tourist attraction and a protected marine environment due to its biodiversity.

👤 In Real Life

Hamilton Island is the largest island in the Great Barrier Reef **archipelago**. It is the only island with a commercial airport, making it easily accessible by plane.

▶ A view of the Hamilton Island from an airplane

The Amazon Rainforest

The Amazon Rainforest is one of the largest and most useful tropical rainforests in the world. It covers over 5.5 million square kilometres, and lies mainly in the basin that is drained by the great Amazon River and its tributaries. The Amazon River is 6,400 kilometres in length, and is the second longest river in the world.

▲ The Amazon Rainforest represents more than half of the planet's remaining rainforests

Location

The Amazon Rainforest is located in the northern part of the continent of South America. It encompasses 40 per cent of Brazil's total area. It is bounded by the Guiana Highlands to the north, the Andes Mountains to the west, the Brazilian central plateau to the south, and the Atlantic Ocean to the east. The Amazon Rainforest has a wider front that stretches for 320 kilometres along the Atlantic and forms a 1,900 kilometres wide belt where the lowlands meet the Andean foothills.

▼ Animals and birds such as the jaguars, different kinds of monkeys, toucan, and many more are inhabitants of this vast rainforest

▲ The Amazon rainforest covers most of the northern portion of the South American continent

Geology

The topsoil in the Amazon Rainforest is several metres deep. However, it does not possess the required nutrients due to erosion over millions of years. Though the soil is lacking in nutrients, lots of plants still grow in this region. The organic matter of the dead plants and animals provides nutrients to the soil and indirectly helps in the growth of the plants. The Amazon basin is made up of clay and sand deposits, and is very thick. Rocks are seldom found here as they wither in their journey from the Andes to the bottom of the river.

💡 Isn't It Amazing!

One square kilometre of the Amazon Rainforest can contain approximately 81,646,627 kilograms of living plants.

Climate

The region experiences very heavy rainfall, high humidity, and high temperature. The temperature is around 27° C round the year. There are no periodic seasons by virtue of the tropics. Thunderstorms are quite common due to the hot and humid weather. This region receives about 150 to 300 centimetres of annual rainfall. The humidity is usually 85 per cent, and at night it can be 95 per cent.

Ecology

The Amazon Rainforest is the world's richest tropical forest in terms of biodiversity. It is home to more than one-third of all species in the world. Here lie thousands of species of plants and various types of trees such as the myrtle, laurel, palm, and acacia. There are also trees such as rosewood, Brazil nut, and rubber. Mahogany and cedar help produce timber for furniture. Presently, around 438,000 species of plants of economic and social interest have been registered in the region.

There are lots of species of insects, plants, birds, and other forms of life in the Amazon Rainforest. Wildlife here also includes jaguars, manatees, tapirs, red deer, capybaras, rodents, and different types of monkeys.

What's So Special?

The Amazon Rainforest is a wonderful place that is full of unique animals, millions of trees, and rare species of plants. There are plenty of things to know about this rainforest other than plants and animals. It is popularly referred to as the 'Lungs of Earth' as it produces over 20 per cent of the world's oxygen supply. The trees in the Amazon Rainforest are so thick that sunlight cannot entirely penetrate into the forest. So, some parts are always in semi-darkness.

The Amazon Rainforest is not only home to plants and animals but to many people. There are 400–500 indigenous local tribes living in the Amazon Rainforest. There are over 50 groups of native tribes who have never met people outside their own tribes.

▲ The well-known tribes of the Amazon Rainforest are the Pigmy, the Huli, and the Yanomami tribes

The Iguazu Falls

The Iguazu Falls are a series of cataracts on the Iguaçu River on the border of Argentina and Brazil. The fall looks like an elongated horseshoe that extends for 2.7 kilometres. It is three times wider than the Niagara Falls in North America, and notably greater than the width of the Victoria Falls in Africa. The Iguazu Falls get their name from the Guarani word meaning 'great water'. There are many rocky and wooded islands on the edge of the steep ledge over which the Iguaçu River plunges. These divide the falls into as many as 275 separate waterfalls that vary in height.

 ## Location

The Iguazu Falls are the largest waterfall system on Earth. The Iguaçu River originates near the city of Curitiba, Brazil, and it divides the river into the upper and lower Iguaçu. The river mostly flows through Brazil, but two-thirds of the falls are on the Argentinian side. The Iguaçu River has a confluence with the San Antonio River, and below that the Iguaçu River forms the boundary between Argentina and Brazil.

 ## Formation

Iguazu Falls were formed as a result of a volcanic eruption, that left a large crack on the Earth's surface. This eruption flooded the region with basaltic lava, which consequently covered the desert that was present there millions of years ago. There were many stages to this lava flow. The base of the falls was formed from the inter-layering of basalt with sandstone. The falls occur along a wide span where the Iguaçu River, flowing westward and then northward, tumbles over the edge of the Parana Plateau before continuing its course in a canyon.

◄ The location of the Iguazu Falls on a map

 ## Features

The Iguazu Falls have a waterfall system that makes up 2.7 kilometres of the Iguaçu River. There are 275 waterfalls which are 197–269 feet high. Countries that have access to the Iguazu River are Brazil, Argentina, and Paraguay.

Iguazu Falls have the highest annual average flow among all the waterfalls in the world; it can reach as high as 450,000 cubic feet per second. One of the striking falls of Iguazu Falls is called 'The Devil's Throat'. It is a U-shaped **chasm** where 14 falls plunge more than 350 feet below. It marks the border between Brazil and Argentina. The width of the falls is 2,682 metres, and it is the widest waterfall in the world.

 ## Isn't It Amazing!

Sometimes a rainbow forms on the waterfalls due to the refraction of light against the mist caused by the thundering waters.

◄ A rainbow appears over the Iguazu Falls

Ecology

The region of the Iguazu Falls has rich and varied vegetation. It features plants from the semi-deciduous to the tropical variety. Plants that grow only in rushing water are found on the ledges of the falls. One common and typical species of plants is the Palo Rosa or the pink stick. It is called pink because of the colour of the wood. Another common species is the palm tree. Other plants common to this region are orchids. However, one must not forget about Ceibo, whose red blossoms are the national flower of Argentina. The plants grow in contrasting ways, for instance, bamboos grow next to palm trees or mosses grow next to lianas and begonias.

There is an abundance of animal life around Iguazu Falls. The most common animals are iguanas. Animals such as ocelots, jaguars, deer, tapirs, and other smaller animals are also found here. There are around 450 species of birds like toucans, magpies, parrots, and teros seen here. There are different species of fish found in this region that include the golden salmon, mandi, and cascudo fish.

▲ *Iguanas are large lizards which are around 6 feet long and weigh approximately 11 pounds*

 # What's So Special?

The Iguazu Falls are among the most beautiful waterfalls in the world and mesmerise all visitors. Spring and fall are the best months to visit this natural wonder. In the winter, the water levels are at their lowest and in summer, it is extremely humid and hot. During the rainy season, from November to March, the rate of flow of water over the falls may reach 12,750 cubic metres per second. The Iguazu Falls are also a UNESCO World Heritage Site.

▼ *The footbridge on the Iguazu waterfalls helps the tourists get a better view of this natural wonder*

The Mount Everest

Mount Everest, popularly known as *Sagarmatha* in Nepal and *Chomulungma* in Tibet, is the highest mountain in the world. It lies in the Himalayan Range in the continent of Asia. Tenzing Norgay from Nepal and Edmund Hillary from New Zealand were the first to reach the summit of this great mountain in 1953. It is at a height of 8,849 metres above sea level.

Location

Mount Everest stands tall at the border of Tibet and Nepal. It is in the Mahalangur Range on the Tibetan Plateau known as Qing Zang Gaoyuan. On the Nepal side, Mount Everest is in the Sagarmatha National Park in the Solukhumbu District. On the Tibetan side, it is in the Tingri County in the Xigaze region.

 **Isn't It Amazing!**

The year 1974 is referred to as a 'Maiden Year' because nobody even attempted to climb Mount Everest, which is very rare.

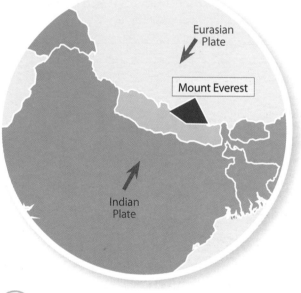

◄ *The image shows the collision of the plates and the emergence of the Himalayas*

Formation

The Himalayan mountain range was formed due to the collision between the Indian Plate and the Eurasian Plate. This movement started some 50 million years ago and is going on till date. 250 million years ago, there was one continent called Pangea. The giant continent broke up very slowly and formed the continents as they are today. It is believed that some 70 million years ago, the Indo-Australian Plate moved northwards towards the Eurasian Plate quite rapidly, 15 centimetres northwards per year. There was an ocean called Tethys that lay between those two plates. Due to the rapid movement of the Indo-Australian Plate, the Tethys Ocean completely disappeared. Presently, the Indian Plate is still moving towards the Tibetan Plateau. The Tibetan Plateau is, therefore, forced to move upwards and amazingly, the height of the Mount Everest is also growing another four millimetres on average, every year.

Climate

The climate of Mount Everest is not at all conducive to living as the temperature is always below freezing point. The temperature is around -19° C in the month of July. In January, the average temperature varies from -36° C to -60° C at its lowest. Fluctuations of temperature and unexpected storms are common. Snowfall is a regular affair and high-speed winds are always attacking the area. These strong winds are dangerous for climbers as they can be strong enough to potentially make them fall. And the windchill cuts through protective clothing, putting them in danger of getting **frostbite**.

Geology

Mount Everest comprises multiple layers of folded rocks. The rocks at the lower level are metamorphic rocks like the schist and gneisse. Just on top of these are igneous rocks. Sedimentary rocks are also found higher up. Due to the collision of the respective plates, marine limestone was thrust upwards to form a prominent band of yellow rocks (the Yellow Band) at the summit. The peak is always covered with snow, all year round.

ⓧ Incredible Individuals

When Yuichiro Miura from Japan scaled Mount Everest for the third time at the age of 80, he became the oldest man to climb Mount Everest. He did this despite the fact that he had a history of heart problems.

◀ *Miura scaled Mount Everest at the age of 70 and 75 as well*

Expeditions and Adventures

Since the time that the Mount Everest was discovered, people have been determined to reach the top of the summit. British surveyors recorded that Everest was the tallest peak in the world in 1856. Although the first to achieve this feat were Tenzing Norgay and Edmund Hillary, many people before them tried to reach the top; for instance, George Mallory and Andrew Irvine made the first attempt in 1924. There have been many famous expeditions to Mount Everest:

- 1963 US National Geographic Expedition
- 1970 Japan Expedition
- 1979 Yugoslav Expedition
- 1990 Earth Day 20 International Peace Climb
- 2000 Nepali Women Millennium Expedition
- 2017 Indian Navy Everest Expedition

◀ *The summit is directly between Tibet and Nepal*

What's So Special?

Due to the continuous collision of the tectonic plates, Everest is growing half a centimetre every year. The amount of oxygen present on Mount Everest is very low. It is about one-third of the amount of oxygen present at sea level. The oxygen levels are low due to low air pressure which makes it uncomfortable while climbing. Practically, there is limited time to climb the mountain as the jet stream hovers on the peak almost throughout the year. The speed of the wind reaches as high as 321 kilometres per hour. **Avalanches** are common and pose problems for climbers.

Most of the climbs are done in May. The only person who has successfully climbed Mount Everest from all the four sides of this mountain is Kushang Sherpa, an instructor at the Himalayan Mountaineering Institute. Few animals can survive in the upper regions of the mountain. However, some unique ones are jumping spiders, bar-headed geese, and yellow-billed choughs.

▲ *The yellow-billed chough belongs to the crow family*

Auroras or Polar Lights

The auroras are a spectacular natural wonder. They are visible in the sky near the poles. They are bright coloured waves of light seen in the evening sky near the magnetic poles on Earth, especially at higher latitudes. In the northern hemisphere the phenomena can be witnessed in countries usually closer to the Arctic Circle. The countries include Alaska, Canada, Iceland, Greenland, Norway, Sweden, and Finland. In the southern hemisphere, it can be witnessed in Antarctica.

Naming the Lights

In the Northern Hemisphere, the Auroras are called the 'Aurora borealis' or the Northern Lights. In the Southern Hemisphere, they are called the 'Aurora australis' or the Southern Lights. These waves of light can be seen in different colours like red, yellow, green, blue, and purple. The lights appear in many forms, for instance, they can appear in patches or scattered clouds of light, or like streamers, arcs, or rippling curtains that light up the sky with an otherworldly glow.

When and Where Do Northern Lights Occur?

The Polar Lights occur between 60° to 75° latitudes and at altitudes of about 100 kilometres. However, they may occur anywhere between 80–250 kilometres above Earth's surface. They can be visible from dusk until dawn, but the best time to witness them is around 2 AM.

In the Northern Hemisphere, the aurora zone extends across the northern coast of Siberia, Scandinavia, Iceland, the southern tip of Greenland, northern Canada, and Alaska. In the Southern Hemisphere, it stretches over Antarctica or the Southern Ocean.

What Causes the Auroras?

The Auroras are formed when electrically charged particles from the Sun during a solar flare penetrate Earth's **magnetic shield** and collide with the atoms and molecules in Earth's atmosphere. This collision produces countless bursts of light called photons, which make up the aurora. The variations in the colour are due to the type of gas particles that are colliding. The atmosphere of Earth is predominantly made up of oxygen and nitrogen. When the solar particles reach Earth's atmosphere, they collide with atoms of these two elements. At this point, they strip away the **electrons** and leave the **ions** behind. In turn, these ions emit radiation at various wavelengths and create the different colours. Collisions of solar particles with oxygen create the red or green lights and the same with nitrogen create the green and purple lights.

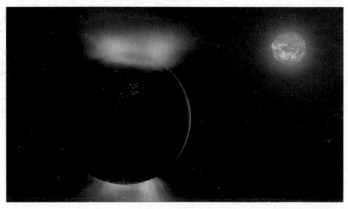

◄ *Earth's magnetic field with solar wind*

👤 In Real Life

The mixture of oxygen and nitrogen produces purple, pink, and white lights. These two gases also emit ultraviolet light, which is not visible with the naked eye. Special cameras on satellites can detect them. Researchers can use the different colours to figure out things like the energy level of the electrons that are bombarding our atmosphere and creating the aurora.

Isn't It Amazing!

No two light displays are the same. The colour and patterns are always different. There is a notion that the Polar Lights only come out at certain times. On the contrary, they are always present. It is just that the sky conditions change, making them visible.

 # Polar Lights

The Polar Lights are a subject of many myths and stories around the world, as people attempted to make sense of what they observed. The lights were not always linked with gods or positivity. The residents of France and Italy considered these lights a bad omen. When the skies visible over the British Isles seemed to have turned red a few week before the French Revolution, the residents later considered this to be a sign of the violence to come. The Japanese on the other hand associate the Aurora borealis with good fortune.

◀ Satellites can take pictures of this breathtaking phenomenon as the Polar Lights are clearly visible from space

 # The Aurora Australis

The Aurora Australis or the Southern Lights occur around the southern magnetic pole. The phenomenon can be seen from Antarctica. However, the best view is possible from Tasmania, Hobart, and the southern tip of New Zealand. The spirals in the aurora sometimes are mirror images of each other at the poles. However, this can only happen when it is fall or winter in Antarctica and summer in the Northern Hemisphere.

▲ The Northern Lights are more famous only because they are more accessible, while their southern counterparts are hard to reach for tourists

 # What's So Special?

It is interesting to know that this phenomenon is visible on some other planets of the solar system as well. Auroras occur on Jupiter, Saturn, Uranus, and Neptune. They usually emit a light that is a mix of yellow and green but colours like blue, red, and violet are also common. The International Space Station is situated at the same altitude as the Polar Lights. Therefore, astronauts are able to see the lights from their side. A pale, yellowish-green is the most common auroral colour that is produced by oxygen molecules located about 96 kilometres above Earth. Red auroras are produced by high-altitude oxygen, at heights of up to 321 kilometres. Nitrogen produces blue or purplish-red auroras.

The Dead Sea

The Dead Sea, also known as the Salt Sea, is a landlocked lake between Israel and Jordan. It is a hyper-saline lake, making it one of Earth's unique places and a natural wonder. It is around 413 metres below sea level and its shoreline is the lowest dry land on the surface of Earth. It is nine times more salty than the oceans and hence life is impossible here. Once the water evaporates, it leaves behind massive amounts of salt.

▲ A map showing the exact location of the Dead Sea

Location

The Dead Sea is located in south-western Asia. The country of Jordan lies on its east, and Israel and the West Bank lie on its west. Its eastern shore belongs to Jordan, the southern half of its western shore to Israel, and the northern half of its western shore lies within the Palestinian West Bank. The Dead Sea receives most of its water from the Jordan River, which flows from the north into the lake.

Climate

The Dead Sea lies within the desert and therefore receives scanty rainfall. The aridness is because of the rain shadow effect of the Judean Hills. Due to the influence of a barrier like a mountain range, that causes prevailing winds to lose moisture before reaching there, it is an area with very little precipitation. This is a rain shadow.

Throughout the year, the weather is sunny, and there is little pollution in the air. Rainfall averages about 65 millimetre in a year. Due to the low elevation, winters are mild with temperatures around 17° C in January. Summers are very hot with temperatures ranging from 34° C to sometimes a maximum of 51° C.

Ecology

Due to the high saline content of the Dead Sea, fish and other aquatic animals and plants cannot live in it. However, the ecosystem is teeming with life. There are migratory birds seen in the skies above the Dead Sea. Animals such as bats, wild cats, camels, ibexes, hares, hyraxes, jackals, foxes, and even leopards are found in the surrounding mountains. The **delta** of the Jordan River formerly had a jungle of papyrus and palm trees. It is interesting to know that in the first century CE, historian Flavius Josephus described Jericho, just north of the Dead Sea, as 'the most fertile spot in Judea'. Valuable crops such as sugarcane, henna, and the sap of the balsamic tree—which was used to make perfume—were once found here. In modern times, the largest crop in the area is dates.

Geography

The Dead Sea was formed from a rift in Earth's crust and is in the Jordan Rift Valley. Initially, before the water level started dropping, the lake was 80 kilometres long, 18 kilometres wide, and had a surface area of about 1,020 square kilometres. Presently, it is 50 kilometres long and 15 kilometres wide. It lies 400 metres below sea level and is known as the lowest water body on Earth.

The Dead Sea is between the hills of Judea to the west and the Trans-Jordanian plateaus to the east. The Judean Hills, to the west of the Dead Sea, rise less steeply and are lower than the mountains to the east. Along with the Jordon River, there are smaller streams and rivers flowing into the Dead Sea. There is no outlet, hence the only way water leaves the sea is through evaporation.

▼ *Dead Sea is one of Israel's most popular tourist destination. It's surface level is dropping by more than one metre every year and can disappear at an alarming rate*

▼ *On the south-western side of the lake, there is a tall halite formation called 'Mount Sodom' which is 226 metres above the Dead Sea level*

In Real Life

The Highway 90 that runs along the Israeli and West Bank shores of the Dead Sea is the world's lowest road. It lies 392 metres below sea level.

What's So Special?

The salinity of the Dead Sea is what makes it unique. The water of this sea is extremely salty because it contains an excess of sodium chloride. The excessively salty water has high density, which helps people stay buoyant. The extreme salinity does not allow any kind of life except bacteria. The Dead Sea is a centre for health research and the centre of treatment for many diseases. Mud from the region is good for the skin. Another amazing fact is that the Dead Sea constantly discharges asphalt (bitumen). The Egyptians used this asphalt for the mummification process.

The Victoria Falls

Victoria Falls is one of the world's mightiest and most splendid waterfalls. It lies in east-central Africa, on the border between Zambia and Zimbabwe (formerly Rhodesia). Victoria Falls is about twice as wide and twice as deep as the Niagara Falls. It is also known as 'Mosioa-Tunya', which means 'the smoke that thunders' in the Lozi language.

Location

The Victoria Falls is located about midway along the course of the Zambezi River, the fourth-largest river in Africa. It is on the border between Zambia and Zimbabwe, in the Livingstone district of Zambia and Hwange district of Zimbabwe.

Formation

This natural wonder formed as a result of soft sandstone filling huge cracks in the hard basalt rock of the plateau. Earlier, as the Upper Zambezi flowed across the plateau, it found the cracks and started wearing away the softer rocks. This created a series of **gorges**. Erosion of the sandstone-filled cracks has been going on for over a million years. These form the zig-zag chasms called the Batoka gorges. Over the millenniums, there has been a steady pounding by the currents of the powerful Zambezi River. This action of the river has cut through the rock faults and fissures and carved out not one but eight successive **precipices**.

▲ The location of Victoria Falls on a map

Description

The waterfall covers the entire breadth of the Zambezi River. An estimated 550 millions litres of water drop for 108 metres within a minute over the cliff. The water then continues to flow downstream as the lower Zambezi River. During the wet season, the width stretches to over 1.3 kilometres, and the mean flow is around 935 cubic metres per second. The mist from the falling water is especially dense during the rainy season.

▲ The Victoria Falls Bridge crosses the Zambezi River just below the Victoria Falls. It is a link between two countries and at both ends, there are border posts on the approaches

Ecology

On the Zimbabwean side of the falls lies the Victoria Falls Rainforest. This region has a variety of unique plants and animals. The area receives rainfall every day. The water vapour from the falls rises and comes down as rain. The natural vegetation around the fall includes species of acacia, teak, ivory palm, fig, and ebony. However, the alluvial flatlands are dominated by mopane. Animals like klipspringers (a type of antelope) and hippopotamuses are commonly seen near the falls. Elephants, giraffes, zebras, gnus (wildebeests), lions, and leopards are seen in the forests and grasslands around the falls. Falcons, eagles, and buzzards can be found in the rock cliffs. There are different species of fish that live in the river above and below the falls. Water birds like the white-backed night heron are common in this region.

Isn't It Amazing!

At sunset, the Victoria Falls host a rare and beautiful sight. A rainbow is formed by the reflection of the moonlight on the water, also called the 'moonbow'. The spectacle lasts from sunset to sunrise and is one of Africa's most distinctive and striking scenes.

▲ A rainbow on the Victoria Falls

What's So Special?

Victoria Falls is approximately twice the height of Niagara and is considered world's largest waterfall because of its width of 1,708 metres and height of 108 metres, resulting in the world's largest sheet of cascading water. There is a natural swimming pool formed in the rocks just above the 108-metres-deep Victoria Falls called the 'Devil's Pool'. The rainforest of Zambezi is the only place on Earth that receives rain 24 hours a day for 7 days a week. In 1989, UNESCO declared Victoria Falls as a World Heritage Site. Approximately one million people visit the falls every year. In 1964, Zambia became free from British rule. They changed names of their cities, streets, buildings but did not change the name of these falls. The official name remains Victoria Falls.

▼ David Livingstone was the first European to discover the waterfall in 1855. He named it after Queen Victoria

The Zambezi River gushes down over the cliff forming the Victoria Falls with a thunder-like sound. It creates a cloud of mist that rises to wet everyone and everything around it.

Mount Kilimanjaro

The highest mountain in Africa is called Mount Kilimanjaro. It is not a traditional mountain but a giant inactive stratovolcano with three volcanic cones, Kibo, Mawenzi, and Shira. While Shira and Mawenzi are believed to be extinct volcanoes, Kibo is dormant. From the surrounding plains, this mountain offers quite a stunning view.

 ## Location

Mount Kilimanjaro is located in north-eastern Tanzania, overlooking Kenya. It lies south of the Equator some 321 kilometres away. The area is not quite mountainous. However, the nearest mountain to Mount Kilimanjaro is Mount Meru, which is 60 kilometres away to the southwest. It is 280 kilometres from the Indian Ocean and just over 400 kilometres from Lake Victoria. Mount Kilimanjaro is located in the Kilimanjaro National Park, which covers 756 square kilometres. From its base, Mount Kilimanjaro rises approximately 5,895 metres from the plains near Moshi, a Tanzanian municipality.

◀ *The Seven Summits are seven peaks in seven continents and Mount Kilimanjaro is one of the 'seven summits' on Earth*

 ## Formation

This stratovolcano began forming millions of years ago. It is made up of many layers of hardened volcanic ash, lava, pumice, and tephra from a volcanic eruption. It was formed, shaped, and scarred due to forces like fire and ice.

Millions of years ago, molten lava escaped through the fractured surface of the Great Rift Valley. This massive eruption forced some of Earth's crust upwards, creating the Shira volcano, the oldest one. However, it stopped erupting five million years ago and collapsed and formed into a caldera. A further eruption led to the formation of the Mawenzi volcano. Finally, four and a half million years ago, a massive eruption happened which resulted in the formation of Kibo. Kibo has erupted quite a few times, forcing the summit to a maximum height of 5,895 metres. A million years later, an enormous eruption from Kibo led to the formation of the shiny black stone—obsidian.

▼ *The tallest free-standing mountain (a mountain that stands alone and is not a part of a range) in the world is Mount Kilimanjaro's highest peak. It is a World Heritage Site declared by UNESCO*

 ## Geography

Mount Kilimanjaro comprises three volcanic cones. They are Kibo the summit, Mawenzi at 5,149 metres, and Shira at 3,962 metres. Uhuru Peak is the highest summit on Kibo's crater and rises upto 5,895 metres. It lies 160 kilometres east of the East African Rift System and 225 kilometres south of Kenya. There is a caldera on the snow-clad dome of Kibo, which is 1.93 kilometres across and 298 metres deep. On the other hand, Mawenzi's cone is jagged and eroded and has seasonal snow. The summit of Kibo, however, has become shorter today due to glacial erosion.

Ecosystem

The vegetation in Mount Kilimanjaro consists of giant lobelia, moss, and lichen. There are different species of bats and antelopes. Elephants, buffaloes, and eland (ox-like antelopes) can be found in the forests of the southern slopes and surrounding areas. Other animals common here are black-and-white colobus monkeys and blue monkeys.

▲ Colobos monkeys are rare, and the most arboreal species of monkey. They rarely descend to the ground, and their mantles and tails act like parachutes

▲ Between 1912 and 2011, nearly 85 per cent of the ice cap on Kibo has disappeared because of climate change

Mount Kilimanjaro's Glaciers

The glaciers on Mount Kilimanjaro are a wonderful sight to watch. It is a common misconception that glaciers can't exist in a region close to the Equator. However, this is untrue, and the glaciers on Mount Kilimanjaro are a sight to behold. The dazzling white colour of the ice reflects most of the heat and the glaciers survive. On the contrary, the black lava rocks on which the glaciers rest absorb heat. Though the heat does not affect the glacier's surface, the heat generated by the rocks below melts the glaciers. Hence, they become unstable, lose their grip and develop in an overhanging form.

Trivia

Mount Kilimanjaro has a unique ecosystem. It contains farmlands, rainforests, alpine deserts, heaths, moorlands, and an arctic summit. Around 30,000 to 35,000 people attempt to reach the summit of Mount Kilimanjaro every year. Coffee grows on Mount Kilimanjaro and is considered to be some of the world's best. Most of the beans are grown in the region's volcanic soils.

⊛ Incredible Individuals

German geographer Hans Meyer and Australian mountaineer Ludwig Purtscheller first reached the Kibo summit in 1889. Of the two, Purtscheller was one of the first mountaineers to climb without the aid of a mountain guide. Novices use their help to learn how to climb safely to the summit. Meyer and Purtscheller are considered to be the first Europeans to reach the summit of Mount Kilimanjaro.

The Sundarbans

The Sundarbans is a magnificent mangrove forest. It is also the largest mangrove forest in the world and a natural wonder. It is a saltwater swamp in the delta formed by the confluence of the rivers Ganga, Brahmaputra, and Meghna on the Bay of Bengal. It gets its name from the 'Sundari' trees in that region. The Sundarbans is famous for the conglomeration of islands. It is an archipelago of not 10 or 20, but 54 islands!

Location

The Sundarbans is located in the state of West Bengal in eastern India and also spreads to southern Bangladesh. This mangrove forest stretches for 260 kilometres from the estuary of the Hooghly River in India to the western portion of the Meghna River estuary in Bangladesh. It comprises dense forests and marshy islands. The total area of the Sundarbans, including both land and water, is approximately 10,000 square kilometres and three-fifths of it is in Bangladesh.

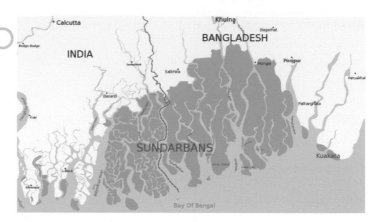

▲ *The Sundarbans on the map*

Geography

The land of the Sundarbans is a low-lying swamp approaching the coast that is made up of sand dunes and mudflats. Mangrove forests constitute about two-fifths of the total area of the Sundarbans with water covering half of it. The landscape is constantly changing through erosion by wind and sea along the coast and also by loads of silt and other sediments that get deposited along many estuaries. The landscape in recent times has been altered by human activities, especially deforestation. There is also a change in the landscape because plenty of river water too has been diverted for agricultural activities, enhancing the damage. Salinity in the mangrove swamps has moved farther inland, especially in the Indian sector of the territory.

Sundarban Mangroves

A mangrove is a tree or shrub that grows in tidal, chiefly tropical, and coastal swamps. They have numerous tangled roots that grow above the ground and form dense thickets. They have the ability to adapt to the salinity of the water.

The Sundarbans has the largest mangrove forest in the world shared between India and Bangladesh. The species that are dominant are the '*Heritiera fomes*' locally known as *sundri* or *sundari*. Mangrove forests have a thick canopy, and the undergrowth is mostly seedlings of the mangrove trees.

▶ *Prolific mangrove vegetation distinguishes the Sundarbans*

Sundarbans Delta

The Sundarbans are part of the world's largest delta. They are areas of vast forestland formed at the lower parts of the Gangetic Delta. This vast delta also called the Bengal delta is formed by the super confluence of the Ganges, Hooghly, Padma, Brahmaputra river in India, and Meghna river across southern Bangladesh.

Ecology

Apart from the Ganga, Brahmaputra and Meghna Rivers, others in this region are the Hooghly, Thakuran, Malta, and Gosaba. This area is prone to frequent cyclonic storms accompanied by tidal waves. Therefore, the region experiences devastating floods from September to November. However, the swampy land and dense forests are still home to plenty of plants and a variety of wildlife.

The dominant flora of the Sundarbans are the *Sundari* and gengwa, nipa palms, and other salt-tolerant species of plants. The region is known for its large variety of animal species. Most of the animal species here today are becoming endangered. It is one of the last preserves of Bengal Tigers, which are found in abundance in this region. Other animals found here are spotted deer, wild boars, otters, wildcats, and Ganges river dolphins. The other species that once inhabited the region are Javan rhinoceroses, guar, and water buffalo, which are now believed to be extinct in the region. Amphibians and reptiles are also found in the Sundarbans. This region is home to many bird species. Of them, some are migratory. They include hornbills, storks and other waders, kingfishers, white ibises, and raptors such as sea eagles.

In Real Life

It is quite interesting to know that the Sundarbans in India are 10 times bigger than the city of Venice in Italy. Of the 102 islands of the Sundarbans Forest on the Indian side, only 54 are inhabited. The rest of the area is mostly forest.

What's So Special?

Apart from the largest mangrove forest, the Sundarbans has the largest number of Royal Bengal Tigers—96 of them. The Sundarbans Tiger Reserve was formed in 1973, and the National Park was established in 1984. Boats are the only means of transport in this area. The evergreen Sundarbans is a World Heritage Site declared by UNESCO.

◀ *Many species of hornbills have a helmet-like structure on their upper mandibles called casques. These add strength to their bills and augments their calls*

▼ *Despite their dwindling numbers, the Bengal Tigers rule the jungles in the Sundarbans*

The Giant Crystal Cave

One of the world's most marvelous natural wonders is the Giant Crystal Cave in Mexico. Two brothers Eloy and Javier Delgado discovered the crystal cave in the year 2000. They were excavating new tunnels in the Naica Mine in search of fresh reserves of zinc, silver, and lead when they discovered the cave. It is one of the most spectacular geographical discoveries on Earth.

Location

The Giant Crystal Cave is connected to the Naica Mine in Naica, Chihuahua, in Mexico. It is 300 metres below the surface in Naica. The cave contains giant selenite crystals, some of the largest natural crystals ever found.

Giant Crystal Cave

Mexico

◀ The location of the Giant Crystal Caves in Mexico

▲ Selenite is a crystallised form of gypsum. It typically appears as a translucent, multifaceted stone

Formation

The Naica mine and cave are above an underground magma chamber. This magma heated the groundwater, which had sulphide ions (S^{2-}). The cool water on the surface was exposed to the heated water but did not mix, as there was a distinct difference in densities. The oxygen slowly circulated into the heated water and oxidised the sulphides (S^{2-}) into sulphates (SO_4^{-2}).The moist sulphate gypsum crystallised at an extremely slow rate, over millions of years, forming the huge crystals found today.

👤 In Real Life

The largest crystal of the Giant Crystal Cave is around 12 metres long, has a diameter of 4 metres and weighs approximately 50,000 kilograms.

▲ The gypsum crystals in Mexico's Giant Crystal Cave

ⓞ Incredible Individuals

Speleology is the study of caves. Edouard Alfred Martel (1859-1938), the father of modern speleology, was a pioneer in cave exploration. He introduced speleology as a scientific study. He also founded the French Federation of Speleology and received the Legion of Honour.

▶ Martel travelled extensively throughout Europe and strongly promoted the study of speleology striving to increase its recognition as a scientific field

🌐 Description

The Giant Crystal Cave is a horseshoe-shaped cavity in limestone. The floor of the cave is covered with perfectly faceted crystalline blocks. There are very big crystal beams that protrude out from both the blocks and the floor. The caves can be accessed today because a mining company has pumped out the water from the caves. Otherwise without the regular pumping operations, the caves would have again been submerged in water. The crystals deteriorate in air, so the Naica Project is trying to visually document them. The selenite crystals measure around 6 metres in length, but some are even 11 metres and are **translucent**. The temperature varies from 45° C to 50° C, and the humidity is 100 per cent.

🌐 What's So Special?

The Giant Crystal Cave has been growing considerably over the past half a million years. It is home to stacks of selenite. The conditions inside the caves are so extreme that being here for more than 10 minutes could be dangerous without proper equipment. The cave is often visited by scientists. One such expedition took place in 2006, led by crystallographer Paolo Forti, of Italy's University of Bologna.

There are more chambers connected to the Giant Crystal Cave, but to reach those would require the destruction of numerous crystals. With the help of **uranium dating**, scientists have determined that the crystals are 500,000 years old. In 2017, researchers found dormant microbes inside them. Researchers believe that these microbes were trapped inside at least 10,000 years ago.

◀ The expedition in 2006 required the invention of special suits for entering the Giant Crystal Cave

The Galápagos Islands

Galápagos Islands or 'Columbus Archipelago' is a group of islands in the eastern Pacific Ocean, a province of Ecuador. Part of the Galápagos Islands was made into a wildlife sanctuary in 1935, and in 1959, it became the Galápagos National Park. These islands were declared a UNESCO World Heritage Site in 1978. The formation of the Galápagos Islands makes them an example of a natural wonder. The islands were formed due to the tectonic activities in the region. These islands are ever changing, new ones emerge and the older ones go back into the ocean.

Location

The Galápagos Islands are located in Ecuador near the Pacific Ocean. These islands lie 1,000 kilometres west of South America. The islands have emerged from the bottom of the sea after major volcanic eruptions. The archipelago consists of 19 islands, dozens of **islets**, and rock formations. It covers an area of 45,000 square kilometres.

Formation

The Galápagos Islands were formed in a unique way. They were basically formed due to the interaction of tectonic plates and hot-spot volcanism. These islands are a result of lava piles. They are dotted with shield volcanoes, some being periodically active. The roughness of the dry landscapes is highlighted by volcanic mountains, craters, and cliffs.

▲ The location of the Galápagos Islands in Ecuador

Isn't It Amazing!

Anyone who visits Floreana Island in the Galápagos, should make a point of stopping by a barrel-shaped post box that was placed there by whaling ships in the 18th century. Tourists enjoy a piece of history that they can relate to in present times, even if it is a bit outmoded in this day and age.

▲ Post Office Bay, Floreana Island, Galápagos

Geography

The Galápagos Islands comprises of 20 islands, 42 islets, and over 250 rocks. The islands have a land area of 8,010 square kilometres. They are scattered over 45,000 square kilometres of ocean. The largest island is Isabela and it is approximately 131 kilometres long and constitutes two-third of the total area of the archipelago. Mount Azul, at 5,541 feet, is the highest point of the Galápagos Islands. Santa Cruz is the second largest island.

Incredible Individuals

Tomás de Berlanga, the Bishop of Panama, discovered the Galápagos Islands in 1535 when his ship drifted away from its route while going towards Peru. He named them Las Encantadas or 'the enchanted'.

Ecology

The ecosystem of the Galápagos Islands is strange but unique. Most of the plant and animal species here are **endemic**. Unlike an equatorial environment, this place does not have tropical vegetation. It is more like an arid region. The different plant species have adapted themselves to the prevailing conditions. Galápagos flora has been classified into three zones. The dry lowlands are covered with cactus forests which are at a higher zone and are dominated by pisonia and guava trees. The moist forest region is dominated by Scalesia forests with dense underbrush. The upland zone is more or less treeless with ferns and grasses.

The archipelago has diverse and unusual animals, one being the Galápagos giant tortoise. Some of these animals are not found anywhere else on Earth. Animals such as Galápagos iguanas, marine iguanas, and Sally Lightfoot crabs are quite common here. There are 15 different species of birds called Darwin's finches. Other birds common to this region are the frigatebirds, waved albatross, and cormorants. A famous creature of these islands is the blue-footed booby.

▲ These tortoises found in the Galápagos Islands are the biggest on Earth and surprisingly can go without eating for a year

▼ The Galápagos Islands have several active volcanoes. Sierra Negra erupted in 2018

Climate

The Galápagos Islands get low rainfall, have low humidity, and low air and water temperature. Since it is near the Equator, the weather remains stable throughout the year. Yet, there are two different seasons. These two seasons are responsible for turning the Islands either into a green and lush tropical land or into a barren tropical desert. The islands experience rainfall during the hot season in the months from December to May. June to November is the dry season with the southeast trade winds bringing a fresh and dry climate to the islands. Air temperature in the Island is around 28° C and average rainfall is measured approximately around 1.9 centimetres.

What's So Special?

The Galápagos Islands attract tourists for their diverse wildlife. It is the only place in the Northern Hemisphere where penguins are found in their natural habitat. Swimming lizards are another unique animal found here. Wildlife here has not been disturbed by human activities, which makes it a serene place. On the Santa Cruz Island is the Charles Darwin Research Station that promotes scientific studies. It works towards protecting the ecosystem of the Galápagos.

▼ Galápagos penguins are found on the western islands of Isabela and Fernandina

The Great Blue Hole

The Great Blue Hole is a large underwater sinkhole off the coast of Belize. A blue hole is a large marine **cavern** that is open on the surface and has developed in an island composed of a carbonate bedrock that is limestone or coral reef.

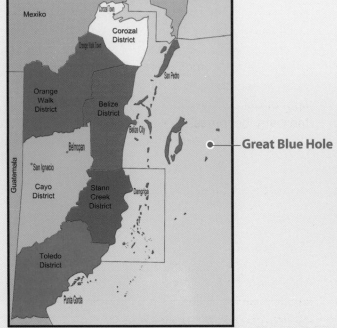

Location

The Great Blue Hole is in the continent of North America. It lies near the centre of the Lighthouse Reef, a small **atoll** that is 100 kilometres from the mainland of Belize, a country located on the northeast coast of Central America. It is bounded by Mexico to the north, Guatemala to the west and south, and the Caribbean Sea to the east. It's coastline runs across 280 kilometres.

Formation

Generally, blue holes are formed from sinkholes that develop slowly over time, with the erosion of rocks. Many blue holes on Earth were formed during the last Ice Age. The sea levels rose and filled existing sinkholes with water. The phenomena has been named the blue hole due to the dark navy blue colour of the water in the deep. However, the shallow waters that surround it are lighter and turquoise blue. The Great Blue Hole was originally formed as a limestone cave during the last Ice Age when the sea level was low. Thousands of years ago, when the oceans began to rise, the cave flooded and the Great Blue Hole was formed. It has a vertical entrance over 300 metres across with a bottom more than 125 metres below the sea's surface today.

Description

The Great Blue Hole is at the centre of the Lighthouse Reef, where a coral island encircles the light turquoise-coloured waters of a lagoon. Water levels there are shallow; therefore, parts of the ring surrounding the dark blue sinkhole can be seen during a low tide. Darker and deeper ocean waters surround the hole. Atolls usually glow in vibrant hues of turquoise, peacock blue, or aquamarine. The combination of pale corals with water creates unique blue-green shades. Within this small sea of light colours lies a giant circle of deep blue called the Great Blue Hole.

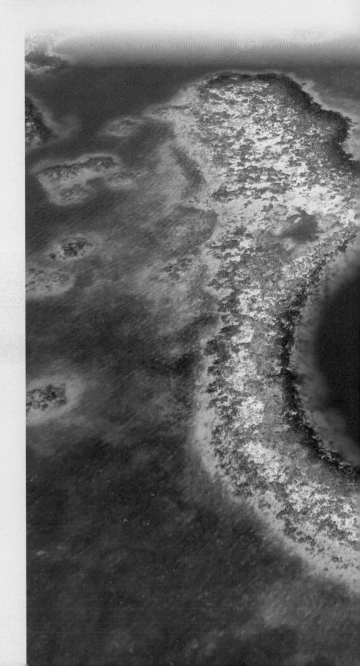

What's So Special?

The Great Blue Hole is part of the larger Belize Barrier Reef Reserve System. UNESCO has designated it as a World Heritage Site. The hole is an opening to a system of caves, and in many places, hanging stalactites are seen, which indicate that it might once have been above water. The Great Blue Hole is visible from outer space and can be identified by its barrier reef. It is a dive spot of Belize. The more one descends the Blue Hole, the clearer the water becomes. This allows a diver to have a good view of the varied marine life inside. Different types of sharks are found within this natural wonder.

Diving in the Great Blue Hole can be exciting, but it requires special skills. Divers are privileged to witness fascinating geological formations that cannot be seen elsewhere. However, the insides are not so colourful, instead, divers witness a dark cave with stalactites. Another special feature of the Great Blue Hole is the famous Blue Hole Monument at the centre of the Lighthouse Reef. Though it does not contain many marine attractions, it is still a diver's delight.

▼ *An aerial view of the Great Blue Hole*

▲ *Divers can explore thousands of stalactites and stalagmites that were formed when the Blue Hole was a series of caverns*

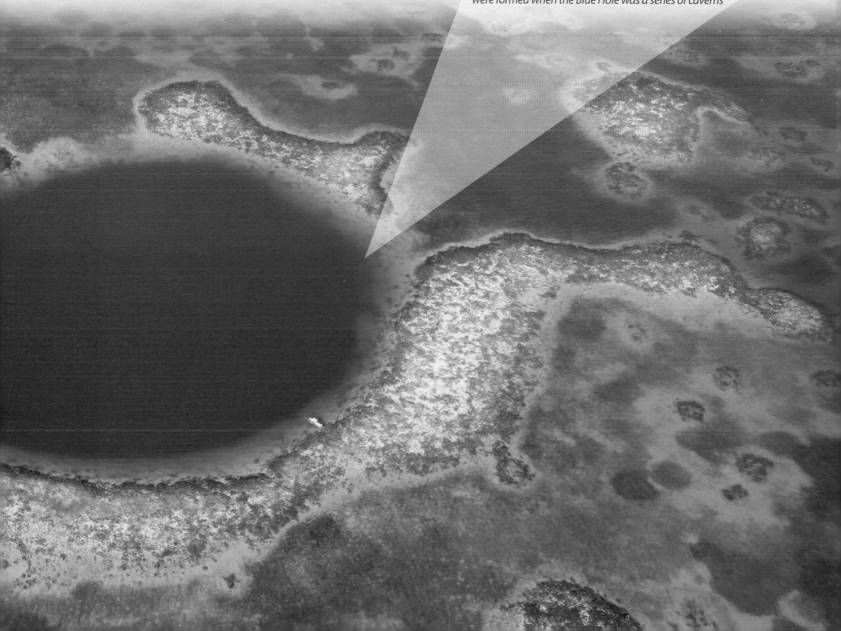

The Ha Long Bay

Ha Long Bay is a beautiful and mysteriously attractive natural wonder. It is located in Vietnam, in Southeast Asia. The meaning of Ha Long Bay is 'descending dragon bay'. According to mythology, gods sent dragons who dropped jewels from their mouths into the bay, forming islands. A beautiful sight here is the cave known as 'Theing Cung Grotto' or 'Heavenly Cave.'

 ## Location

Ha Long Bay is located on the northwest coast of the Gulf of Tonkin, near the city of Ha Long, in the Quang Ninh province of northern Vietnam. This bay lies 164 kilometres to the southeast of Hanoi. The area of the bay is 1,500 square kilometres and it has some 3,000 rocky islands. They are in the form of jagged limestone pillars jutting out from the sea. There are also some caves and **grottoes**. All of these together make a picturesque seascape of Ha Long Bay.

● — **Ha Long Bay**

◀ *The bay extends 120 kilometres along the coastline*

Geology

Three things have worked simultaneously to develop the **karst** topography of Ha Long Bay. These landforms have thick limestone layers, hot and moist climate, and slow tectonic plate movements. Presumably, this went on for 20 million years. For millions of years, Ha Long Bay has undergone several geological processes. 500 million years ago, it was a deep sea. However, around 340 million years ago, it became shallow.

🔍 In Real Life

A cave known as the Hospital Cave served both as a secret, bomb-proof hospital and a safe house for Vietnamese leaders during the America-Vietnam War. It was used until 1975.

▲ *The Hospital Cave*

Description

There are 1,600 limestone islands in the Ha Long Bay. Most of the islands in Ha Long Bay are limestone, which have been forming for over 500 million years. These limestone islands make the Ha Long Bay unique. However, most of the islands are not inhabited, as the limestone topography makes it difficult. The bay has huge caves on some of the islands. Hang Dau Go (translated as the 'wooden stakes cave') stands as the largest grotto (natural or artificial) in the Ha Long area. There are many islands that have not been named. On the other hand, some are named according to their shapes, for example, Voi Island means 'elephant island'. Due to the steep edges and heights, some have not been explored yet.

▲ A cave on the Ha Long Bay island

Ecology

There are two types of ecosystems in the Ha Long Bay. One is a tropical, moist, evergreen rainforest, while the other is a marine and coastal ecosystem. The temperature here is between 15° C–25° C. Rainfall measures upto 2,000–2,200 milimetres. Ha Long Bay has the typical diurnal tide system. The salt content in the waters is higher in the dry season and lower in the rainy season. The bay is 33 feet deep and rich with marine life. The Ha Long Bay has 450 different **molluscs** and 200 different species of fish.

The World Nature Conservation Society has discovered that seven plant species of the Ha Long Bay are found only on limestone islands and nowhere else on Earth. They are 'Livistona halongensis', 'Impatiens halongensis', 'Chirita halongensis', 'Chirita hiepii', 'Chirita modesta', 'Paraboea halongensis' and 'Alpinia calcicola'. There are also species other than those mentioned here. The rare and endangered Cat Ba Langur is found here. There are plenty of monkeys too. The variety of birds here includes hawks, cuckoos and hornbills. Unfortunately, many species of fish here are being threatened by the game fishing, i.e., fishing for pleasure that occurs near the coral reefs.

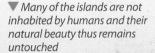

▼ Many of the islands are not inhabited by humans and their natural beauty thus remains untouched

◄ The Cat Ba Langur is on the brink of extinction as merely 70 such animals remain on earth

What's So Special?

Nguyen Tai, a scholar and poet called it 'rock wonder in the sea', some 500 years ago. UNESCO classified the core of Ha Long Bay as a World Heritage Site in 1994.

OCEANS
&
WATERBODIES

THE GREAT OCEAN

Earth is the only planet in the solar system to have stable bodies of liquid water on the surface. 70 per cent of its surface is covered with water. This vast, salty, and continuous body of water is called the ocean. Apart from the ocean, there are other waterbodies on Earth. They come in different shapes and sizes from seas to rivers, lakes, ponds, bays, gulfs, and straits. These are much smaller than the oceans and each of them contain a different ecosystem with plants, animals, and fish unique to their environment.

Most of the above-mentioned waterbodies are naturally formed geographical features with some exceptions. There are some small waterbodies that are artificial and contained. These along with some smaller waterbodies that are not contained are navigable and referred to as waterways.

▼ *The ocean is a great resource for human beings as it provides water, food, and a source of transportation*

What is an Ocean?

Oceans make a continuous body of salt water covering 70 per cent of Earth's surface. Oceans contain almost 98 per cent of all water on Earth. Ocean water is salty due to the presence of a chemical substance called **sodium chloride** or salt. More than 95 per cent of our oceans are still unexplored.

▲ There is so much salt in the ocean that if you took it all out and spread it evenly over the planet's surface, it would form a layer more than 152 metres in height

▼ There is enough water in the oceans to fill up a cube whose edges are 1,000 kilometres in length

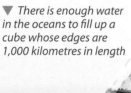 Formation

This vast body of water makes Earth different from other planets in the solar system. Oceans have been present on Earth's surface for about four billion years, carving the coastline, driving the climate, and controlling life. However, 4.5 billion years ago, when Earth was born, it was a molten **inferno**. There was no place for liquid water, but the elements to create water were present deep within the newly formed planet. When the first volcanoes erupted, the gas that came out was steam. Later, molten rocks cooled and clouds formed. Consequently, it rained for centuries and filled the basins that are now our oceans.

In Real Life

Half of the oxygen present in the atmosphere is produced from ocean water.

Threat to Oceans

Despite the fact that oceans provide useful materials, they are prone to damage due to overfishing, pollution, etc. **Overfishing** means that people take too many fish from the water, too quickly; even faster than they can naturally be replaced. It is important to take care of aquatic ecosystems because their loss spells consequences for all living beings. The climate and weather, the air we breathe, the food we eat, all depend on oceans. Oceans are the most important source of nourishment for all the different kinds of life on Earth.

▲ The ocean, which is home to many species of fish, has been polluted by human activities over the years

Names of Oceans

There are five major oceans. These are the Pacific Ocean, the Indian Ocean, the Atlantic Ocean, the Arctic Ocean, and the Antarctic or Southern Ocean. The fifth ocean is the newest one considered by the International Hydrographic Organisation (IHO). However, the three major oceans of the world are the Pacific, the Atlantic, and the Indian Oceans. They are called the three great oceans. Different cultures had different names for them through the ages, but the current names were first made a long time ago—as early as 450 BCE for the Atlantic, and in the 1500s for the others.

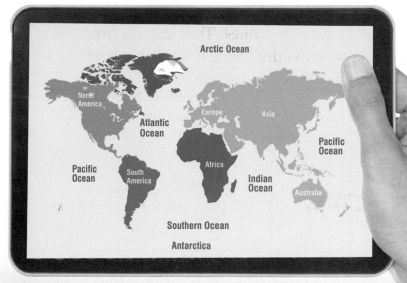

▲ The map marks all the continents and the surrounding oceans. Actually, Earth has only one continuous ocean but it is demarcated according to landmasses

Isn't It Amazing!

Water in the ocean is constantly and continuously moving. It is like a conveyor belt in a factory. So, the global ocean conveyor belt is the name given to the system of constantly moving and circulating water. This movement is driven by salinity and temperature.

▼ Over the years, ports have come to be hubs of human activities

Releasing Water

Rainfall made up only half of our present oceans. According to some scientists, the rest of the water came from space. During Earth's formative years, it was hit by thousands of **comets** which were made of ice. When the downpour stopped, Earth filled up with thousands of litres of water.

Water has always been present in Earth's mantle. It was gradually released after volcanic eruptions. In fact, water is still being released from Earth's mantle after volcanic eruptions.

The water in the oceans is attracted to the surface due to the gravitational pull of Earth. It cannot leave the planet through natural means.

▲ A comet is filled with dust, rock, and ice. They are informally called "dirty snowballs"

Peeling Back Layers

Scientists have divided the ocean into five main layers. These layers are known as zones. They extend from the surface to the most extreme depths where light cannot penetrate.

The ocean deep zones are where some of the most fascinating creatures are found. As the depth of an ocean increases, the temperature drops at an extraordinary rate. However, the pressure increases. Each of the ocean's layers have their own characteristics.

▶ *Kelp is a seaweed found underwater near coastal regions*

 ## Epipelagic Zone

The epipelagic zone, also known as the sunlight zone of the ocean, starts from the water's surface and extends for 200 metres. There is plenty of light and heat within this layer and most oceanic life and human activities occur here. However, both light and heat decrease as the depth increases. The pressure here is low, but it increases with depth. Coral reefs can be found in this layer. Photosynthesis for aquatic plants can only happen in this level.

Epipelagic Zone
(0–200 metres)

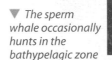 ## Bathypelagic Zone

The next layer is called the bathypelagic zone, also known as the midnight zone. This zone is dark, with the only visible light coming from its aquatic animals. Some examples of the animals found here are the pelican eel and humpback anglerfish. The penetration of sunlight is very low, hence many animals in this layer are either black or red. This is for their defence because only minute amounts of blue-green light reach this zone. The colour red and black are not reflected in this light. Some whale species, such as the sperm whale, spend some time at this level in search of food.

Wolf eel

▼ *The sperm whale occasionally hunts in the bathypelagic zone*

Bathypelagic Zone
(1,000–4,000 metres)

👤 In Real Life

The lowest and the deepest point on Earth is the Mariana Trench. It is found in the floor of the western North Pacific Ocean. The Mariana Trench stretches for more than 2,550 kilometres with a mean width of 69 kilometres. The greatest depths are reached in the Challenger Deep at 11,034 metres. The Mariana Trench was designated as US national monument in 2009 as it is within the territories of US dependencies.

Dumbo octopus

Hadalpelagic Zone
(6,000 metres onwards)

💡 Isn't It Amazing!

Earth's longest chain of mountains, the Mid-Ocean Ridge, is almost entirely beneath the ocean. It is a continuous range of underwater volcanoes that wraps around the globe like seam on a baseball. It stretches nearly 65,000 kilometres. The majority of the system is underwater, with an average water depth to the top of the ridge of 2,500 metres.

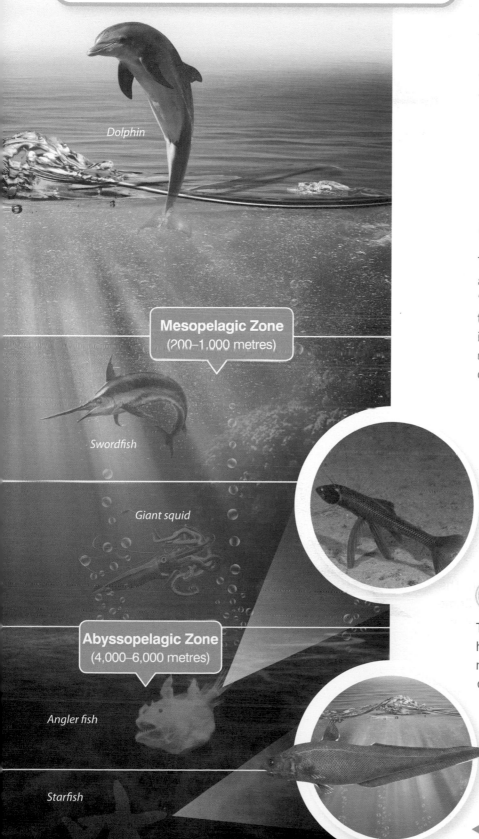

Dolphin

Mesopelagic Zone
(200–1,000 metres)

Swordfish

Giant squid

Abyssopelagic Zone
(4,000–6,000 metres)

Angler fish

Starfish

Mesopelagic Zone

Below the epipelagic zone lies the mesopelagic zone or the twilight zone. It starts 200 metres from the surface and extends to 1,000 metres from the surface. This twilight or mid-water zone is home to some aquatic animals like the swordfish and wolf eel. Sunlight here is sparse, but the light of bioluminescent creatures is visible. A diverse set of fish including swordfish, squid, and cuttlefish, can be found here.

Abyssopelagic Zone

The abyssopelagic zone is also known as the abyss. The name originates from the Greek word 'abyssus' meaning 'bottomless'. In this zone, the temperatures are near freezing point and there is no penetration of natural light. As there is no sunlight, there are no plants. Three-fifths of the ocean floor falls within this zone.

◄ Animals like the abyssal octopus and tripod fish, etc., are found in the abyssopelagic zone

Hadalpelagic Zone

The ocean trenches are found in the hadalpelagic zone. This zone begins 6,000 metres from the surface and extends to the deepest parts of the ocean floor. The depth of this layer depends on the trenches and valleys in the area. In Puerto Rico, fish were discovered as deep as 8,369 metres. The pressure exerted at this zone is equal to that of 48 jet planes.

◄ The grenadier fish are the most abundant fish found in this zone

The Five Major Oceans

There is only one true ocean on Earth. This connected body of water surrounds the seven continents. It has been demarcated into five oceans by scientists so that they can study and understand them better. These are the Pacific, Atlantic, Indian, Arctic, and the Southern Ocean.

🌐 Why are Oceans Blue?

The water in the ocean appears blue because sunlight falls on it. Sunlight is white light. The water absorbs the red, orange, and yellow wavelengths from this white light more strongly than it does the blue wavelengths. In fact, it even reflects these blue wavelengths. That is why the ocean water and sky appear blue.

⭐ Incredible Individuals

Film director James Cameron has made a number of trips and expeditions to the ocean deep. He has dived on the wreck of the Titanic multiple times, and is 1 of 4 people who have made their way to the depth of the Challenger Deep, the deepest point in the Mariana Trench.

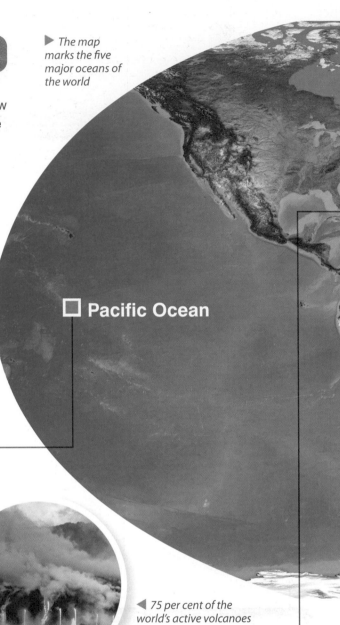

▶ *The map marks the five major oceans of the world*

 Pacific Ocean

🌐 The Pacific Ocean

The Pacific Ocean is the biggest ocean in the world. It covers more than 30 per cent of Earth's surface. The name 'Pacific' comes from the Latin word '*pacificus*', meaning 'peaceful ocean'. However, it is not that calm and peaceful, as the Ring of Fire is located near it. There are too many volcanoes in this region, and volcanic eruptions occur quite frequently along with earthquakes.

◀ *75 per cent of the world's active volcanoes are located in the Pacific Ocean basin*

▼ *The photograph shows a part of the Atlantic Ocean Road, an 8.3 kilometres road that connects the island of Averøy, Norway, with the mainland*

🌐 The Atlantic Ocean

The Atlantic is the second-biggest ocean in the world and lies between the continents of America, Europe, and Africa. It is about half the size of the Pacific Ocean, covering roughly 20 per cent of Earth's surface. It was mentioned for the first time in 450 BCE as '*Atlantis thalassa*' in the book *The Histories* by Herodotus, meaning the 'Sea of Atlas'.

🌐 The Arctic Ocean

The Arctic ocean is the smallest and shallowest among the major oceans. It is located entirely within the Arctic Circle and covers around 4 per cent of Earth's surface. It occupies the region of the North Pole. Once called the Frozen Ocean, most of the Arctic Ocean is covered with ice throughout the year.

▼ *The Arctic Ocean's name is derived from the Greek word 'arktikos', which means 'bear'*

Arctic Ocean

Atlantic Ocean

Pacific Ocean

Indian Ocean

Southern Ocean

🌐 The Southern Ocean

The Antarctic Ocean was recently renamed as the Southern Ocean. The Atlantic, Indian, and Pacific Ocean basins merge into icy waters around Antarctica. It is the fourth-largest ocean located at the southernmost point of the planet and surrounds Antarctica. The Southern Ocean is the least explored and least understood marine region in the world.

▶ *The deepest point in the Indian Ocean is the Sunda Trench with a depth of 7,725 metres*

▶ *The Southern Ocean has the largest ocean current flowing from the west to the east, and is called the Antarctic Circumpolar Current*

🌐 The Indian Ocean

The Indian Ocean covers one-fifth of the world's oceans and is the third largest after the Pacific and the Atlantic Oceans. It is geologically the youngest and physically the most complex among the three major oceans. The Indian Ocean is bounded by Australia in the East, by Africa in the West, by Asia in the North and the Atlantic Ocean in the South. It is said to be the warmest ocean of all.

Life in the Ocean

The term 'marine life' refers to all the living organisms living in Earth's waters. These include a diverse array of plants, animals, and other organisms such as **bacteria** and **archaea**. It is believed that about one million species of animals live in the ocean. Among these, 95 per cent are invertebrates such as jellyfish and shrimp.

Incredible Individuals

Marie Lebour (1876–1971) was a British marine biologist (a person who studies marine life in great detail). She researched the life cycles of different marine animals like molluscs and microplankton. She discovered 28 new species of microplankton which she described in her written works. She also conducted research on the eggs and larval stages of herrings and sprats.

▲ Some species of jellyfish are immortal. For example, the immortal jellyfish—*Turritopsis dohrnii*—found in the Mediterranean Sea and in the waters of Japan cannot die of old age

🌐 Flora

An ocean is a large and deep body of water. Plants and animals are found in all different parts of the oceans except for regions where there is no sunlight. Marine plants provide food, shelter, and protection for the animals. One can find great diversity in the flora of the ocean, from **microscopic** plankton to the *Nymphaeaceae*, a giant species of the water lily plant.

There are two types of plants found in the ocean—rooted plants and floating plants. Rooted plants, as the name suggests, are plants whose roots are attached to the ocean floor. They need sunlight, so they grow near the shores and in shallow waters. Floating plants drift freely without attached roots. They grow on the water's surface.

A majority of the plants are tiny algae called phytoplankton. All these microscopic plants have a big job to do. They produce half the world's oxygen, which human beings and all other organisms require for survival. There are some bigger algae in the water called seaweed and kelp. We can even find forests in the ocean called kelp forests. They are present in cold and shallow waters. These big plants provide food and shelter to a variety of marine life.

◀ Seaweeds are used in foods, fertilisers and cosmetics. They also have medicinal value

 ◀ Sea lily

Fauna

Fish, sponges, sea anemones, and corals are some examples of marine animals. Crustaceans are invertebrates that have exoskeletons. They are also considered to be marine animals. Crabs, shrimp, and lobsters are examples of crustaceans. But marine diversity is not just limited to fish and crustaceans, even some mammals live in the water. Dolphins, porpoises, and manatees are examples of marine mammals. A common vertebrate found in the ocean is the bristlemouth fish. It is a tiny ocean fish that glows in the dark and has needle-like fangs.

▲ Shrimp caught from the ocean

Marine animals can be divided into three groups—zooplankton, nektons, and benthos. The word plankton originates from the Greek word '*planktos*', which means 'wandering'. Zooplankton, such as jellyfish, are drifting or floating animals. They are very small. It is difficult to see these creatures with the naked eye. Nektons are free swimmers and most of the ocean animals belong to this class. Octopuses, dolphins, whales, eels, squids, and sharks are examples of nektons. Benthos are the animals that spend their entire lives at the bottom of the ocean. Lobsters, oysters, and some species of worms and snails are examples of benthos.

▶ Nekton, such as dolphins, can live in both shallow and deep ocean waters

▼ Coral reefs show some of the greatest bio-diversity in the world, enough so that we are still finding new species

Isn't It Amazing!

The eel uses its shock to stun its prey, and keep predators at bay. The shock of an electric eel has been known to knock a horse off its feet. Now that's shocking!

▲ Electric eel

The Ocean in Motion

The water in the ocean is never still. It is constantly moving from north to south, east to west, and up and down the shores around the world. These movements can be influenced by the movement and force of local winds. The ocean's movements can also be influenced by the Earth's rotation and revolution, as well as the position of the Moon and the Sun in relation to the Earth. These different movements are categorised as waves, tides, and ocean currents. The movements are also influenced by the temperature, salinity, and **density** of water.

▲ *The waves hit a road built over the ocean*

Waves

Waves create oscillatory movements that cause the rise and fall of surface water. These are horizontal movements. Waves are created by energy, which moves across the ocean's surface. This energy is provided by the winds. The winds transfer energy to the water on the ocean's surface.

The transfer of that energy may create tiny ripples that disappear when the winds die down. Or, the energy may create larger waves that continue until they reach the shore. Each water particle moves in a circular manner in waves. There are two parts of a wave, the raised part is called the crest and the lower part is called the trough. Waves are measured by their wavelengths, that is the horizontal distance between the crests.

Ocean Currents

An ocean current is a continuous, directed movement of ocean water generated by a number of forces acting upon the water, such as the wind, the Earth's rotation, temperature, and salinity. The ocean currents that are driven by winds move clockwise in the Northern Hemisphere and counter-clockwise in the Southern Hemisphere. As the water moves in these ocean currents, it brings cold water towards the Equator on the west coasts. At the same time, it brings warm water towards the poles on the east coasts. Ocean currents occur in all the major oceans. The Gulf Stream in the Atlantic Ocean is an ocean current.

▼ *The diagram shows the flow of the warm and the cold water currents in the ocean*

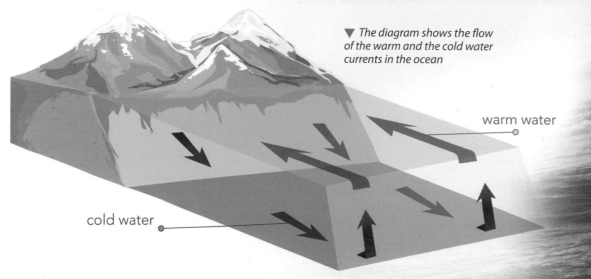

warm water

cold water

Types of Ocean Currents

There are two types of ocean currents—warm ocean currents and cold ocean currents. Ocean currents that flow from the equatorial regions towards the poles and have a higher surface temperature are called warm ocean currents. They move warm waters to the cool regions. In the Northern Hemisphere, they are found on the west coasts of the continents in the higher latitudes, for example, the Alaskan and Norwegian Currents.

Ocean currents that flow from the polar regions towards the Equator and have a lower surface temperature are called cold currents. They carry cold water towards the warmer regions. They occur on the west coasts of the continents in the low and middle latitudes of both hemispheres. In the Northern Hemisphere, they are found on the east coast in the higher latitudes, for example, the Labrador, East Greenland, and Oyashio Currents.

Isn't It Amazing!

Earth tides are deformations of the solid earth caused by the sun and moon's periodic gravitational attractions. They occur on a regular basis due to the Earth's rotation in the solar and lunar gravitational fields. The lunar-solar attractions often cause elastic deformations in the solid earth, causing the Earth's shape to change and the vertical to be distorted.

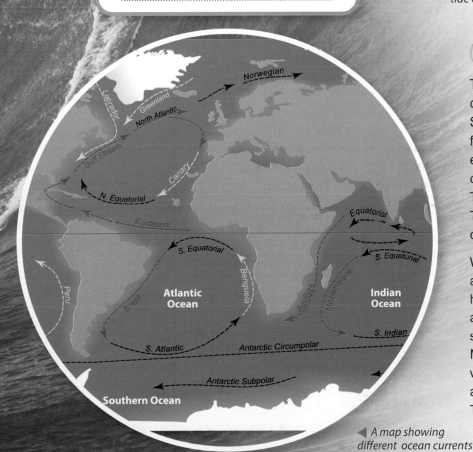

A map showing different ocean currents

 ## Tides

▲ High tide meter

The movement of a tide is the periodic rise and fall of water, which occurs once or twice in a day. These are vertical movements of water caused mainly due to the gravitational pull of Earth's Moon. The greatest height reached as the water rises is known as high tide or flood tide. The lowest level reached as the water falls is known as low tide or ebb. Tides are classified according to their frequency or the position of the Sun, Earth and Moon when they occur.

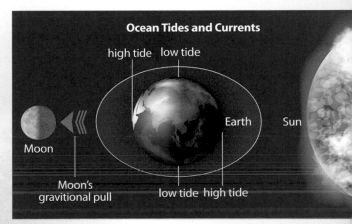

▲ The diagram shows how the position of the moon and its gravitational pull influence high tide and low tide on Earth

 ## Types of Tides

Tides based on frequency are the semi-diurnal tide, diurnal tide, and mixed tide. Semi-diurnal tides are the most common, featuring two high tides and two low tides each day. The diurnal tides feature only one high tide and one low tide each day. The mixed tides have variations in heights. These are common along the western coast of North America.

When the Sun, Moon, and Earth are in a straight line, the height of the tide is higher than normal. This is known as a spring tide. On the other hand, after seven days of the spring tide, when the Moon and the Sun stand at right angles with regard to Earth's position, the tides are lower than normal.
This is known as the neap tide.

Importance of Oceans

Oceans cover roughly three-fourths of our planet. They are of great importance not only to human beings but to each and every living organism on Earth. Surprisingly, oceans are the world's largest producer of food. They also provide minerals, oil, and natural gas. They produce more than half the world's oxygen and absorb carbon dioxide. It is estimated that oceans produce around 50–80 per cent of the oxygen on Earth and absorb almost one third of the carbon dioxide emitted. Oceans and ocean currents maintain the global climate by absorbing heat from the Sun.

70%
WATER

Food Source

Oceans are a great source of protein as they contain many different species of fish that are consumed by billions of people. Algae and sea plants are used for cooking delicacies such as sushi. It is believed that there are more than 2.2 million different species of animals that live underwater. It is possible that there are species of animals yet to be discovered.

Occupation

Statistics reveal that 59.6 million people around the world are engaged in fishing and **aquaculture**. Therefore, oceans are a source of income for many. However, our oceans are facing major threats due to global warming, pollution, habitat destruction, invasive species, and a dramatic decrease in ocean fish stocks. These threats to the oceans are so extensive that more than 40 per cent of the ocean area has been severely affected and no area has been left untouched. It is therefore important for us to protect oceans.

Regulating Climate

Oceans regulate the climate on Earth in many ways. The water soaks up heat and transports the warm water from the Equator to the poles, and cold water from the poles to the tropics by the movement of the ocean currents. Without these movements, the global climate would have been inhospitable.

In Real Life

There is a component in phytoplankton known as beta-carotene. It can protect the corneas of our eyes and has a lot of minerals that can improve our vision.

◀ *Phytoplankton is incredibly nutritious*

Oxygen

Though there are no trees in the oceans, algae and phytoplankton act as trees and fill the atmosphere with ample oxygen. These organisms may be microscopic, but they do a very important task.

▲ *The fishing industry worldwide employs around 200 million people*

Sources of Water

There are many types of waterbodies on Earth. They may be saltwater or freshwater. Some of these may be moving and some are contained. They can be distinguished by their shapes, sizes, and vegetation. Sources of water can be broadly divided into two categories: surface water and groundwater. Surface water is found in oceans, seas, lakes, rivers, ponds, and reservoirs. Groundwater lies under land surface that travels through and fills openings in the rocks. The rocks that store and transmit groundwater are called aquifers.

▲ Seawater is salty, like ocean water

Surface Water

It is a body of water that is above the ground, such as oceans, streams, rivers, lakes, wetlands, reservoirs, and creeks. Surface water moves to and from the Earth's surface through the water cycle. Precipitation and water runoff feed bodies of surface water.

There are three types of surface water: perennial, ephemeral, and man-made. Perennial type of source is permanent that persists throughout the year and is refilled with groundwater when there is little precipitation. Rivers, lakes, streams, and ponds are some examples of perennial surface water.

Ephemeral (semi-permanent) surface water exists for only part of the year. This surface water includes small creeks, lagoons, and water holes. Man-made surface water is found in artificial structures, such as dams and constructed wetlands.

The availability of surface water is naturally more than the groundwater. Therefore, it can be used for drinking, cooking, bathing, and agricultural activities. Wetlands with surface water are also important habitats for aquatic plants and wildlife.

▲ A view of the Bay of Bengal

Groundwater

These sources are found beneath the land surface, such as springs and wells. In the water cycle we can observe that when rain falls to the ground, some water flows along the land to the streams or lakes, other water evaporates into the atmosphere, while some is taken up by plants, and the remaining seeps into the ground. Water that seeps deep into the ground is called groundwater. It is formed as water flows through the earth's surface and passes through rock voids. Groundwater and surface water are also reservoirs that can feed into one another. Groundwater can resurface on land to replenish surface water, while surface water can seep underground to become groundwater. These are the places where springs form.

▲ Ponds support two-thirds of all freshwater species

The Splendid Seas

A sea is a large area of salt water that may or may not connect to an ocean. The Caribbean Sea connects to the Atlantic Ocean. However, the Caspian Sea is landlocked. Many consider the Caspian Sea to be a lake because like other seas it does not drain into the ocean but it is sea-like in its size and depth. Some of the major seas of the world are the Mediterranean Sea, the Black Sea, and the Arabian Sea.

▲ Previously, the Black Sea was named 'inhospitable sea' by the Greeks as it was difficult to navigate

🌐 The Black Sea

The Black Sea is oval-shaped and lies in south-eastern Europe. Though it lies deep inland, it is connected with the Atlantic Ocean through a series of waterways. They are the Bosporus Strait and the Sea of Marmara. The Dardanelles Strait links the Black Sea to the Aegean Sea, the Mediterranean Sea, and the Atlantic Ocean. The Black Sea is located at the point where Europe and Asia meet. Its bordering countries are Ukraine, Russia, Georgia, Turkey, Bulgaria, and Romania. Rivers like the Danube, Dniester, Bug, Dnieper, Don, and Kuban empty into the Black Sea.

🌐 The Mediterranean Sea

The Mediterranean is a large, intercontinental sea that separates Europe from Africa. It stretches from the Atlantic Ocean in the west to Asia in the east. This sea is called the sea between lands.

The Mediterranean Sea is deep and almost landlocked. It lies between latitudes 30° and 46° N and longitudes 5°50′ W and 36° E. The Strait of Gibraltar connects the Mediterranean Sea with the Atlantic Ocean. The area of the Mediterranean is 25,12,000 square kilometres. It is of historical importance as many early civilisations developed in the Mediterranean region. Therefore, it is also described as the cradle of civilisation.

◀ The picture shows a coast of the Mediterranean Sea in Europe. It is active with beachgoers and boating enthusiasts

In Real Life

The Caspian Sea receives water from the Volga, Ural, Emba, Kura, and Terek Rivers, among others, but has no outlet. About 130 rivers drain their waters into the Caspian Sea.

▶ *The Caspian Sea lies east of the Caucasus Mountains at Europe's south-easternmost extremity*

🌐 The Caspian Sea

As it is landlocked, the Caspian Sea is the world's largest inland body of water. It lies between Europe and Asia, bordering Russia and Azerbaijan in the west, Kazakhstan in the north, Turkmenistan in the east and Iran in the south. It dominates west-central Asia. The area of the Caspian Sea is approximately 3,86,400 square kilometres, which is larger than Japan. The sea was named for the Kaspi, the ancient people who once lived on its western shores. Among its other historical names, Khazarsk and Khvalynsk were derived from the former people of the region, while Girkansk stems from Girkanos, which means the 'country of wolves'.

🌐 The Arabian Sea

The Arabian Sea is located in the north-western part of the Indian Ocean. It covers an area of 38,62,000 square kilometres and its depth is 8,970 feet. It forms a part of the principal sea route between Europe and India. It is also bounded on the north by Pakistan and Iran, and on the west by the Horn of Africa. In Roman times its name was Erythraean Sea. Some of the islands in the sea are Socotra in Yemen, Lakshadweep in India, and Kuria Muria off the coast of Oman. The Indus and the Narmada are two major rivers that drain into the Arabian Sea.

▲ *Mumbai, India, is one of the busiest ports in the Arabian Sea*

💡 Isn't It Amazing!

The Baltic Sea is almost landlocked, but its outlet is quite shallow. This is why it is a freshwater sea. Its waters have a low rate of evaporation. The water further remains fresh because of the spring snowmelt that swells the waters of the Baltic Sea. The Baltic Sea has very low salinity as a result of these factors.

▶ *A view of the Baltic Sea at sunset*

Home to History

Early civilisations grew along rivers. Since the pre-historic age, rivers attracted human beings looking to settle in one place. Early settlers realised that lands along rivers were fertile enough to cultivate crops. They grew crops and stored the surplus, eliminating the need to move from place to place in search of food. They formed permanent settlements which grew into famous ancient civilisations like the Mesopotamian, Indus Valley, Nile River Valley, and the Yellow River civilisations. These further became the basis for states, nations, and empires.

◄ *The land around Rivers Tigris and Euphrates is still very fertile. As there was an abundance of water, people of the Mesopotamian Civilisation developed farming and irrigation systems*

▼ *The Nile River flooded every year in August and provided nutrients to the soil for growing crops in the dry desert land of Egypt*

▲ *The Euphrates River rises in eastern Turkey and flows through Syria and Iraq*

Tigris & Euphrates Rivers

The Tigris-Euphrates river system in southwest Asia constitutes these two rivers. They flow parallel to each other through the Middle East. Their source is in Turkey, 80 kilometres apart. They travel through northern Syria and Iraq towards the Persian Gulf. The length of River Euphrates is 2,800 kilometres. On the other hand, River Tigris is not as long as the Euphrates. It is about 1,850 kilometres long. Many civilisations have grown along the banks of these rivers. The most famous and prominent one was the Mesopotamian Civilisation which stretched from c. 5000–3500 BCE.

The Nile River

The Nile River is located in southeast Africa and has been recognised as the longest river on Earth. It rises south of the Equator and flows northward through northeast Africa to drain into the Mediterranean Sea. It has a length of about 6,650 kilometres. This mighty river has two main tributaries which meet to form the Nile. One tributary is called the White Nile, which starts in South Sudan. The other is called the Blue Nile, and that starts in Ethiopia.

This river has been very important from the perspective of human history. It provided a fertile soil for cultivation. The river therefore played an essential role in the growth of the ancient Egyptian Civilisation around c. 3100 BCE.

The Indus River

The Indus River, also known as Sindhu in Sanskrit, is a river in South Asia. It is one of the longest rivers in the world, with a length of 3,200 kilometres. It flows from Tibet, into Jammu and Kashmir, and then into Pakistan. The main tributaries of the Indus River are the Rivers Kabul and Kurram on the right bank; and the Jhelum, Chenab, Ravi, Beas, and the Sutlej Rivers on the left bank. The Indus Valley Civilisation grew around this river around c. 4000–3000 BCE. It had highly developed cities with a famous underground drainage system.

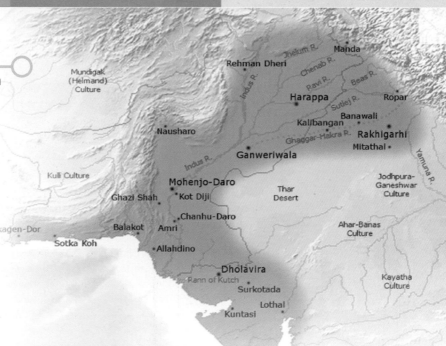

▲ The map shows the extent of the Indus Valley Civilisation at its peak, with clear markings of River Indus and its tributaries

▲ Ruins of two big cities of the Indus Valley Civilisation, Mohenjo-Daro and Harappa

▲ The length of the Yellow River is 5,463 kilometres. The area of its drainage basin is around 750,000 square kilometres

In Real Life

The Indus River displays a unique phenomenon called **tidal bore**. It is a giant wave which moves forward from the sea onto the rivers along with an unusual tide. It enters shallow and narrow inlets and can cause a lot of destruction.

The Yellow River

The Hwang Ho River in China, also known as the Yellow River, is the third largest river in Asia. It is the principal river in China and is called the 'cradle of Chinese civilisation'.

The Hwang Ho River rises on the plateau of Tibet and flows eastward, emptying into the Yellow Sea. It stretches across China for more than 4,667 kilometres. It carries yellow-coloured silt all the way, hence the name. The river and its tributaries played a vital role in shaping the Chinese civilisation.

The Grand Rivers

A river is a large, natural stream of flowing water. There are many rivers flowing through the continents. However, some rivers flow throughout the year, whereas there are some that are filled only in the wet seasons. Rivers that have uninterrupted flow throughout the year are called perennial rivers, while the rivers that flow in the monsoon season are called seasonal rivers. Rivers Mississippi, Amazon, Indus, Congo, and Ganga are all perennial. Rivers Mahanadi, Godavari, Krishna, and Kaveri are seasonal rivers.

▼ *An arch constructed on the banks of the Mississippi River, USA*

The Mississippi River

The Mississippi River is one of the world's longest river systems and the second longest in North America. The river flows through an area of 5,887 kilometres from its source at Lake Itasca in northern Minnesota to the Gulf of Mexico. The name is derived from a native American word that means 'father of waters'. This river system has many creeks, bayous, and other natural drainage networks. The Missouri River is such a tributary. It is about 160 kilometres longer than the Mississippi River. The Mississippi-Missouri combination is the fourth longest river in terms of length. Agriculture is dominant along this river and agricultural industries have developed here.

260 species of fish and 145 species of amphibians and reptiles inhabit the Mississippi River basin. 60 per cent of North American birds use this river basin as their migratory flyway.

The Amazon River

The Amazon River is located in the continent of South America. It drains practically 40 per cent of South America, thus it is the greatest river of the continent and the largest drainage system in the world. This is because of the volume of its flow and the area of its basin. The total length of the river, as measured from the headwaters of the Ucayali-Apurímac river system in southern Peru, is at least 6,400 kilometres, slightly shorter than the Nile River. It is as long as the distance between New York City and Rome. The mouth of the Amazon River is in the Atlantic Ocean, on the northeastern coast of Brazil.

▲ *There are around 400–500 indigenous Amerindian tribes that live in the Amazon Rainforest. It is believed that about 50 of these tribes have never had contact with the outside world*

The Congo River

The Congo River lies astride the equator in West Central Africa. This is the second-longest river in Africa. Formerly, it was known as the Zaire River. It drains almost the whole of the Republic of Congo, Democratic Republic of Congo, the Central African Republic; and some parts of Zambia, Angola, Cameroon, and Tanzania. Its source lies in the highlands of North Zambia. It flows into the Atlantic Ocean, at Banane. The Congo River is the main mode of transportation in Central Africa. It is home to a variety of fauna, animals like the Congo peafowl, dryas, crocodiles, elephants, monkeys, and 700 species of marine life.

◀ *The Congo River is the deepest river on Earth. It reaches depths of over 750 feet*

In Real Life

The Amazon Rainforest is the largest rainforest in the world. It is of great ecological importance as its biomass is capable of absorbing enormous amounts of carbon dioxide. This region is home to thousands of plants and millions of animal species. One-fifth of all of the world's species of birds can be found here. However, deforestation has taken a toll on this lush rainforest. An estimate says that over one-fifth of the total area of the rainforest has been cut down.

The Amur River

The Amur River is the third-longest river of China. It rises in Russia, flows along the path to Mongolia and reaches China. In China it is called the Heilong Jiang River or 'black dragon'. China and Russia both benefit economically from this river as fishing is the main occupation practised on its waters.

◀ *An aerial view of the Amur River and the Khabarovsk city bridge; the Trans-Siberian railway is built near this river*

The Paraná River

The Paraná River is located in south-central part of South America. It runs through Brazil, Paraguay, and Argentina. Paraná River, together with its tributaries, forms the larger of the two river systems that drain into the Río de la Plata. It is 4,880 kilometres long and extends from the confluence of the Grande and Paranaíba Rivers in southern Brazil. The Paraguay-Paraná river system covers an area of more than 2.5 million square kilometres. It is the second largest river system in South America, after the Amazon River. The Itaipu Dam on this river was once the largest hydroelectric power station in the world, before the Three Gorges Dam in China came online and replaced its position.

▶ *The Itaipu Dam on the Paraná River*

Famous Rivers

History shows us how rivers have been integral to civilisation. They also play a vital role in the geopolitics, economies and cultures of their bordering regions, and so some rivers are famous across the world today. Let us take a look at a few such rivers.

The Brahmaputra River

▲ *The Brahmaputra River originates from the Chemayungdung Glacier in the Himalayas*

The Brahmaputra River has different names as it flows through different countries. The river flows in the continent of Asia. It is 2,900 kilometres long.

The name 'Brahmaputra' is used in India. It translates to 'son of Brahma' in Sanskrit; Brahma is a Hindu god. The Brahmaputra rises in the Himalayas, and flows through southwest Tibet, where it is called 'Yarlung Zangbo', and enters India in its northeast border, through the Yarlung Tsangpo Canyon. In India, the Brahmaputra flows from Arunachal Pradesh. It gets the name Brahmaputra from Assam where it flows through the Assam Valley. Here it joins the River Ganga in Bangladesh as Jamuna and drains in the Bay of Bengal. The river forms a vast **delta** here.

The total area drained by this river is approximately 5,80,000 kilometres. The river is important for both irrigation and transportation. It is the lifeline of Assam. However, flooding of this region is also very common. During spring, when the snowcaps melt in the Himalayas, floods are inevitable. They cause destruction of crops and property, and lead to many deaths.

The Ganga River

The River Ganga (also known as Ganges) runs along the plains of northern India. This river is also a good example of a perennial river. It rises in the Himalayas and drains into the Bay of Bengal. Its length is about 2,510 kilometres, relatively shorter than the other great rivers of the world. But it is of massive importance. It flows through the most fertile and densely populated regions of the world. Millions of people use its water for bathing, drinking, and industrial production.

It is the holy river for the Hindus, and plays an important role in many cultural and religious rites. The River Ganga has a unique ecosystem with 140 species of freshwater fish, 90 amphibian species, and 315 bird species. These are mainly found in the mangroves of the Sundarbans delta in the Bengal Basin.

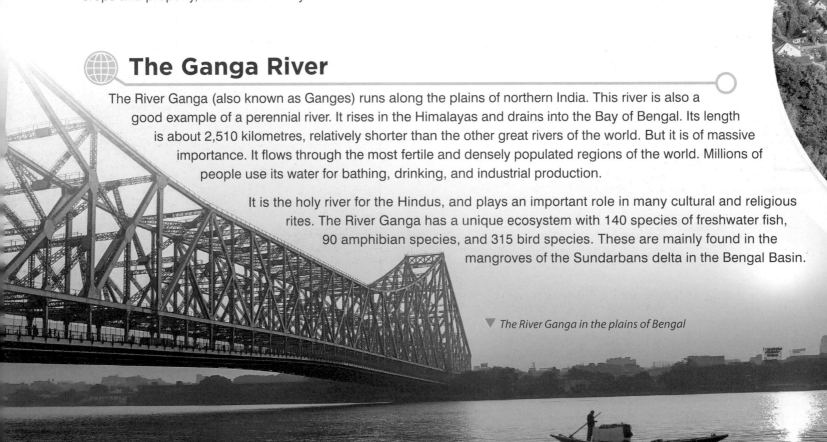

▼ *The River Ganga in the plains of Bengal*

The Volga River

The Volga River is located in Europe. It is the longest river of the continent. The river is 3,692 kilometres long and drains almost two-fifths of the European part of Russia. It rises in the Valdai Hills which are in the northwest of Moscow. It discharges into the Caspian Sea. River Volga ranks among the world's greatest rivers due to its immense economic, cultural, and historic importance.

The river valley provides a large amount of wheat. It is also rich in other minerals. There are around 127 species in the river. The Volga **estuary** is the largest in Europe. The river remains frozen for three months in a year during winter.

 River Volga has more than 200 tributaries. The prominent ones are the Rivers Kama, Oka, Vetluga, and Sura

The Danube River

The River Danube is the second-longest river in Europe after Volga. It rises in the Black Forest mountains of western Germany and flows for some 2,850 kilometres to its mouth on the Black Sea. It passes through Germany, Ukraine, Hungary, Moldova, and six other European countries. It is also of great economic value to these 10 countries as it is used for fishing, transport, and hydroelectricity. This river played a vital role in the settlement and political evolution of central and southeastern Europe. Its banks, that are lined with castles and fortresses, formed the boundary between great empires, and its waters served as a vital commercial highway between nations.

The Zambezi River

The Zambezi River drains the southern portion of Central Africa. It is the fourth-longest river in this continent, flowing for 2,540 kilometres from the Central African Plateau. It empties into the Indian Ocean. On its route, it flows through six African nations including Zambia, Zimbabwe, and Mozambique. Indeed, several disputes have broken out among these countries over the claim to its waters.

 The Danube River is a graveyard for sunken German warships from WWII. Sensing defeat, rather than letting the Allies capture their vessels, the Germans scuttled many of them in the river

💡 Isn't It Amazing!

More than seventy countries celebrate World Rivers Day on the fourth Sunday of September. This global event raises awareness of the importance of rivers and how we can protect them for our better future.

The Victoria Falls on Zambezi River has an output of 550 million litres of water every minute—as much as 200 Olympic-sized swimming pools!

Cascading Waters

A waterfall is a place where water flows vertically from a river or another waterbody. It is a steep fall over a rocky ledge into a plunge pool below. Cascades is another name for waterfalls. When water flows over underlying rocks, it naturally erodes softer rocks like limestone faster than harder rocks like granite, leaving the hard rocks behind. The granite that remains when the soft rock is worn away creates cliffs and ledges.

▲ *The formation of land causes a waterfall. If there is a cliff or ledge naturally, rushing river waters will simply fall over the edge*

Niagara Falls

Waterfalls are beautiful physical occurrences. There are some that are grand and make our planet even more beautiful. One such waterfall is the Niagara Falls. It is on the Niagara River in North America and is one of the spectacular physical features of the continent of North America. The falls lie on the border between Ontario, Canada, and New York State, USA.

There are two main parts of the falls and they are separated by the Goat Island. It comprises three waterfalls, from largest to smallest, they are: the Horseshoe Falls (also known as the Canadian Falls), American Falls, and Bridal Veil Falls. The height of the Horseshoe Falls is 56 metres and the length of its curving **crest line** is about 670 metres. The American Falls, adjoining the right bank, are 58 metres high and 320 metres across. A huge amount of water flows over Niagara Falls, as much as 5,525 cubic metre per second. This water is used to generate hydroelectric power.

▲ *The length of the Canadian, or Horseshoe brink is 2,600 feet. The horseshoe shape makes the waterfall look smaller, but it is just the opposite*

Incredible Individuals

Annie Edson Taylor was the first person to go over the Niagara Falls in a barrel on 24 October 1901. She was a school teacher and a brave lady to do this. She died in 1924 and is buried at Oakwood Cemetery in Niagara Falls in an area called Stunter's Rest.

Victoria Falls

Victoria Falls is another magnificent waterfall. It is also one of the world's mightiest waterfalls located in east-central Africa, on the border between Zambia and Zimbabwe. It is located midway along the course of the Zambezi River. Victoria Falls is about twice as wide and deep as the Niagara Falls. The mist from the falling water is especially dense during the rainy season. It is considered to be the biggest curtain of falling water in the world. The waterfall spans the entire breadth of the Zambezi River and is twice as wide and deep as the Niagara Falls. Approximately, 550 million litres of water drops 93 metres every minute over the cliff at Victoria Falls, and continues flowing downstream as the lower Zambezi River.

▲ *The width of Victoria Falls in the wet season is a bit over 1,609 metres wide*

Small Waterbodies

Apart from the vast oceans, large seas and big rivers, there are some smaller waterbodies on Earth which might be salt water or freshwater. Some of these are moving and some are contained. They can be distinguished by their shapes and sizes and by the kind of vegetation that thrives within them. The different smaller waterbodies are lakes, ponds, gulfs, bays, and straits.

▲ *Lakes regulate the flow of river water. During the monsoon season they prevent flooding*

Lakes

A lake is a body of water that is full of freshwater. It is surrounded on all of its sides by land. The great lakes in the northern parts of the USA are much larger than the average lake. Some lakes however are salt waterbodies, such as Utah's Great Salt Lake.

Lakes are found everywhere in the world and in all kinds of environments. There are different sizes of lakes and some are so big that they are referred to as seas, for example the Caspian Sea.

Bay

A bay is a body of water which is partially surrounded by land. It is usually smaller and less enclosed than a gulf. The mouth of the bay, where it meets the ocean, is typically wider than that of a gulf. The Bay of Bengal and the Hudson Bay are examples of bays. Bays are called **lagoons** sometimes. Lagos, the capital of Nigeria, is a bay-side city. It sits on Lagos Lagoon, on the Bight of Benin.

Strait

A strait is a narrow body of water that acts as a passage between two navigable landmasses. It is formed by natural process. A strait can connect two bigger waterbodies also if it is formed by a fracture in an **isthmus**. These straits are usually formed because of tectonic activity, a matching example being the Strait of Gibraltar. This is the only link between the Mediterranean Sea and the Atlantic Ocean. When fractures in an isthmus are created by human activity, they are usually called canals.

▲ *Ponds support two-thirds of all freshwater species*

Ponds

A pond can be formed by natural or artificial methods, as compared to seas and lakes. It is a smaller body of water. They are by all means smaller than lakes, though there is no standard or fixed measurement of how big a pond should be. Therefore, many times a big pond can be mistaken for a lake. Ponds are fresh waterbodies and arise naturally in floodplains.

Gulf

A gulf is a portion of the sea that is surrounded by land on all sides except for one where there is a narrow opening. They are generally larger than bays and are more indented. Gulfs are formed by movements in Earth's crust.

Gulfs can also have wide openings and sometimes cannot be differentiated from larger bodies of water.

▼ *The Suez Canal has made transportation between Europe and Asia easier as it is no longer necessary to go around the entire continent of Africa*

Natural Lakes

A lake is a waterbody that is surrounded by land. There are hundreds and thousands of lakes on Earth. There are two distinct types of lakes—natural and artificial. Natural lakes were formed by glaciers that once covered Earth some 18,000 years ago, during the most recent ice age. Lakes were also formed due to the movements of tectonic plates and as a result of volcanic eruptions. Some lakes are also formed by rivers and landslides. Some of the famous natural lakes are Lake Superior, Lake Victoria, and Lake Baikal.

▶ *The Michigan State Tree and White Pine, along with some 60 species of orchids are native to the Lake Superior area. This lake was formed 1.2 million years ago*

Lake Superior

One of the greatest natural lakes in the world is Lake Superior in the USA. There are five great lakes in North America, of which Lake Superior is the largest, coldest, and deepest. It is also one of the world's largest bodies of freshwater. It got its name from the French words '*lac supérieur*', which mean 'upper lake'.

Lake Superior is situated on the northern edge of Wisconsin and is bounded by Michigan, Ontario, and Minnesota. The lake is about 257 kilometres wide and 563 kilometres long. The deepest point in Lake Superior is 400 metres below the surface. It is mostly covered with ice in the winters but does not freeze completely. It is the cleanest and clearest of the Great Lakes. Visibility can be about 27 feet. There are many streams and rivers that empty into this lake.

▼ *Lake Superior holds 10 per cent of the Earth's freshwater supply*

👤 In Real Life

Over 200 rivers feed Lake Superior. The Nipigon River is one of the largest among them. It has had high waters in the months of October and November. In the months of March and April, it has had low waters.

Lake Victoria

Lake Victoria is another famous natural lake. It is the largest in the continent of Africa and is the reservoir of the River Nile. It lies mainly in Tanzania and Uganda. This lake was formed during the upheavals that created the Great Rift Valley 12 million years ago. It is approximately 410 kilometres long and 250 kilometres wide. It is not very deep and occupies a shallow depression (75 metres deep) on the Equatorial Plateau, whose altitude is 3,725 feet. The lake has an irregular shoreline and many small islands. Numerous streams, including the Kagera River, lead into Lake Victoria. This lake is said to be relatively young as its current basin formed only 400,000 years ago. Lake Victoria supports the lives of millions of people living around its shores, in one of the most densely populated regions on Earth.

▲ *Lake Victoria covers an area of 68,800 square kilometres, making it one of the largest lakes by area, and one of the largest tropical lakes in the world*

▼ *There are between 1,500 and 1,800 animal species and hundreds of plant species found in Lake Baikal*

Lake Baikal

Lake Baikal is one of the deepest lakes in the world, and is located in Russia. It is the largest in terms of volume. Its surface area is 31,500 square kilometres and it has a length of 636 kilometres and depth of about 1,637 metres.

Lake Baikal is actually located in Siberia within the Republic of Buryatia and the Irkutsk province of Russia. It is the oldest existing freshwater lake on Earth, formed around 20–25 million years old. There are more than 330 rivers and streams that flow into Lake Baikal. It lies in a deep structural hollow surrounded by mountains, some of which are 2,000 metres above the lake's surface. It produces hot mineral springs in the area where there are breaks in the Earth's crust. Occasionally, earthquakes also occur in this region. An earthquake in 1862, in the northern Selenga delta, created a new bay in Baikal known as the Proval Bay.

Artificial Lakes

Artificial lakes are created by humans. They are made by digging basins or by damming rivers and springs. These artificial lakes can become reservoirs for storing water for irrigation, hygiene, and industrial use. Artificial lakes are also used for recreational activities such as boating, swimming, and fishing. Some famous artificial lakes are Lake Volta, Lake Williston, and Lake Naseer.

Lake Volta

Lake Volta is an artificial lake in Ghana. It was formed by the Akosombo Dam whose construction began in 1961 and ended in 1965 on the Volta River. During its construction, a lake was created flowing upstream from the Akosombo Dam to Yapei. Lake Volta is one of the largest artificial lakes in the world. It is about 400 kilometres long and covers an area of 8,502 kilometres. The lake has been used to navigate from the northern Savanna to the coast of Ghana. It is also an important fishing and irrigation source for the fishermen and farmers in the dry Accra Plains lying immediately below the dam.

Lake Oahe

The Lake Oahe is created by the Missouri River, in USA. It stretches for 231 miles from Oahe Dam near Pierre. It is also the largest of the four Missouri River reservoirs. Its maximum depth is 205 feet. It is good for boating and fishing. The most commonly found species here are smallmouth bass, white bass, northern pike and perch. This is the largest man-made lake in the continent of North America.

Lake Bhojtal

Lake Bhojtal is situated in the west central part of Bhopal, Madhya Pradesh, India. It is surrounded by Van Vihar National Park in the south, human settlements in the east and north, and agriculture fields in the west. The lake has an area of 31 square kilometres. Fishing is an important occupation of inhabitants around the lake and is mainly done on its south-eastern shores. It also serves as the source of water for irrigating a large area.

▼ A view of Lake Volta

▼ A view of Lake Oahe

▼ A view of the sunset in Lake Bhojtal

In Real Life

There are two possible burial sites located near Lake Oahe's shoreline. These are of the Sitting Bull, a Sioux leader. The shoreline is actually known for containing several cultural artefacts important to different Native American tribes. US law prohibits collecting or damaging them.

▼ *A view of Lake Nasser*

▼ *A road built over Williston Lake*

▼ *Kariba Dam wall*

Lake Nasser

Lake Nasser, also called Lake Nubia, is a reservoir on the Nile River, in Upper Egypt and North Sudan. This artificial lake was created by the construction of the High Dam at Aswan. The dam was built in 1960s. Lake Nasser is 479 kilometres long and 16 kilometres wide at its widest point. It has a gross capacity of 168,900,000,000 cubic metres. Water that is discharged downstream can irrigate 800,000 acres of land. This lake has a major role to play in Egypt's fishing industry.

Isn't It Amazing!

During its creation, Lake Nasser threatened to submerge the archaeological sites at Abu Simbel and Philae in Egypt. These sites could have been lost under water had the Egyptian government not intervened by making an appeal to UNESCO, thus saving the loss of these sites.

Lake Williston

The W.A.C. Bennett Dam led to the formation of Lake Williston, which is one of the largest artificial lakes in the world. It is located in Columbia, Canada. Williston Lake covers an area of 250 kilometres in the Rocky Mountain Trench. It is a man-made lake created when the large hydro-electric project, the W.A.C. Bennett Dam was built in 1968. Williston Lake, is the dam reservoir on three different rivers, the Peace, Parsnip, and Findlay.

Lake Kariba

Lake Kariba is a lake in central Africa that lies between Zambia and Zimbabwe. It was created by damming the Zambezi River in the Kariba Gorge, 400 kilometres below Victoria Falls, where the river narrows between hills of hard rock. The Kariba Dam's hydroelectric facilities served Zambian cities, the Harare and Bulawayo districts, and the southern part of Zimbabwe after 1960.

Global Warming

Global warming is defined as the increase in the average temperature of Earth's air and oceans due to the rising levels of greenhouse gases. Carbon dioxide is an example of a greenhouse emission. Global warming is leading to drastic and alarming changes in the climate.

▼ There was a time when thick ice sheets covered the land. This period was called the ice age. The first ice age took place 570 million years ago

 ## Changes in Climate

The climate of Earth has gone through many changes such as the melting of glaciers during the ice ages, a period when glaciers covered most of Earth. In recent time, the temperatures have increased and that has caused the sea levels to rise. Global climate has also gone through extremely warm periods. However, all these changes happened gradually, at a very slow pace over thousands of years. The changes happening presently are taking place faster than some living beings can adapt to them. Scientists believe that most of the temperature increase since the mid-20th century is likely due to human activities. The temperature since 1880 has been rising every year by about 0.8° C.

Greenhouse Effect

Greenhouse gases let the Sun's light shine onto Earth's surface, but they trap the heat that reflects back up into the atmosphere. In this way, they act like the insulating glass walls of a greenhouse. The greenhouse effect keeps Earth's climate comfortable, otherwise the temperature would have been cooler than required and many life forms would freeze, finding it difficult to survive. Greenhouse gas emissions have a wide range of environmental and health consequences. They lead to respiratory diseases caused by smog and air pollution, as well as contributing to climate change by trapping heat.

▼ Toxic factory emissions contribute negatively to the greenhouse effect

◀ The diagram shows the greenhouse effect

 ## 👤 In Real Life

Some other consequences of climate change exacerbated by greenhouse emissions include extreme weather, food supply shortages, and increased wildfires.

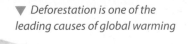
▼ Deforestation is one of the leading causes of global warming

Causes of Global Warming

Human beings are responsible for and contribute to global warming by aggravating the greenhouse effect. The effect occurs when certain gases fill up Earth's atmosphere. These include carbon dioxide, methane, nitrogen oxide, and fluorinated gases. Large amounts of these gases are emitted from factories burning fossil fuels such as oil, coal, and natural gas. Even fuels used in transport vehicles add to the problem. Forested areas reduce the amount of carbon dioxide in the atmosphere, but deforestation is cancelling out their effects. In this way, human activities increase the emission of greenhouse gases in the atmosphere, causing global warming. Household appliances such as refrigerators and air conditioners use a lot of energy and emit **refrigerants** that deplete the ozone layer and further contribute to global warming.

Effects of Global Warming

Effects of global warming are clearly visible today. Human beings, plants and animals are severely affected by changes in their environment. The global ecology is changing too quickly for anyone to adapt. It is triggering natural disasters like floods, tsunamis and earthquakes.

Glaciers are melting and shrinking throughout the world. If the temperature increases, they will continue to melt, which is an alarming sign for wildlife in the polar regions. As the glaciers melt, the ocean levels will rise. This rise in the sea level consequently will lead to frequent floods. Another effect of global warming is the warming of the polar regions due to melting of glaciers. This is making the habitats of some animals warmer. Therefore, these animals are migrating to cooler places. This is also putting some species in danger of extinction.

70 per cent of the Earth is water, so when the oceans heat up, more water evaporates into the clouds which results in heavy and untimely downpours. Storms like hurricanes and typhoons occur much more frequently. Due to untimely rains, crops get destroyed and affect life. Therefore, it is vital to tackle this problem quickly. Otherwise our planet will become a tough place to live in. It is of utmost importance to plant enough trees to counter the greenhouse effect. To reduce emission of greenhouse gases, people should drive less and walk or cycle more. However, changes by individuals are not enough. There needs to be a serious overhaul in our methods of production and consumption.

▲ Owing to global warming ice breaks off in the polar regions causing the sea levels to rise

ROCKS
&
MINERALS

A Rocky Planet

Our planet Earth is a terrestrial planet, just like Mercury, Venus, and Mars. It means that these planets are made up of **silicate** rocks or metals so we can find minerals like feldspar and metals such as magnesium and aluminium within their cores, and on their surfaces. Pluto, a dwarf planet, is comprised of rocks. Jupiter, Saturn, Uranus, and Neptune are gas giants, which means that they are composed of gases such as helium and hydrogen, but they still have a solid or rocky core. They are different from terrestrial planets as gas giants do not have a well-defined surface. They do not have a clear boundary between where the atmosphere ends and the surface starts.

Earth is made up of rocks and minerals from the core to crust. But what exactly are these rocks and minerals? First, rocks and minerals are naturally occurring solids. Rocks are solid mineral materials, forming Earth's surface. Minerals are naturally occurring **crystalline** solids, so the atoms of the minerals have a crystal form.

▼ *Vinicunca Mountain (5,200 metres) also called Montaña de Siete Colores or Rainbow Mountain is located in the Andes, Peru, South America*

What Are Rocks?

Rocks are made up of one or more minerals. Unlike minerals, they lack a uniform or crystalline structure. Therefore, two rocks might have different physical properties depending on how many minerals they are made of. Rocks are classified based on how they are formed. There are three major types—igneous, sedimentary, and metamorphic.

Igneous Rocks

During a volcanic reaction, magma is released from beneath the Earth's crust. This magma flows out onto the surface as lava. The magma cools down and becomes hard when it reaches Earth's surface. When it solidifies, it forms igneous rocks. Sometimes, it solidifies within Earth's crust.

The **atoms** and **molecules** of melted minerals make up magma. These rearrange themselves into mineral grains as the magma cools down. Basalt and granite are examples of igneous rocks. Large slabs of Earth's crust are made of granite. It contains the minerals quartz and feldspar. Basalt is more commonly found on the seafloor. It is a volcanic rock, rich in magnesium and iron. Volcanic rocks are formed when lava cools and solidifies on the earth's surface. Volcanic rocks are also known as 'extrusive igneous rocks' because they form from the 'extrusion,' or eruption, of lava from a volcano. Granite and basalt are also found in the lava erupted from volcanoes in Hawaii, Iceland, and some parts in the northwest of the USA.

▲ Basaltic lava flow in Hawaii

▶ A basalt rock structure in Russia

Sedimentary Rocks

Sedimentary rocks are formed mainly by the deposition of sediments carried by a river or stream to seas and oceans. Sediments are composed of minerals or organic matter. These sediments settle at the bottom of oceans and seas over a long period. Eventually, they harden into solid rocks. Some examples of sedimentary rocks are shale, limestone, and sandstone. They are also formed from eroded fragments of some other types of rocks and the remains of plants and animals.

Metamorphic Rocks

Metamorphic rocks are formed due to excessive heat and pressure on the existing igneous and sedimentary rocks. The name 'metamorphic' means 'to change form'. Therefore, as the name suggests, metamorphic rocks are transformed from sedimentary or igneous rocks because of heat, pressure, and **obtrusion** of fluid. The heat can come from magma or hot water from hot springs. These rocks are mainly found in the interior of Earth's crust where they are subjected to such intense pressure and heat that they transform. For example, slate is a metamorphic rock formed from shale, which is a sedimentary rock.

▲ *Cliffs made of metamorphic rocks are commonly found in Northwest Scotland and the western Isles of United Kingdom*

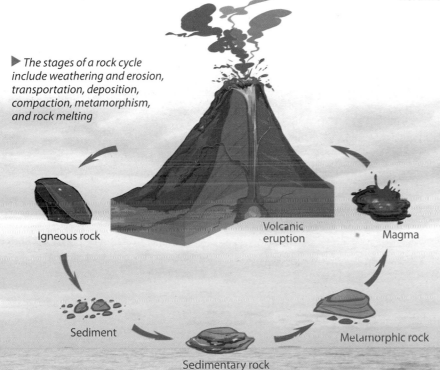

▶ *The stages of a rock cycle include weathering and erosion, transportation, deposition, compaction, metamorphism, and rock melting*

Igneous rock

Volcanic eruption

Magma

Sediment

Sedimentary rock

Metamorphic rock

The Rock Cycle

Rocks are always changing. However, a rock takes millions of years to transform into another type of rock. The rock cycle is a geological process where all three types of rocks undergo gradual changes. For example, magma from a volcano cools down and hardens to form igneous rocks. These rocks are sometimes broken into sediments (fragments) by the forceful action of river water, harsh winds, or extreme weather. Over the years, these sediments accumulate and compress to form sedimentary rocks. Then, because of heat and pressure, the sedimentary rocks transform into metamorphic rocks. This cycle is repeated again but not necessarily in the same order. In the rock cycle, changes can occur in any order.

⊛ Incredible Individuals

▲ *A portrait of James Hutton painted in 1776*

James Hutton (1726–1797) is considered to be the father of modern geology. He came up with the theory of uniformitarianism. This gives an explanation about the processes that Earth's surface has been through in 'geologic' time. It means that Earth has changed so much over a long period that some rock types that were formed in the past cannot form today. This theory helped future geologists understand how to study rocks.

Igneous Rocks

Igneous rocks are different kinds of crystalline rocks. They are formed by the cooling and solidification of magma or lava that emerges from beneath the Earth's crust. The word 'igneous' means 'fire' as its origin is the Latin word '*ignis*'. For instance, a lot of hard rocks found in northern Canada are actually igneous rocks.

 ## Types of Igneous Rocks

There are basically two types of igneous rocks—**extrusive** and **intrusive**. When the molten substances cool and harden on the surface of Earth, they are called extrusive. As the lava comes in contact with the cool temperature of the atmosphere, it cools down faster. This is the reason these rocks have fine grains. Rocks such as basalt, pumice, obsidian, tuff, andesite, and dacite are all examples of extrusive rocks.

▲ *Granite is an example of intrusive igneous rock*

Intrusive igneous rocks are those where the magma solidifies deep inside Earth's crust. The magma takes a long time to cool and this process goes on for millions of years. Intrusive igneous rocks vary from thin sheets to huge and irregular masses. Diorite, gabbro, granite, pegmatite, and peridotite are examples of intrusive rocks.

◀ *Pumice is an extrusive igneous rock. It has a porous surface which is the result of gas-rich frothy lava quickly solidifying*

 ## Formation of Igneous Rocks

Due to immense pressure and heat, magma flows up to the surface of the Earth during volcanic eruptions. At this point, the temperature of the molten magma can be around 700–1300° C. Over the years, this magma crystallises and becomes a hard, igneous rock. Igneous rocks are composed of one or more minerals. If the magma cools down too quickly, then it leads to smaller-sized crystals, whereas if the cooling is slow, it forms large crystals. Therefore, the cooling process of the magma determines the size of the rocks.

In Real Life

Obsidian forms quickly with a microscopic crystal growth and is known as volcanic glass. Because obsidian has very sharp edges, it was used to make cutting tools and arrowheads. Even today, there are some surgeons who like to use scalpels made of obsidian, because they can be made 3 times sharper than diamond, and 500-1000 times sharper than a steel blade.

Texture

The extrusive and intrusive igneous rocks differ in **texture**. Extrusive rocks cool quickly and have **microscopic** grains. Igneous rocks are said to have an aphanitic texture. The word aphanitic is applied to igneous rocks whose surface texture is so fine-grained that it is difficult to understand their mineral composition by simply looking at them.

On the other hand, intrusive rocks that cool slowly have a texture where the grains are visible and there is significant crystal growth. This is referred to as a **phaneritic** texture.

Some igneous rocks have different textures depending on the way they are formed. Obsidian has a glassy texture because it is formed when lava cools quickly. Pumice and scoria are formed when there is an explosive volcanic eruption where the magma breaks as it reaches the surface releasing gas bubbles. Due to this, they have a **vesicular** texture. On the other hand, tuff has a pyroclastic texture as it is formed from volcanic ash. Pyroclastic rocks are formed from the broken materials ejected from the volcano.

▲ *Obsidian rocks have a glassy lustre and are harder than window glass*

Classification and Identification

Igneous rocks can be classified on the basis of their chemical composition, especially the different types of minerals present in the rocks. They are often named on the basis of the proportion of the different minerals they contain

Geologists identify these rocks by their texture and formation. The way the magma cools down dictates the texture of the rock. For example, magma that solidifies beneath Earth's crust and forms intrusive igneous rocks will surely have a different texture from the magma that forms on Earth's crust. This magma comes into contact with ash flow as a result of volcanic ash spewing up from an eruption, flowing across and settling down to form rocks.

◀ *These basalt rock formations are called 'trolled toes'. According to Icelandic folklore, the basalt rock formations off the coast of Vik were once trolls*

▼ *A grey lava field near a Hawaiian volcano. A lava field, is a large expanse of nearly flat-lying lava flows*

Examples of Igneous Rocks

Some common igneous rocks are basalt, granite, pumice and obsidian. These rocks are very useful in real life (e.g., in construction, for decorative, building statues and as cosmetic processes). However, these igneous rocks are different from each other in composition and texture.

▼ *Basalt is a dark black rock but its colour changes to yellow-brown due to weathering*

▼ *Obsidian is also called nature's glass for its glossy appearance*

🌐 Obsidian

Obsidian is an extrusive igneous rock formed with the rapid cooling of lava on the Earth's surface. Obsidian forms when lava cools quickly above ground. It is usually dark and has a glassy appearance. These rocks have sharp edges and early human beings of the Stone Age used obsidian to make cutting tools and tips for their arrows and spears. While many rocks formed in the Earth's crust are very old, obsidian is just 20 million years old, which is young for a rock. Obsidian is extremely rich in silica and low in water. It has a glassy **lustre** and is slightly harder than window glass.

▼ *Obsidian blades have a cutting edge that is much sharper than high-quality steel surgical blades*

🌐 Basalt

Basalt is an extrusive igneous rock formed when lava cools down quickly. It is a dark-coloured, fine-grained rock. Basalt makes up most of the Earth's surface than any other type of rock. Much of the ocean floor is made up of basalt rocks. For example, most of the Hawaiian Islands are comprised of basalt, as they are based around basaltic volcanoes which are above an oceanic hotspot. This type of igneous rock is also found in abundance on our Moon. Much of the Moon's surface contains basalt, and it can also be seen on Mars and Venus. The areas where basalt is predominant on the Moon are called 'lunar maria'.

Basalt is rich in iron and it is very hard. It is mainly used as an ingredient in concrete. Earlier, basalt was used as a grinding stone. Crushed basalt is used to layer and surface roads or pavements along with asphalt. It is used to filter stones in drain fields and as the base of any road. Sometimes thin slabs of basalt are used for making objects of stone.

▲ *Basalt has continuously been used in roads and pavements since 600 BCE*

Isn't It Amazing!

Around 55 million years ago, the Giant's Causeway in Northern Ireland was made from a lava flow. As the lava cooled down, it split and formed 40,000 salt pillars or columns. The columns are hexagonal and look like huge stepping-stones.

▼ *Thousands of tourist visit the Giant's Causeway every year. Its name has been derived from a local Irish folklore that claimed this natural wonder was built by giants*

Pumice

Pumice is a heated molten rock that escapes from a volcano. The frothy lava cools quickly and solidifies to form this rock. Little pockets of air can be seen on the surface which is why it is considered to be a porous rock. This type of rock has a very low density and can float in water. The lightness of this rock is the result of air spaces, which are caused by fast cooling, and a loss of atmospheric pressure. Powdered pumice is used as an abrasive, a substance used to grind, polish, or clean a hard surface. It is also used as decorative landscape stone.

▲ *Pumice stones are used to clean one's feet as well*

▼ *Granite is considered to be a dimension stone, which refers to a natural rock that is mined for the purpose of meeting specific size and shape requirements. A dimension stone is mostly used for construction*

Granite

Granite is an intrusive igneous rock formed when magma solidifies underground and cools slowly. It originates from the Latin word 'granum' meaning 'a grain'. Granite is made up of many small bits of quartz and feldspar stuck together. It comes in different colours, such as white, pink, grey, or black. As it is extremely hard, it is used for building statues. These statues can stand for decades despite the weathering effects of the environment. Granite is also used for construction purposes. As it can be smoothed by polishing, it is used in monuments, carved decorations on buildings, and even as slabs covering the counters in modern kitchens.

▲ *A granite kitchen slab*

Sedimentary Rocks

Sedimentary rocks are formed by the consolidation of sediments. Sediments carried by rivers, glaciers, and winds generally form them. These rocks are deposited in layers and sometimes contain fossils of plants and animals. Sedimentation is the collective name for the processes that cause these particles to settle in place.

◀ Some sedimentary rocks are made of gravel and pebbles and are cemented by calcium carbonate

Formation of Sedimentary Rocks

Sedimentary rocks are the most commonly found rocks on Earth. They are generally formed from rocks that experience constant weathering and erosive action by wind, water, or other forces. All rocks are subject to erosion. This happens due to the force of rivers, gravity, winds, and thermal expansion of pre-existing rocks. Under their influence, these rocks are broken down into pieces. The small pieces that have broken off from the rock are then carried away over long distances. Eventually, they are deposited in layers somewhere like on the banks of a river. These layers are converted into new rocks by **compaction** (squeezing) and cementation (binding). Therefore, sedimentary rocks are formed by sediments that are collected in one place after breaking off through the process of weathering, erosion, deposition, compaction, and cementation. Sandstone, limestone, mudstone, coal, and shale are sedimentary rocks. Some sedimentary rocks may be either organic or chemical, depending on how they formed. Limestone, for example, may be created from either organic or chemical processes.

Types of Sedimentary Rocks

There are three types of sedimentary rocks—**clastic**, chemical, and organic.

Clastic
The deposits of broken rocks due to weathering form clastic sedimentary rocks by compaction and cementation. Sandstone, shale, siltstone, and breccias are examples of clastic sedimentary rocks.

Chemical
Chemical sedimentary rocks are formed when the water that the sediments are mixed with evaporates and leaves behind dissolved minerals. These rocks are quite common in arid lands or deserts due to lot of wind erosion. Examples include rock salt, flint, iron ore, and chert.

Organic
These sedimentary rocks are formed from organic debris such as roots, leaves, or animal matter. This debris has calcium minerals, which pile on the sea floor over time. Gradually, organic sedimentary rocks are formed. Examples include coal, chalk, and dolomite.

▲ Clastic sedimentary rocks are named according to the grain size of the sediment particles

▲ Halite is an example of a chemical sedimentary rock. It is also known as table salt

▲ Coal is an organic sedimentary rock formed from the remains of plants squeezed deep beneath the ground over millions of years

Classification and Identification

Over the years, geologists have attempted to classify sedimentary rocks on the basis of their origin and composition. However, there is a lack of universal acceptance for any of the proposed classification systems. This is because there is a great variation in the mineral composition, texture, and other properties of sedimentary rocks.

Texture

Texture is the physical makeup of any rock, and covers the size, shape, and arrangement of the various grains or particles present in its composition. Two main textural groupings for sedimentary rocks are clastic or fragmental, and nonclastic or crystalline. Sedimentary rocks with a clastic texture are made up of grains or clasts that do not interlock, instead, they are piled together and cemented. This type of rock is porous and not very dense.

Chemical sedimentary rocks are crystalline, which means that they are made of crystals interlocked with each other. However, the same type of texture is also seen in igneous and metamorphic rocks. The textures of sedimentary rocks are not too varied as they are formed from existing rocks.

▲ *Layers of a sedimentary rock*

▼ *Mud cracks and ripple marks are features of sedimentary rocks that often contain fossils*

Examples of Sedimentary Rocks

There are quite a few different types of sedimentary rocks found around us on Earth. They all have distinct characteristics. Some common sedimentary rocks we are familiar with are sandstone, limestone, coal, and rock salt.

 As sandstone is porous, it can serve as a filter in nature by filtering out pollutants from running water

🌐 Sandstone

Sandstone is a type of sedimentary rock comprising stony grains cemented together over a significant period. It is formed in two stages from the beds of sand under the sea. Initially, layers of sand build up as sediments from water or air. Then the sand particles are glued together by minerals such as calcium carbonate. This sand is also rich in **quartz**. Sandstone can be found in different colours such as red, white, yellow, grey, and brown. Sandstone is gritty to touch, like sandpaper. It is used as a construction material or as a raw material in manufacturing. Sandstone is also used to construct buildings and statues. It is quite common to find natural gas in sandstone as it is porous and can trap the gas.

▲ *Sandstone is used for construction as it is resistant to weathering*

▼ *Limestone mostly forms the floor of shallow tropical seas*

🌐 Limestone

Limestone is a sedimentary rock which is made up of more than 50 per cent calcium carbonate. Its texture is usually granular. It can have minerals other than calcium carbonate. The colour of the stone depends upon what other elements are combined with the calcium carbonate. Limestone is mainly considered to be an organic sedimentary rock because there is an accumulation of shell, coral, algal, and fecal debris in its composition. Some types of limestone are chemical sedimentary rocks because it is formed by the precipitation of calcium carbonate from the oceans and lakes.

Limestone is used to provide nutrition to plants as it contains the remains of marine animals. In construction, limestone is added to paints as thickening agents. When heated and mixed with other chemical compounds, limestone can be used to make decorative glass. It makes the glass sturdier. This becomes very useful when thick cooking utensils are made.

▲ *Stalactites and stalagmites are pointed formations found in limestone caves. They consist of leftover limestone that remained after the water evaporated*

Rock salt

Rock salt, also known as Halite, is a chemical sedimentary rock formed due to the evaporation of salty waters in oceans or saline lakes. The halite rocks are found in some other types of sedimentary rocks, salt domes, and dried lakes. Halite is colourless, though the minerals and purity can affect the colour, with a glassy lustre. It is not always found so easily, except in areas that have a very dry climate. Rock salt is found where large now-extinct seas and salt lakes existed millions of years ago. These left behind thick deposits of salt.

▶ Farmers use rock salt as salt for cattle, which is essential for their health

▲ Salt fields in Thailand

In Real Life

Rock salt is used as a seasoning for food and for making ice creams. This is because it lowers the freezing point when packed with ice in an ice cream maker, thus making ice cream cold.

Coal

▲ Coal also has elements such as hydrogen, oxygen, sulphur, and nitrogen apart from carbon

Coal is an organic sedimentary rock. It is black or brown in colour and often called a fossil fuel because it is formed from the remains of dead plants and animals. Usually, when these organisms die, they decay and are converted into organic matter, bones, water, and carbon dioxide. Sometimes, the dead plants and animals only decay partially. These remains eventually become coal, oil, and natural gas, which are all fossil fuels.

The plants and animals that usually die in a swamp environment are deposited in layers. Due to the accumulation of the debris and the influence of extreme heat and pressure, coal is formed. This process of coal formation from the remains of organic material takes millions of years.

Coal is combustible and is a major source of fuel. When burned, it releases energy in the form of so it is primarily used to generate electricity. Coal is also used in the production of other materials such as cement, other fuels, and coke-not Coca Cola, a material that is one of the most important ingredients for steel manufacturing.

▲ Coal is found in most areas of the world and it has a high-energy content

Isn't It Amazing!

The world's longest stalactite is 28 metres (92 feet) long, and is found in the Gruta do Janelao, in Minas Gerais, Brazil. The world's longest stalagmite is 70 metres tall. It is found in the Son Doong Cave in Vietnam. Remember, stalactites and stalagmites always come in pairs!

Metamorphic Rocks

Metamorphic rocks are those that are made up of other existing igneous and sedimentary rocks. They are usually formed due to certain changes in temperature, pressure, and the addition and subtraction of chemical components through a process called metamorphism, which means 'change in form'. These metamorphic rocks cover 12 per cent of Earth's surface.

▲ *Layers within metamorphic rocks, also known as foliation*

Formation of Metamorphic Rocks

Metamorphic rocks are formed when the physical or chemical composition of the existing rocks is altered due to heat and pressure into a denser form. The movements of the tectonic plates force the pre-existing rocks to move and shift. In the process, the rocks that are buried in the interior are subjected to immense pressure and heat and are subsequently warped and deformed.

As this phenomenon goes on for many years, a plate comprising of sedimentary or igneous rocks might become subducted under another plate. The weight above can cause the rocks under it to go through the process of metamorphism. The heat from magma and the constant friction along a fault line can also bring about this type of change. In this case, rocks do not melt fully but there are definite changes in their chemical composition, texture, and even their physical structure. Pressure or temperature can even change previously metamorphosed rocks into new types. Metamorphic rocks contain the same minerals as the original rocks, but their structures are just rearranged.

◀ *Granite metamorphosed into gneiss. The process of metamorphism it goes through makes the new rock denser than the original rock and less vulnerable to erosion*

Types of Metamorphism

There are three ways that metamorphism in rocks occurs: Contact, regional, and dynamic metamorphism. This can lean to either foliated or non-foliated rocks, which are separated on basis of texture and strength.

Contact, or thermal, metamorphism occurs when magma comes in contact with existing rock. This causes the temperatures to rise while the fluid from the magma seeps into the rock. It produces non-foliated rocks.

Regional metamorphism is caused by large geologic processes such as mountain-building. It occurs over a much larger area, and as the rocks are exposed to the surface, with huge pressures acting on them, they are bent and broken. It produces foliated rocks.

Dynamic metamorphism also occurs due to mountain-building, and the forces of pressure and heat cause the rocks to bent, be crushed, flattened, folded, and sheared.

Classification and Identification

Metamorphic rocks are classified by their texture, which is either foliated or non-foliated according to their parent rock. A metamorphic rock that is formed from more pressure than heat is foliated. This type of metamorphic rock has a distinct texture. It usually has a banded and layered appearance. Rocks that are formed due to tectonic movements are called nonfoliated. They do not have a layered appearance and their formation is dependent on pre-existing conditions. These rocks have a uniform look.

▼ *A cross-section of a gneiss rock with red veins*

How They Look – Texture

Foliated texture refers to the parallel arrangement of certain mineral grains, which give the rock a striped appearance. For example, gneiss, schist, slate, and phyllite have a banded appearance. These rocks develop a sheet-like structure that tells us the direction in which the pressure was applied.

Non-foliated rocks have a different texture than foliated rocks owing to the different ways these rocks are formed. Hornfels, marble, quartzite, and novaculite are good examples of non-foliated metamorphic rocks.

▼ *Metamorphic rock formations in Montana, USA*

🔆 Isn't It Amazing!

Schist is a metamorphic rock that originates from slate, another metamorphic rock. In Australia, houses that were built using schist in the 1800s are still standing today. Presently, schist is used as a decorative stone as well as for jewellery.

▲ *Here, schist stones have been piled up to form a wall*

Quartzite

As its name suggests, quartzite is a metamorphic rock composed of quartz grains. It is formed from sandstone or chert by the action of heat and pressure. Quartzite that is deeply buried underground is formed through metamorphosis of sandstone.

▶ *Quartzite is comprised of a high degree of quartz, almost 90 per cent*

 ## Formation

Quartzites are the highly concentrated, purest part of silica on Earth. They are created when two continental plates collide with each other to form mountains. The movement of the plates forces sedimentary rocks upwards into a series of folds. That is why quartzite is found in folded mountain ranges throughout the world. Quartzite has silica in high amounts.

 ## Uses

Being a tough rock, quartzite has many kinds of uses. Early human beings used this extremely hard rock to make weapons. They made axe heads and scrapers out of quartzite. However, as it has a coarse texture, tools with fine edges could not be made with quartzite. It was then used as a replacement for flint.

In modern times, quartzite is used to make bricks and other building materials. It is a versatile rock and is used as flooring, roofing, and also in decorative wall coverings. The soil around the region where quartzite develops does not have enough nutrients to sustain the growth of plants.

▲ *Quartzite used in construction*

▼ *A quartzite rock formation at the Pipestone National Monument, Minnesota, USA*

 ## Features

Quartzite is one of the most physically durable and chemically resistant rocks found on the surface of Earth. It is usually snowy white or light grey in colour. Occasionally, some come in colours like yellow or light brown. If there are impurities such as stains created from iron, then it can be pink, red, or purple in colour. Some other impurities can even cause quartzite to be yellow, orange, brown, green, or blue. However, very rarely is it dark. It has a smooth structure, granular appearance, and a glassy lustre. Quartzite is generally gritty to touch. Mountaintops that have quartzite never change, as quartzite is resistant to weathering. The difference between quartz sandstone and quartzite is that when the latter is broken, the fracture will cut right through its granular structure. Whereas quartz sandstone will break around the grains rather than through them.

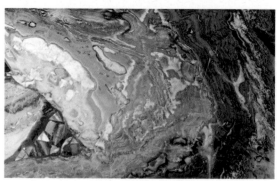

▲ *Coloured quartzite formed as a result of some impurities*

Marble

Marble is a hard crystalline metamorphic rock formed from limestone. It is composed mainly of a mineral called calcite. It also comprises minerals such as mica, quartz, iron oxides, and graphite. When the original limestone is a calcite limestone, then the marble is a calcite marble and if the original limestone is dolomitic limestone, then the marble is dolomitic.

▲ *Even though marble is hard, it is easy to carve*

▲ *The word 'marble' originates from the Greek verb 'marmar', which means 'to glisten'*

Formation

Marble is a metamorphic rock formed through metamorphosis from limestone. This happens when limestone is subjected to great pressure and heat. This high pressure results in re-crystallisation, changing the properties of the original limestone rock and converting it into marble. It does not have foliation, which is normal in case of rocks that are formed by the pressure created from a convergent plate boundary. It takes over thousands of years for the limestone to transform into marble under constant pressure and heat. As a result, the marble becomes harder, denser and more colourful than the original stone.

Uses

Marble is a very hard stone, but polishing gives it a smooth texture. Marble is used for creating sculptures and statues. After polishing, it becomes shiny and is used to beautify homes, hotels, buildings, and castles. It is used to make the structure of a building or as supporting columns. Limestone can be damaged relatively faster by water and moisture in the air. However, marble is a much more resistant stone. This is the reason why old structures made from this stone still stand tall against the various damages that time inflicts upon them.

Features

Marble is found naturally in large deposits. It is a light-coloured rock. Usually, marble does not contain impurities. However, marbles with impurities like clay minerals and iron oxides can be grey, pink, yellow, or black in colour. These colours are caused by impurities that appear in patches in marble, making it beautiful. One quality of marble is that it is heat-resistant – it does not heat up quickly. Hence, in warm climate, marble can have a cooling effect. It is a durable stone of average hardness.

Isn't It Amazing!

The Taj Mahal a mausoleum in India, one of the Seven Wonders of the World, is entirely made of marble.

Incredible Individuals

Giovanni Maria Benzoni (1809-1873) was an Italian neoclassical sculptor whose most famous work is the Veiled Rebecca. Described as a melody in marble, the statue was created in 1876, and is simply stunning.

◄ *4 copies were made by Benzoni, and they all still exist in different museums around the world*

Crystals and Gemstones

Crystals are a kind of solid material where the molecules fit together in a repeating pattern. Due to this pattern, the solid material can form different kinds of unique shapes. Crystals are often used as decorative items or to make jewellery because of their attractive appearance.

Formation of Crystals

Crystals are formed when a liquid such as magma cools down and begins to harden. This process is called **crystallisation**. To become stable, the molecules in a liquid gather. The molecules do this in a uniform and repeating pattern as they try to become stable. Thus, crystals are formed. Diamonds, emeralds, and rubies are examples of crystals. Crystals are also formed when water evaporates from any mixture. Salt crystals are a great example of this as they are formed when salt water evaporates.

▲ Crystals are three-dimensional arrangements of atoms, molecules and ions

Features

Crystals generally come in geometrical shapes such as triangles, rectangles, and squares. They have flat surfaces called facets. The shape depends on the type of molecules and atoms that make up the crystal. Crystals may be small or large, but if they are formed from the same molecule, their shape will be the same. Seven basic crystal shapes are also called lattices. They are cubic, trigonal, triclinic, orthorhombic, hexagonal, tetragonal, and monoclinic.

Some Splendid Crystals

Snowflakes are made of beautiful ice crystals. They are formed high up in the clouds when water freezes. They always have six sides and display a delicate six-fold symmetry. Each one of them is unique.

Quartz is quite common, and the hardest of all minerals and crystals. It has a specific chemical component called silica. It also has a particular crystalline form and a hexagonal structure. It can be found in all types of rocks, be it igneous, sedimentary or metamorphic. Quartz is resistant to weathering both chemically and physically.

Diamonds are one of the hardest substances on Earth. They are also the most valuable minerals in the world. Besides jewellery, diamonds are also used in special tools like diamond saws.

▲ Colombia is the largest producer of emeralds and contributes 50 per cent of all emeralds in the world

▲ Every snowflake has approximately 200 snow crystals

▲ Quartz is used in the internal parts of watches

▲ There are white dwarf stars in space, each containing a diamond core

Diamonds

Diamonds are the hardest natural substances on Earth. They are formed under extremely high pressure. They are found in few places in the world and hundreds of kilometres under the ground. Diamonds, themselves, and jewellery made from diamonds are precious because of their high demand across the world.

▲ *Volcanic activities bring the diamond crystals closer to Earth's surface*

Isn't It Amazing!

Coloured diamonds are a rarity. The rarest of them all is the red diamond found in Brazil, Africa and Australia. According to scientists, only 20–30 such diamonds have been discovered to date and most of them are less than half a carat.

► *Rubies in great demand are generally deep red with a hint of blue and this colour is referred to as 'Pigeon's blood'*

Rubies

Rubies are another precious gemstone formed from a mineral called corundum. Rubies comprise aluminium oxide. They are red in colour because of the element chromium. Corundum also forms sapphire in many colours, which generally come from trace mixtures of iron, titanium, and chromium.

Emeralds

Emeralds are basically green precious stones formed from a mineral called beryl, which is a mix of beryllium, aluminium, silicon, and oxygen. The green colour comes from additional traces of chromium and vanadium. Aquamarine, a semi-precious gemstone is also formed from beryl.

Gemstone

Our planet Earth has many kinds of minerals that form splendid crystals. The most valuable ones are gemstones. They are precious or semi-precious stones that are cut, polished and used in jewellery. Uncut stones look like ordinary rocks, but when cut and polished; they obtain a magnificent lustre, which can be used to make beautiful jewellery.

Gems are classified according to their physical properties such as hardness, lustre, colour, density, and magnetism. They are also classified according to the way these gems break, or by the type of mark they leave when rubbed on a laboratory tool called a streak plate.

Gems are divided into precious and semi-precious categories. Amber, amethyst, garnet, onyx, tanzanite, and turquoise are some of the semi-precious gems. Precious gems include diamonds, rubies, sapphires, and emeralds.

▲ *Gemstones are highly priced for their beauty, durability and rarity*

Soil

Soil is the uppermost layer of Earth's crust where plants can grow. It is a mixture of organic matter such as decaying plants and animals, and fragmented rocks and minerals. This layer is not as solid as rock but has small spaces known as pores that are capable of holding air and water. It looks like dirt. Are soil and dirt the same? No, dirt is soil that has lost its ability to support life.

Formation of Soil

Soil takes a long time to form. It is believed that it can take thousands of years to form one inch of soil. However, other factors influence its formation. All living organisms such as plants, fungi, animals, and bacteria help in the process. Other factors like the **topography** of a place and the climate are also vital in soil formation. One important factor, of course, is the parent material. It refers to the kind of rocks and minerals that slowly disintegrate to form soil. Soil is vital for the sustenance of life on Earth.

👤 In Real Life

You can grow different plants based on the soil that is available. Gardeners and professional landscapers choose their plants according to the soil. For example, if sandy soil is abundantly available, a gardener would plant broom shrubs that do not need more water and can grow well in sunny places. In peaty soil, a gardener might grow the heather shrub that grows low on the ground and spreads across the available area.

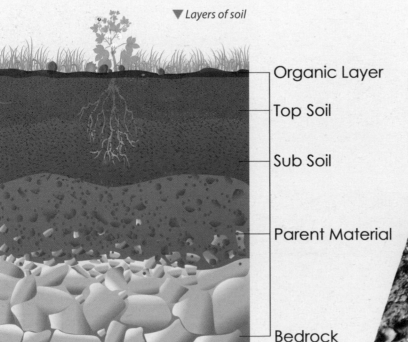

▼ *Layers of soil*

- Organic Layer
- Top Soil
- Sub Soil
- Parent Material
- Bedrock

Types of Soil

There are different types of soil: sandy, clay, loamy, silt, peat, and chalk. Soil is differentiated on the basis of its composition.

Sandy soil: This type of soil is light and not very rich in nutrients. The particles are fine and hard. Sandy soil does not bind well and cannot hold water for a long time. It is formed mainly from the weathering of bedrock such as shale, limestone, granite, and quartz.

Clay soil: It is smoother than sandy soil. The particles of this type of soil are fine and bind well. It is a wet and sticky soil. While wet, it can be moulded into different shapes. However, dry clay soil is quite hard. Clay soil, unlike sandy soil, does not drain well.

Chalky soil: It is not acidic, always alkaline. It is a strong soil containing chalk or limestone. It can hold little water and gets dry quickly. This type of soil is fertile, but not all the nutrients are present in it.

Silt soil: It has a smooth texture and holds water better than sandy soil. This type is good for cultivation. Silt soil is formed when sediments carried by water or ice get deposited. Sometimes, the silt that gets deposited becomes silt stone over time.

Loamy soil: It is a mixture of sand, silt, and clay particles. It can retain water. This type of soil is ideal for cultivation as it is full of nutrients from decomposed material.

Weathering, Erosion, and Conservation

Weathering refers to the breaking down of rocks and minerals on Earth. The agents of weathering are water, ice, acids, **salts**, plants, animals, and changes in temperature. The process of weathering takes place over millions of years to produce a thin layer of soil.

 ## Types of Weathering

There are three types of weathering—physical, chemical, and biological. Physical weathering occurs due to the effect of temperature changes on rocks, which causes them to break. Sometimes, water can help this process along. It takes place mainly in mountainous areas and deserts where there is little soil and scarce vegetation to cover the soil.

Chemical weathering is caused by rain water that reacts with mineral grains in rocks to form new minerals. The water, in this case, is acidic in nature. This phenomenon can only take place when there is sufficient water. It happens at higher temperatures. Therefore, warm and humid climates suit it the most.

Plants and animals cause biological weathering. They produce acid-forming chemicals that cause weathering and, in the process, break down rocks.

▲ *The effects of physical weathering created this great natural structure*

Erosion

After the rocks are broken down, they form soil. Erosion happens on this soil. It is the process by which weathered soil, rocks, and other materials on Earth's surface are dispersed by the actions of gravity, water, ice, and wind. In short, it is the transportation of weathered rocks.

Erosion happens when streams and rivers wear down rocks and carve caves and crevices. The minerals behave like sandpaper and rub off the rocks. As the smaller pieces move downstream, they scrape larger rocks and soften them. Winds in the desert send tiny particles flying through the air. These particles can change the shape of rocks and landscapes. Glaciers can rip away fragments of rocks when they move. They can even create a valley.

Conservation of Soil

Earth is a beautiful planet with natural resources like air, water, soil, minerals, fuels, plants, and animals. Conservation is the practice of caring for these resources for the benefit of all living beings. Soil is one of the natural resources. It is instrumental in the production of food. A certain quality of soil is required for the cultivation of crops to feed human beings and animals. Therefore, it is vital to conserve soil for the well-being of all living things.

Sowing the same crop repeatedly in one place can reduce the nutrients in the soil. This is called 'monoculture'. To avoid this, the conservation method known as 'contour-strip cropping' can be applied. Plants such as wheat, corn, and clover should be planted in alternate strips across the path of prevailing winds. Different crops have different types of leaves and root systems that slow down erosion. Another method of soil conservation is 'selective harvesting'. It is the practice of removing certain individual trees or small groups of trees while leaving others rooted in place to anchor the soil. It is important to conserve soil to save it from harsh weather and erosion. Proper conservation yields more nutritious soil.

In Real Life

Soil is alive but it can also die. Due to the allure of short-term gains, excessive use of chemical pesticides and fertilizers causes long-term damage to soil. The best example of this phenomenon is the American Dust Bowl in the 1930s. 100 million acres of fertile grasslands were destroyed at that time because of poor land management.

◀ *Soil blown by dust bowl winds piled up in large drifts on a Kansas farm*

▼ *Bank erosion is a natural process without which rivers would meander or change their course*

▶ *Contour-strip cropping is used when there is no alternative method for soil conservation while farming on a slope*

Minerals

Minerals are solid, inorganic crystalline substances. They are formed naturally, and each mineral has a specific chemical composition. Minerals that are made up of one element are called native minerals, for example, gold, silver, copper etc. However, when a mineral has more than one element, it is a **compound** mineral. Being made up of silicon and oxygen, quartz is an example of compound mineral.

▲ *Most minerals have a specific arrangement of atoms and ions that defines the characteristics of their crystal forms*

Occurrence and Formation

Minerals are formed in all kinds of environments and under a varied range of chemical and physical conditions. There are four methods of mineral formation. They are igneous where minerals crystallise from a rocky or molten magma. They are sedimentary when the minerals are the result of sedimentation. They are metamorphic when new minerals form from already existing ones. This metamorphosis occurs due to the change in temperature and pressure (or both) on some existing rocks. Minerals can also be formed from a hydrothermal process, wherein minerals are left over from hot-mineral laden water.

▲ *Green Torbernite Mineral in its pure form*

Structure

A mineral is pure and has a uniform structure. Solids that occur naturally are considered true minerals. Rocks consist of minerals that are grouped together. The combination of minerals determines the type of rock formed. Minerals and rocks affect landform development and form natural resources such as gold, tin, iron, marble, and granite. Minerals can be written as a single chemical formula because they are pure. However, there are some impurities too. There are over 3,000 known minerals, and the list is still growing. Some commonly found minerals are quartz, mica, olivine; while emerald lies at the more precious end of the range.

Incredible Individuals

 Friedrich Mohs (1773–1839) was a German mineralogist and geologist. In 1812, he developed a decimal scale to measure the hardness of minerals. This scale is used till date. The Mohs hardness scale takes the rough measure of the resistance put up by a mineral when there is scratching or abrasive action on its smooth surface. There are numerical values assigned to the hardness. For example, talc has the value of 1 because it can easily be scratched even by a person's fingernail. Diamond has the value of 10 because you need to use a glass cutter to make changes to it.

Physical Properties of Minerals

The physical properties of minerals are determined by their chemical structure. To identify minerals, we must first identify their physical properties clearly, which are as follows—(i) colour of the mineral, (ii) streak, which is the colour of the mineral powder, (iii) lustre or the appearance of minerals in reflected light, (iv) cleavage or the tendency of a mineral to break along smooth planes parallel to the zones of weak bonding, (v) fractures or the way a mineral breaks along curved surfaces without a definite shape, (vi) hardness or the mineral's resistance to **abrasion**, (vii) specific gravity or the ratio between the weight of a substance and the weight of an equal volume of water, (viii) tenacity or the resistance to breaking, crushing, bending and tearing.

▲ *Streak is determined using a streak plate*

▲ *Magnesium covered with a black oxide layer*

Grouping Minerals

Mineralogists group minerals according to their chemical composition. However, the most commonly followed grouping system is the one devised by Professor James Dana of Yale University, way back in 1848. Dana system divides minerals into the following basic classes— silicates, oxides, sulphides, sulphates, halides, native elements, carbonates, phosphates, and mineraloids.

 ## Oxides

Oxides are chemical compounds which are made up of oxygen and other chemical elements. A majority of Earth's crust consists of oxides. They are formed when elements are oxidised by air, i.e. when oxygen in the air reacts with the element. Water is the oxide of hydrogen. Nitrous oxide is an oxide of nitrogen, commonly known as laughing gas. Many metals form oxides, for instance, those of iron, aluminium, tin and zinc. These are also important as **ores**.

Some simple oxides are hematite (Fe_2O_3)and zincite (ZnO). Oxides are economically important and are the principal sources of tin (SnO_2), iron (Fe_2O_3, Fe_3O_4), chromium ($FeCr_2O_4$), titanium (TiO_2), manganese (MnO_2) and aluminium (Al). Oxides occur in association with igneous rocks and are high-temperature minerals. Magnesium oxide (MgO) is a basic oxide and is a good thermal conductor and electrical **insulator** used in firebricks and thermal insulation.

 ## Silicates

Silicates are the largest group of minerals found on Earth. They are found in abundance and comprise silicon and oxygen. There are more silicates than all other minerals put together. They also have in them one or more metals like aluminium, calcium, potassium, sodium, barium, iron, and magnesium. Almost all of the igneous-rock-forming minerals are silicates. Igneous rocks make up over 90 per cent of Earth's crust. Naturally, 40 per cent of common minerals are silicates but only 25 per cent of all known minerals are silicates. Each group of silicate minerals conveys something about the environment where it was formed. Some of the common silicate minerals are feldspar, quartz, granite, asbestos, hornblende, clay, and mica. All these minerals have a chemical formula. The symbol for the chemical element of silicon is Si.

▲ *A specimen of a feldspar rock*

In Real Life

Silicon's melting point is 1,414° C, and its boiling point is 3,265° C.

▼ *Mica and feldspar are two examples of silicate minerals*

Incredible Individuals

 Jacob Berzelius, a Swedish chemist, discovered silicon in 1824. He discovered it by heating chips of potassium in a silica container and then carefully washing away the residual by-products. He is considered to be one of the founders of modern chemistry. He also developed chemical symbols and noted the atomic weights of many elements. He discovered several new elements, such as Cerium (Ce) and Thorium (Th).

Native Elements

Native elements are chemical elements that may occur in nature uncombined with any other elements. They are composed of atoms from a single element. Elements that are present in the atmosphere are not included in this category.

Classification

Native elements are divided into three categories. The first category is metals. It includes platinum, iridium, osmium, iron, zinc, tin, gold, silver, copper, mercury, lead, and chromium. The second category consists of semi-metals like bismuth, antimony, arsenic, tellurium, and selenium. The third category is that of non-metals such as sulphur and carbon.

Native elements can form under contrasting conditions and in all types of rocks. Some metals and non-metals are found in abundance on Earth. They are of great commercial importance. For example, gold, a metal, and carbon, a non-metal, are of great importance.

▼ Copper

The Mineral Gold

Gold is the most well-known mineral on Earth. It is known for its value from the earliest times. There are traces of silver in the natural form of gold. Sometimes, traces of copper and iron are also found along with gold. Mineral gold is bright yellow, but if the silver content is more, then it appears whiter. Gold is mined from ores like iron-stained rocks or huge white quartz. The colour of the ore is generally brown. It is crushed and then the gold is extracted from it.

◀ Gold is a metal that can resist natural weathering processes

Features of Gold

Gold is one of the heaviest and most expensive metals. It is a **malleable** substance and can be hammered into thin sheets. It is also a resistant metal and does not tarnish or become discoloured. These thin sheets are used to add a gold design to furniture, picture frames, and many household items. Gold is used to make medals, medicines and jewellery. Astronauts have a thin film of gold on the visor of their helmets, which reflects solar radiation. However, as gold is soft, it is usually alloyed with other precious metals like copper, silver and platinum when it is used in jewellery. This increases its durability.

Isn't It Amazing!

There is enough gold in Earth's core to coat the planet's surface to a depth of 1.5 feet.

In Real Life

Our bodies contain about 0.2 milligrams of gold, most of it is in our blood.

The Mineral Silver

Silver has a white, metallic lustre known for its decorative beauty and electrical conductivity. Similar to gold, silver is also a valuable metal. It is found widely in nature, but when compared with other metals, the amount seems to be quite small. It constitutes 0.05 part per million of Earth's crust. Silver is the best reflector of visible light and is used to make mirrors. It has the tendency to stain or become discoloured. It becomes dark grey when it meets air, and needs to be polished intermittently.

▲ *The world's top producers of silver presently are Mexico, Peru and China*

Isn't It Amazing!

Gold and silver have played an important role as currency across the world. In 550 BCE, King Croesus of Lydia (now in Turkey) was the first to order the use of gold coins. However, silver was used as coins some years before, i.e., 600 BCE, in the same kingdom. Silver, being less valuable than gold, was used to make coins of a lower denomination and that could for everyday transactions.

◄ *Gold and silver are two of the most expensive metals in the world*

▼ *Silver is widely used by dentists to make caps to repair a decayed tooth and prevent it from further decay*

Features of Silver

Silver is the best conductor of thermal and electrical energy. Like gold, pure silver is also too soft to use to make jewellery or tableware. Therefore, forks and knives are usually made from sterling silver, an alloy of 92.5 per cent silver and 7.5 per cent copper. Sometimes other metals are used instead of copper. Throughout history, silver has been used to make coins, jewellery, musical instruments, and medicines.

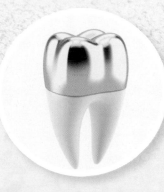

Sulphides

Sulphide is a member of a group of compounds of sulphur with one or more metals. Most sulphides are structurally simple and have many of the properties of metals such as metallic lustre and electrical conductivity. They have a striking colour, less hardness, and a high specific gravity. Sulphides are generally **opaque**, dense, and have distinct streaks. They are an important group of minerals, which include the majority of ore minerals like iron, copper, nickel, lead, cobalt, zinc, and silver.

 ## Sulphide Minerals

Sulphide minerals are the source of various precious metals, especially gold, silver, and platinum. They are the most important group of ore minerals. The metals from these ores are used by many industries. For example antimony, bismuth, copper, lead, nickel, and zinc are used for industrial purposes. Other industrially important metals such as cadmium and selenium are found in numerous common sulphides. They are recovered through refining processes. Sulphides are economically valuable as most metal ores are processed to obtain lead, copper, and silver. This is because of their tendency to bind with metals. A few examples of sulphides are galena, lead sulphide, chalcopyrite, copper, and iron sulphides.

▼ *Lead sulphide or galena*

◀ *Galena is a soft mineral with cubic cleavage, grey streaks, and metallic lustre*

▼ *Arsenic sulphide or auripigment*

 ## Uses

Sodium sulphide is an industrial chemical used for manufacturing dyes, tanning leather, processing crude petroleum, etc. Several metal sulphides are used as **pigments**. Zinc sulphide is used for optical devices. Zinc sulphide with a trace of copper is used for photoluminescent strips for emergency lighting and luminous watch dials. Calcium polysulphide is also commonly known as lime sulphur. It is used in gardening as a fungicide.

◀ *Crystals of sodium sulphide*

Sulphates

Sulphate is a salt of sulphuric acid. A sulphate ion is a group of atoms with the chemical formula SO_4^{-2}. They are formed by replacing hydrogen with a metal, for example sodium. When the hydrogen atoms are replaced, then it becomes a normal sulphate. When one hydrogen atom is replaced, it is called a bisulphate. Mostly, metal sulphates are easily soluble in water, whereas calcium and mercuric sulphates are only slightly soluble. Sulphates can be found quite in abundance in nature, for example, barium sulphate occurs as barite and calcium sulphate occurs as gypsum and alabaster. Soluble sulphates comprise a central sulphur atom. They are bonded to four oxygen atoms and should be distinguished from sulphide minerals. Sulphates like gypsum $(CaSO_4 \cdot 2H_2O)$ and magnesium sulphate $(MgSO_4)$ have great industrial uses.

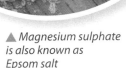

▲ *Magnesium sulphate is also known as Epsom salt*

▼ *Zinc sulphide*

The bubbles in the mud indicate the release of hydrogen sulphide gas

Pyrite is an iron sulphide ... is the most common ...ong sulphide minerals

Marcasite iron sulphide

🔆 Isn't It Amazing!

Sulphur is a bright yellow element, known in the Bible as 'brimstone'. It is abundant in nature and was used for a variety of purposes in the ancient times. Sulphur is used for making car batteries and manufacturing fertilizers.

▶ *Sulphur, also known as brimstone*

🌐 Uses

Sulphates have varied uses. Most commonly, they are used in detergents and as foaming agents. Sulphate compounds are also found in personal care products like toothpastes, sprays, lotions, soaps, and shampoos. Sometimes they are added to products to make them more effective cleaners.

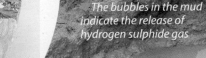

Other Mineral Groups

Other mineral groups are carbonates, phosphates, halides, and mineraloids. Carbonates are minerals made of carbon and a metal. Calcium carbonate is the most common in this group. Inorganic phosphates are compounds of phosphorus and oxygen that occur naturally in many forms and are combined with other elements like metals. Halides are minerals that are made up of sodium and calcium. A mineraloid is a naturally occurring mineral-like substance that does not demonstrate crystallinity.

◀ *Calcium carbonate*

Carbonate

A carbonate is a chemical compound that is made of carbon and oxygen. It produces carbon dioxide, water, and a chemical salt when added to an acid. It is found naturally on Earth. Widely used carbonates are sodium carbonate (Na_2CO_3), sodium bicarbonate ($NaHCO_3$) and potassium carbonate (K_2CO_3).

A very common carbonate is ammonium carbonate, popularly known as smelling salt. Calcium carbonate is found in the shells of animals and in rocks like Iceland spar, limestone, and marble. It is also used in the production of lime or calcium oxide. Ammonium, potassium, and sodium carbonates are easily soluble in water. Carbonates give off carbon dioxide when treated with dilute acids like hydrochloric acid.

▼ *Water pools capped with calcium carbonate in Pamukkale in Central Turkey*

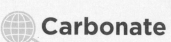
◀ *Rock phosphate*

Phosphates

A phosphate is a salt of phosphoric acid. The most important phosphate is calcium phosphate, which is available in abundance on Earth. It is not very good for plants, as it is slightly soluble in water. When it is treated with sulphuric acid, a superphosphate of lime is formed. Another inorganic phosphate is ammonium phosphate, which is used as a fertiliser. Trisodium phosphate is used in detergent and to soften water. Disodium phosphate is sometimes used in medicines and making baking powder.

Phosphate rocks are the main source of phosphorous, which is not found freely in nature. Phosphate rocks are found in North Africa, Russia, and in several places in the United States. Did you know that phosphorus glows in the dark and in moist air? The name is derived from the Greek word 'phosphoros', which means 'light bearing'.

▲ *A phosphate mine processing mill*

▼ *Crystals of Himalayan halite salt*

◀ *A piece of fluorite*

Halides

Halides are compounds comprising halogens. A halogen element is one of the five non-metallic elements that make up a mineral group. The name halogen originates from the Greek roots 'hal' meaning 'salt' and '-geh' meaning 'to produce'. Halides produce salt. They are basically formed by combining a metal with one of the five halogen elements such as chlorine, bromine, fluorine, iodine, and astatine. As most of these compounds are soluble in water, they occur under special conditions. Halite (NaCl) or rock salt is an exception. It is very common and found in huge deposits all over the world. It is a mineral that has many uses, including the production of table salt.

Another common halide mineral is fluorite (CaF_2) or calcium fluoride. It is generally used in the manufacturing of steel and aluminium. It serves as a **flux**, making molten metal flow more easily. It comes in nearly every colour of the rainbow and has a striking appearance. Sylvite is similar to halite and contains potassium, which is used as a fertiliser.

◀ *Opal*

Mineraloids

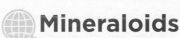

A mineraloid is a naturally occurring, inorganic solid that does not present crystallinity. It looks like a mineral but does not have the required atomic structure to be defined as a mineral. Some even do not have the necessary chemical compositions.

Some familiar materials can be described as mineraloids. For example, opal is an hydrated silica with the chemical composition $SiO_2.nH_2O$. The 'n' in its formula indicates that the amount of water is variable. Therefore, opal is a mineraloid. Another example of a mineraloid is obsidian.

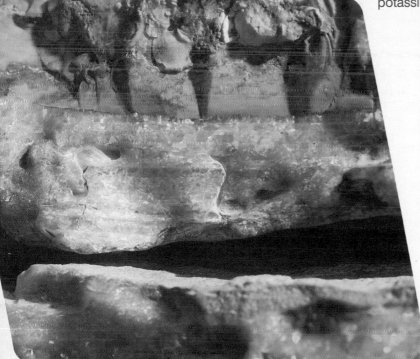
▲ *A rare opal boulder in Coober Pedy, Australia*

⊛ Incredible Individuals

In 1669, Hennig Brand discovered phosphorus, by extracting it from buckets of urine. With this, he became the first person known to discover an element. He named this element 'phosphorous' or 'light-bearer' because it glowed in the dark. He spent a large part of his life looking for something called the 'philosopher's stone', which could allegedly convert base metals to gold. Such an element does not exist, but is often depicted in books and films.

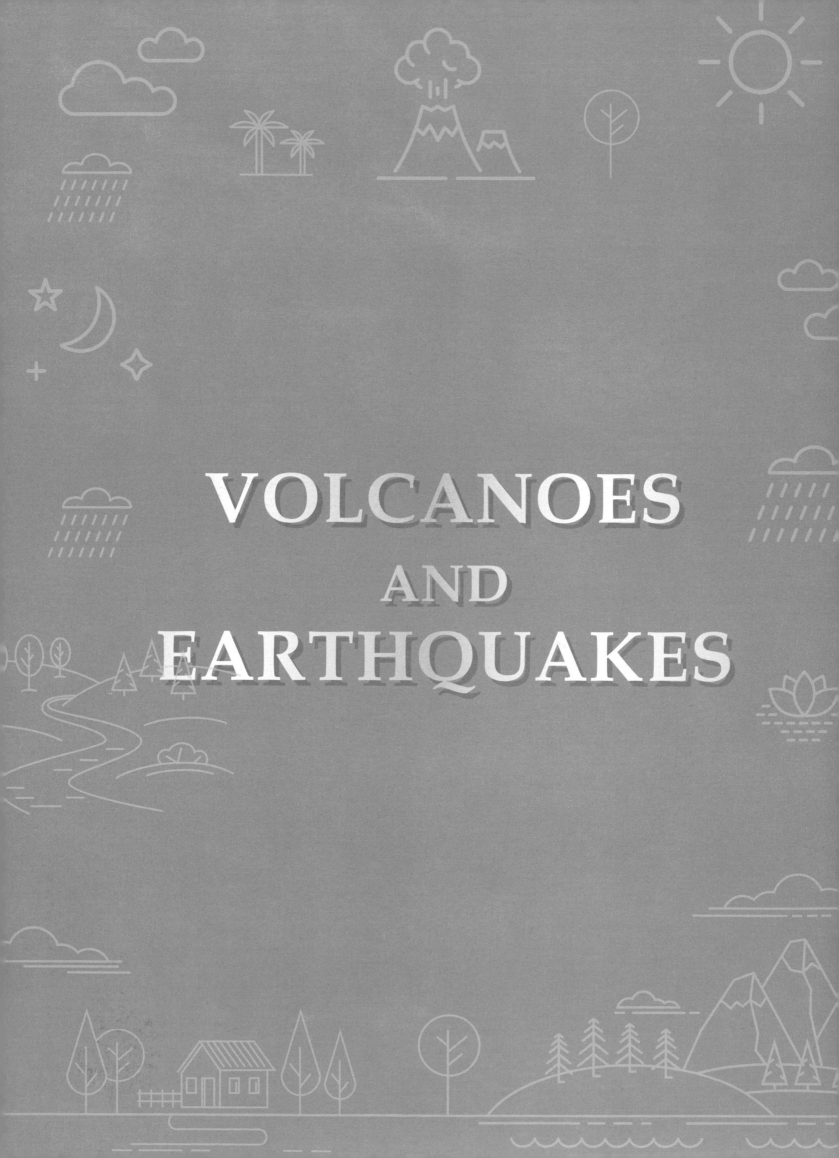

VOLCANOES
AND
EARTHQUAKES

DEADLY DISASTERS

Earth is a magnificent planet with varied natural features and natural phenomena. Volcanoes and earthquakes are such natural phenomena. Earth's crust is made up of huge slabs called **tectonic plates**, which resemble the pieces of a jigsaw puzzle. These plates are constantly moving, and the resulting friction causes earthquakes and volcanic eruptions.

A volcano is an opening in Earth's crust through which **lava**, hot gases, and ash come out. Volcanic eruptions can be very destructive but can sometimes also lead to the creation of new landforms. Earthquakes are the sudden shaking of Earth's surface due to the movements underneath it. Volcanic eruptions and earthquakes are natural disasters that can cause great destruction to life.

▼ *Earthquakes can have disastrous consequences such as triggering landslides, tsunamis, and possibly volcanoes*

What Is a Volcano?

The word 'volcano' is derived from the word 'Vulcan', the Roman god of fire. A volcano is a vent in Earth's crust through which molten lava, gases, ash, and rock fragments escape into the air. Hot gases and melted rock or **magma** are ejected from deep within Earth's crust that find their way up. This material within Earth's crust can flow slowly out of a **fissure** in the ground, but can also erupt suddenly into the air.

 ## Volcanic Eruptions

Volcanoes have played an important role in the formation of the oceans and continents. Volcanic activity is the process by which the materials from Earth's interior reach the surface. Eruptions mainly occur when excessive pressure builds up within Earth's innermost layer, and most volcanoes have a volcanic **crater** at the top through which these materials come out.

▲ *Iceland's Kerid crater lake stands out because it is surrounded by rare red volcanic earth*

Strong volcanic eruptions throw bits of magma into the air, which cool into tiny pieces of rock called volcanic ash. Winds carry this volcanic ash thousands of kilometres away. Steam and poisonous gases also escape from volcanoes. Sometimes these gases are mixed with ash and other hot **debris**. This mixture travels outward in destructive fiery clouds called **pyroclastic flows**. Millions of years ago, hot gases like carbon dioxide streamed from within and out through countless volcanoes to form the atmosphere around the Earth and oceans.

▶ *An eruption creates a vertical column of ash and smoke. Depending on the strength of the eruption, the plume can go from under 100 metres all the way to over 40 kilometers high*

In Real Life

▲ *Gases emerging from Mount Aso in Japan*

Japan experiences frequent volcanic eruptions. There are around 60 active volcanoes in the country, and there have been three major volcanic eruptions since 1980. The reason for all of this stressful activity is the movement of tectonic plates near Japan.

How Are Volcanoes Formed?

Volcanoes do not just form anywhere on our planet. There are certain locations where these openings are formed. The main three places where they originate are divergent plate boundaries, convergent plate boundaries, and hot spots.

Divergent Plate Boundaries

Earth's crust is made up of massive, irregularly shaped slabs of solid rock known as tectonic plates. These plates are constantly moving but in slow motion, and most volcanoes lie along the boundaries between the plates. Some volcanoes form when two plates pull apart and form divergent plate boundaries. The molten rock rises between these two plates, causing fissure eruptions in which lava flows out over the ground without any explosions. This type of volcano is found along the Mid-Atlantic **Ridge**. Volcanoes in the northern part of this ridge formed the island country of Iceland.

◀ *Lava usually emerges from the Earth at 700°C–1250°C*

▼ *Molten rock is known as magma while underground, becoming lava when it reaches the surface. Both produce igneous rock after cooling down*

 ## Convergent Plate Boundaries

Sometimes oceanic and continental plates collide. The oceanic plates are thinner and more dense, and are sometimes forced beneath the continental plates, which are thicker and less dense. This is how convergent plate boundaries form. The process by which the plate is forced down is called **subduction**.

When this happens, violent eruptions take place and force magma to rise to the surface, creating explosive volcanoes. These types of volcanoes are found around the edges of the Pacific Ocean.

 ## Hot Spots

A small number of volcanoes form at the 'hot spots' in the Earth's crust where molten rock rises from deep below the crust. Hot spots occur in mantle plumes that are unusually hot areas and not at the boundaries of tectonic plates. The volcanoes of Hawaii are the best examples of hot-spot volcanoes.

▶ *A mud pit formed in a volcanic hot spot*

Parts of a Volcano

In this world, we can see many types and shapes of volcanoes. But all of them basically have the same parts and layers. These are either located in the mountainous regions or within the Earth. Scientists have discovered volcanoes on the moon and other planets as well, but even those have the same basic parts. These parts are magma chamber, dike, lava, main vent, side vent, throat, crater, pyroclastic flow, and ash cloud.

 Lava

Lava is molten rock or semi-fluid rock that erupts out of a volcano. When lava erupts from a vent it comes out at a temperature of between 700°–1250° C. As it flows down the volcano, it is called lava flow. It eventually cools and hardens when it comes in contact with air. This solidified form is also referred to as lava. This should not be confused with magma, which is hot liquid rock that is found just below the surface of Earth.

▶ *Lava from a vent or crater is accompanied by dangerous gases such as sulfur dioxide and hydrogen sulfide*

Magma Chamber

It is a large pool of molten rock found underneath Earth's crust, and are usually found 1-10 km below the surface. Magma is formed when the temperatures in Earth's crust or mantle increase and air pressures decrease. It is composed of molten rock, dissolved gases, and crystals. The molten rock itself is made of oxygen, aluminium, silicon, magnesium, calcium, iron, etc. As the magma (which is a liquid) cools, it forms crystals of different metals. Eventually, it solidifies and becomes igneous or magmatic rock. When a volcano erupts, or a deep crack occurs in the crust, the magma rises and overflows from the magma chamber.

▲ *If lava cools at a faster rate, the rock it forms will have a fine grain and a glassy appearance. If it cools slower, it will have larger grains and be more coarse*

Volcanic Ash and Ash Cloud

Volcanic ash is formed during explosive eruptions when gases in magma expand and escape violently into the atmosphere. Hence, an ash cloud is created when this ash is propelled into the air. Volcanic ash consists of particles of rock, minerals, and glass.

Crater

The crater is a bowl-shaped opening at the top of a volcano. The outward explosion of rocks and other materials during a volcanic eruption causes the formation of craters.

▲ *Ash cloud is seen rising from the crater*

Dike

Magma inside the mountain exerts a lot of pressure on the crust as well as on the volcano itself. The magma pushes its way through small cracks in the crust and ultimately reaches the surface, creating dikes in the process. Therefore, a dike is an **intrusion** of magma that cuts through the existing rocks and then solidifies. A volcano can have hundreds of dikes.

Main Vent

It is the weak point on Earth's crust where hot magma rises from the magma chamber and reaches the surface. It is an opening through which lava, gases, ash, and other explosive materials come out.

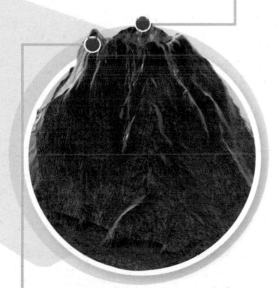

◀ *Parts of a volcano*

Throat

The uppermost section of the main vent is called the throat of a volcano. It is from here that the lava is ejected.

Conduit

This is the main passage for the magma to reach the surface. It is like a pipe or tube that is located at the main vent where all materials pile up. These materials move from the magma chamber to the surface from the conduit tube. A large volcano could have a network of conduit pipes where materials travel. After an explosion, some lava cools at the mouth of the conduit pipe, creating a plug.

Side Vent

A side vent is an opening in the side of a volcano through which volcanic materials like lava, gases, and pyroclastic debris come out.

Categories & Types of Volcanoes

Volcanoes are a magnificent phenomenon of nature and play an important role in shaping our planet's geography. There are three categories of volcanoes: active, dormant, and extinct. This categorisation is based on the recent activity of a particular volcano and its frequency of eruption, size, and potential impact. They can be further differentiated by types as well.

▶ An erupting volcano

 ## Extinct Volcanoes

An extinct volcano is one that has erupted thousands of years ago and no one expects another eruption presently. One such volcano is located on Hawaii's Big Island and its name is Mount Kohala. This volcano last erupted approximately 60,000 years ago. Scientists believe that it will never be active again.

It is quite difficult to differentiate between a volcano that is not active presently and one that has remained inactive. The Fourpeaked Mountain, Alaska, USA for example, erupted once in 2006. Before that though, it had been marked as an extinct volcano as it had not erupted for about 10,000 years.

In Real Life

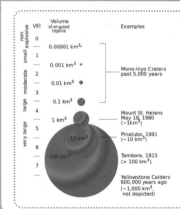

The Volcanic Explosivity Index (VEI) is a numerical scale that assesses the explosiveness of past volcanic eruptions. The explosivity value of an eruption is calculated using the volume of materials, the height of the eruption cloud, and qualitative observations (using words ranging from "gentle" to "mega-colossal").

◀ Some volcanic eruptions of the past on the Volcanic Explosivity Index

Volcanoes that have got cut off from their magma supply are termed as extinct. The Hawaiian-Emperor seamount chain in the Pacific Ocean, the Shiprock volcano in Navajo Nation territory in New Mexico, and the volcanoes of Edinburgh Castle in Scotland are examples of extinct volcanoes. However, it is difficult to determine if a volcano is extinct. So, **volcanologists** often describe extinct volcanoes as inactive as these were active at some point in time. Whereas, some volcanoes once known to have become extinct are now termed as dormant. Hence, it is quite complicated to figure out whether a volcano is active, dormant, or extinct.

▼ This is Mount Kirkjufell, an extinct volcano in Iceland. Note that in an extinct volcano, the magma chamber is empty

▼ The Fourpeaked Mountain in Alaska is a dormant volcano. Note that dormant volcanoes or sleeping giants who still have access to magma, unlike the extinct ones

Incredible Individuals

People who study or research volcanoes are referred to as volcanologists. Maurice and Catherine 'Katia' Krafft were volcanologists who dedicated their lives to the study of volcanoes. They were attracted by erupting volcanoes and saved up money to travel to Mount Stromboli to take pictures. They visited hundreds of volcanoes around the world in their lifetimes. They were nicknamed 'Volcano Devils'. Unfortunately, they lost their lives when they were hit by pyroclastic flow of the Mount Unzen volcano in Japan.

▶ *A crater of the volcano Piton de la Fourmaise on the Island of Reunion called 'M and K Kraft' has been named after this couple*

Dormant Volcanoes

A **dormant** volcano is one that has not erupted for a while but can erupt in the near future. Sometimes, there is very little difference between a dormant volcano and an active one. This is because even though a volcano can remain dormant for hundreds of years, there is always a chance that it can erupt at some point in the future.

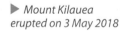 Active Volcanoes

An active volcano is one that has erupted in the recent past, and can erupt in the future. One of the best examples of active volcanoes is Mount Kilauea, which has been erupting continuously from 1983 to the present day.

An active volcano can be quite dangerous and destructive. However, when passive, the soil it enriches can become fertile and perfect for agricultural settlements. According to scientists, when a volcano shows signs of unrest (gas emission and unusual tectonic activity) it can be called active as it is about to erupt.

▶ *Mount Kilauea erupted on 3 May 2018*

Cinder Cone Volcanoes

They are the simplest and smallest type of volcano, and are also the most common type found. These generally circular volcanoes usually have small footprints, with gentle slopes that are between 30–40 degrees.

 ## Types of Volcanoes

Volcanoes can also be classified into five major types according to the nature of their eruption, the basis of their formation and how they developed with time. The five types of volcanoes are: cinder cone volcanoes (circular or oval cones), composite volcanoes (tall and thin), shield volcanoes (flat), calderas, and lava dome volcanoes (dome-shaped).

 ## Isn't It Amazing!

▲ *Paricutin Volcano*

The Paricutin volcano, also known as the 'Volcan de Paricutin,' is located in Michoacan, Mexico. It is one of the world's seven natural wonders. It is well-known for being the youngest volcano in the Northern Hemisphere, and is forming in a farmer's cornfield.

 ## All About Cinder Cones

They are formed when magma that contains an enormous amount of dissolved gas approaches vents in the Earth's crust. When it breaks through, the building pressure of the gas is suddenly let free. This results in an explosive eruption that launches a spray of magma into the air. This molten rock cools as it travels through the air, and comes back to the Earth as cinders. Over time, this builds up a circular or oval-shaped cone, with a bowl-shaped crater at the top. Cinder cone volcanoes are fairly small, generally only about 300 feet tall and not rising more than 1,200 feet.

The cinders here are small fragments of igneous rock that are very similar in composition to basalt, and are formally called scoria. Scoria is very **vesicular**, and range in colour from black, to deep reddish brown, to dark grey. Volcan Rumoka is a cinder cone volcano in the Virunga Mountains in Nord Kivu, Democratic Republic of Congo. Volcan Rumoka last erupted in December 1912, and the lava continued to flow till March 1913.

▲ *Scoria is used for decorative landscaping and for insulation*

▼ *Mount Bromo is an example of a cinder cone volcano*

Composite Volcanoes

The word 'composite' means 'made up of several elements'. As the name suggests, composite volcanoes are made up of multiple eruptions. These eruptions might occur over a period of hundreds or even thousands of years.

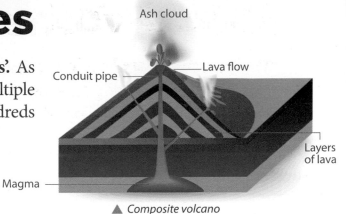

▲ Composite volcano

Formation

Composite volcanoes are sometimes also called stratovolcanoes as they are steep-sided volcanoes composed of many layers of volcanic rocks. These layers are usually made from high-**viscosity** lava, ash, and rock debris. The lava cools down and forms a thick layer of crust in the vent or opening, giving it a conical shape.

Sometimes the lava forms small dome volcanoes over the vent in the crater of a stratovolcano or on its steep sides. They are usually formed in the Earth's subduction zones, where tectonic plates slide under each other.

▲ Kawah Ijen is a composite volcano in Indonesia

Features

Composite volcanoes represent more than 60 per cent of the volcanoes present on Earth today. Mount St Helens, for example, is located in the state of Washington, USA. Infamous for being a dangerous volcano, it once continuously erupted from September 2004 to January 2008.

Composite volcanoes vary in size, and the base of a composite volcano can be as large as 8 kilometres across. The size is based upon how long they have been active, how many eruptions they have undergone, and how much they have eroded with time. Mount Shasta, in the Cascade mountain range in northern California, stands 14,163 feet above sea level. In comparison, Mount Vesuvius is only 4,203 feet tall, and the Krakatau volcano sits only 2,667 feet above sea level. When stratovolcanoes erupt, they comprise some of the most dangerous instances of volcanic activity.

They remain dormant for long periods of time, during which the solidified lava around the vents collapses inwards, blocking the vents up. This increases the pressure, and the eventual explosion can be lethal. When Mount St. Helens erupted in 1980, the eruption killed people and crops were destroyed. This was the deadliest and most economically destructive volcanic event in the history of the US.

▲ Before Mount St. Helens erupted in 1980, it had a pointed top. Now it has a bowl shape where its peak once stood

Shield Volcanoes

Shield volcanoes are large and broad. The world's largest volcano, Mauna Loa in Hawaii, is the best example of a shield volcano. Hawaii lies over an island chain made up of five volcanoes that stand very close to each other.

Flood Basalts

Shield volcanoes resemble a warrior's shield in shape. They have wide diameters, with steep middle slopes and flat summits. The lava that pours out of shield volcanoes is thin. It can travel for great distances down the shallow slopes of the volcano.

Basalt lava flows from these volcanoes. As basalt lava is very fluid, it does not settle in one place long enough to pile up and so it runs downhill. Volcanoes that are formed like this are called flood basalts. The eruption that occurs in shield volcanoes is similar to the flow of water from a fountain. It is not explosive. However, if it comes into contact with water, it becomes explosive. The intervals between eruptions are shorter, and the explosions are less intense.

Features

The name 'shield volcano' comes from the shape of these mountains, which resembles low shields. In these volcanoes, while the lava flows fluidly, the gases are in short supply. Yet, they are among some of the largest volcanoes in the world. Basaltic shield volcanoes do not actually look like volcanoes as they are not steep. They are characterised by low explosiveness, which forms cinder cones and **spatter** cones at the vent. Shield volcanoes are the result of a greater quantity of magma. The lava is hot and it barely changes after its formation.

In Real Life

Shield volcanoes are the result of hot-spot volcanism. The 'hot-spot' refers to a part of Earth's mantle where heat rises upwards from deep within its core. Near the tectonic plates in the crust, it results in hot temperatures and low pressures. Eventually, this melts the rock and forms magma which rises through the Earth's crust and creates volcanoes. Even if the tectonic plates move over this area, new volcanoes eventually form here. The Hawaiian Islands are a chain of shield volcanoes that were formed in this way.

▼ Erta Ale is an example of a basaltic shield volcano. It is located in eastern Ethiopia

Calderas

Sometimes a volcano will partially collapse after an eruption. This is because it has emptied all of the contents of its magma chamber during the eruption. More often than not, the eruption that has occurred is explosive, creating a caldera or depression where the volcano has collapsed.

▲ Usually, water fills up in the depressed region of the caldera

 ## Features

The caldera might be bowl-shaped as the land around the vent of the erupting volcano has collapsed inwards. Depending on the intensity of the eruption, and how long it lasted, volcanic eruptions can create calderas as wide as

100 kilometres. The terms crater and caldera are often used synonymously, but calderas are larger than craters. A crater can occur inside a caldera, but the reverse cannot happen.

▲ The Kilauea caldera radiates a glow because of the lava present in its crater

 ## Formation

A caldera is formed when the magma chamber beneath a volcano is emptied in a large eruption. Sometimes, a volcanic eruption occurs so quickly that the empty chamber beneath does not have the strength to support the weight of the volcano. So, the vent collapses inwards. This can happen in a single **cataclysmic** event, or over the course of several eruptions. A very good example of the latter is the **supervolcano** over which the Yellowstone National Park is located. The supervolcano erupted three times. It last erupted 6,40,000 years ago. It released 1,000 cubic kilometres of rock, covering much of North America in 2 metres of debris.

▼ A diagram showing the calderas created in the famous Yellowstone National Park

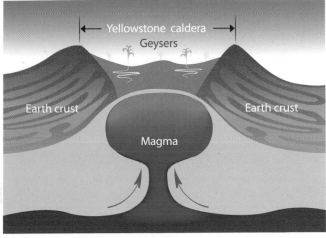

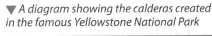

The Torfajokull volcano has not had a large eruption since 1477, but its 18x12 kilometre caldera is home to Iceland's largest geothermal areas with steaming sulphur, mud pools, and hot springs. On the northern edge of the caldera, the hot springs at Landmannalaugar have temperatures of 36–40° C.

◀ A geyser in Yellowstone National Park, which lies over a supervolcano

Lava Domes

Lava domes are also called dome volcanoes. These are formed by small masses of lava which are too thick to flow very far. Unlike shield volcanoes, with low-viscosity lava, the magma from volcanic domes just piles up near the volcanic vent. Sometimes the lava might be viscous, but it is forced out of the vent in short bursts, almost resembling how an ointment is forced out of a tube. The dome shape comes from the expansion of the lava within. The mountain forms from material spilling off the sides of the growing dome.

Features

Lava domes can explode violently, releasing a huge amount of hot rock and ash. The eruption of Mount St. Helens was caused in part by a lava dome shifting to allow explosive gas and steam to escape from inside the mountain.

▲ A lava dome during an eruption

A lava dome can form on any kind of landform that experiences a lot of volcanic activity. Usually, they can be found in the crater of larger volcanoes like Mount St. Helens. Some lava domes are flat and circular in shape, while others are tall and pointed towards the top. Most have steep sides. They can reach a height of 800 metres.

Lava domes can be very dangerous. When such a structure grows high and has steep sides, or when it spreads onto a steep slope, it becomes unstable.

ⓞ Incredible Individuals

The name Lassen Peak comes from a Danish explorer and homesteader Peter Lassen who lived in the area during the mid 19th century. He aided newly arrived European settlers through the surrounding areas. However, this lava dome was originally named San José by a Spanish officer who became the first among European settlers to see this peak back in 1821. The name changed several times after that.

After the Explosion

Novarupta is an example of a lava dome. It is found in Alaska, USA. It once erupted, leading to the largest volcanic eruption of the 20th century. The eruption began on 6 June 1912, and ended after 60 hours. Even though no deaths were reported, the surrounding animals, plants and fishery industries did not recover for several years.

Lassen Peak, or Mount Lassen, is another example of a lava dome in northern California, USA. It is the southernmost active volcano in the Cascade Range. It was believed to be extinct until it suddenly erupted on 30 May 1914. Even after this, there were many minor eruptions reported over the course of the next year.

On 22 May 1915, more explosive eruptions occurred here. This forced a stream of molten lava 1,000 feet down the mountain called a lahar, melting snow and causing mudflows.

◀ Lassen Peak is the largest volcano in California, and was active periodically until 1921

▼ Lava domes or their formative eruptions commonly occur on convergent plate boundaries. These eruptions are quite common

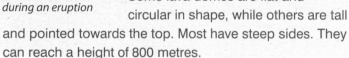

The Great Eruption

Mount Vesuvius is an active volcano located on the Bay of Naples in Italy. In fact, its western base sits on the bay. In 2013, the height of this volcano was recorded to be 4,203 feet. A volcano's height changes after every major eruption—and Mount Vesuvius has had many eruptions. The most famous among them was the great eruption of 79 CE that wiped out the population of Pompeii.

 ## The Lost City

Pompeii was a thriving city in what is now southern Italy about 2,000 years ago. In 79 CE, the eruptions possibly began with a thundering blast that warned the nearby residents of what was coming. Then, volcanic rocks flew out of the vent. As soon as the residents saw these rocks, they ran for their lives. Entire villages were abandoned as people ran towards the neighbouring forests for cover.

Sadly, they were running right towards the danger zone where volcanic stones and ash descended upon them. Those running for their lives might have experienced breathing problems because of the ash. They also would not have been able to see too far ahead. Many people died instantly, without even realising why or how they had lost their lives. Pompeii—and many of its 10,000 inhabitants—disappeared almost instantly under a cloud of ash.

When Mount Vesuvius erupted, volcanic rocks and gases flew out of the vent to a height of 33 kilometres!

 ## Discovered Again

Study of Mount Vesuvius only began in the 18th century. In 1995, Italian archaeologists were digging in the area to see if it was fit to build a gas pipeline to reach the nearby town of San Paolo Bel Sito. There they found the skeletons of a woman and a man and put the pieces together to understand the volcano and the disasters it had caused.

Surprisingly, Mount Vesuvius was dormant for hundreds of years before the great eruption of 79 CE. This eruption killed 3,360 people with its mud and lava flow. Again, in 1631 CE it erupted and killed 3,500 people with the mud flow. Yet, it is considered to be a young volcano as it was only formed 200,000 years ago.

 ## Disaster Zone

Nearly 2,000 years ago, the great eruption destroyed the cities of Pompeii, Herculaneum, and Stabiae among others. The volcano, however, has remained active to this day. It was most active between 79 and 1037 CE, as around nine eruptions were recorded from this volcano. Besides volcanoes, this area also experienced earthquakes for six months. Then on 16 December 1631, another eruption took place that killed 3,000 people. After this eruption, the skies above turned dark from the ash rising from the volcano and remained dark for months.

Today, people visit Pompeii to see the site of the great eruption

History's Deadliest Eruptions

Though Mount Vesuvius is remembered by many, perhaps the deadliest volcanic eruptions occurred in Indonesia. During the 1815 eruption of Mount Tambora, 92,000 people were killed. Again, in 1883 when Mount Krakatau erupted, it killed 36,417 people.

The Tambora Eruption

Mount Tambora is 13,000 feet in height. When this massive volcano erupted it released gas, dust, and rocks that cloaked the entire island of Sumbawa and went further still. The ash and lava that spilled down the mountains destroyed entire forests. The nearby Java Sea experienced a tsunami, that went on to kill 10,000 people.

As a result of this volcanic eruption and tsunami in Indonesia, many parts of Europe and North America suffered a famine. Volcanic ash that settled on Earth's surface after the eruption caused the destruction of the vegetation and crops. This was the reason behind the consequent famine. Climate scientists suspect Tambora played a role in the unseasonably cold spell that hit most of the Northern Hemisphere in 1816, dubbed the "year without a summer." The telegraph had not yet been invented at the time of this eruption, so many people had no idea about it.

▲ Its huge caldera is 6 km in diameter, and 1,100 metres deep

The Krakatau Eruption

Though Mount Tambora's eruption was deadlier than the Kratakau eruption, more people knew about the latter because the telegraph had been invented by then. Krakatau erupted in 1883. It is an island volcano that lies between the islands of Sumatra and Java, a hotbed of volcanic activity.

When Krakatau erupted, the explosions were heard 4,653 kilometres away, all the way across the Indian ocean on Rodriguez Island. This distance is nearly one-thirteenth of the Earth's circumference. The surrounding waters rose 40 metres in height. These fearsome sea waves killed thousands. Only one-third of the island of Krakatau remained above sea level, but new islands of pumice and ash were formed in the north.

▲ The Krakatau explosion was the loudest sound ever recorded by humanity

Effects of Volcanic Eruptions

Volcanic eruptions can affect human beings in many ways. Lava flows, pyroclastic flows, hot gases, and ash can cause breathing problems and kill people. Buildings, roads, and fields get covered with ash; and if this ash is not cleared off, then the buildings might collapse. In an eruption, entire forests can be covered by ash and lava. However, volcanic soil is rich and fertile, so when it cools off, it is easy for vegetation in the area to recover quickly.

Livestock and other animals are killed during an eruption by the lava flows. They also die due to forest fires and earthquakes caused during an eruption. As plant life is destroyed, there is a drop in food production. This might lead to famine and cause even more deaths.

Mount Thera

The eruption of Mount Thera in Greece was a catastrophic volcanic eruption that took place approximately 3,500 years ago. It devastated the island of Thera, which got buried under a thick layer of ash and pumice after the eruption. It resulted in a layer of **ash plume** that was approximately 30–35 kilometres long, and which extended into the **stratosphere**. Then, a devastating tsunami occurred on the north coast of Crete. The explosion was equivalent to the blast of 40 atomic bombs. It blew out the interior of the island and forever changed its **topography**.

The caldera of Thera and the town formed near it

Huaynaputina Volcano

Huaynaputina is a young volcano located in southern Peru. It was the site of a catastrophic eruption—which was preceded by several earthquakes—in 1600 CE. The eruption is notable, not only because the summit elevation of this volcano is 4,800 metres, but also because it is the only major explosive eruption in the history of the Central Andes. It also had a great impact on the global climate. It has been recorded as the largest volcanic explosion, destroying villages many kilometres away and agriculture worldwide. Ash fall was reported 250–500 kilometres away, throughout southern Peru.

▶ *While the actual eruption only lasted 12-19 hours, the air was not clear of ash from February to April*

Mount Pelee

Mount Pelee is an active volcano on the Caribbean island of Martinique in West Indies. It erupted on May 1902, killing approximately 30,000 people. Casualties were mainly caused by the fast-moving pyroclastic flows.

▲ *The summers following the Mount Pelee eruption were the coldest compared to the previous five centuries*

💡 Isn't It Amazing!

According to reports, only two people survived the 1902 eruption of Mount Pelee, one of whom was a prisoner trapped in an underground cell.

The Aftermath

A volcanic eruption has a large effect on the planet as a whole. An eruption has the potential to destroy wide stretches of land, human, plant, and animal life, as well as the surrounding environment for years.

The Ring of Fire

Though it is called the 'Ring of Fire', it is actually a horseshoe-shaped area that is home to a string of volcanoes. Of the earthquakes that have occurred on our planet's surface, 90 per cent take place in the Ring of Fire. It is home to 70 per cent of the Earth's active volcanoes. No doubt, it is a hotbed of seismic activity.

▲ The Pacific plate is the largest tectonic plate on Earth. It spreads over an area of 103 million square kilometres

What is the Ring of Fire?

The Ring of Fire is a chain of volcanoes and other sites of seismic activity around the borders and edges of the Pacific Ocean, extending for 40,000 kilometres. This area consists of 452 volcanoes that begin at the southern tip of South America and end at New Zealand, covering North America and Japan. There are some active and dormant volcanoes along Antarctica that are also a part of this area.

Formation

The Ring of Fire was formed by the movements of tectonic plates. These plates are constantly moving on a layer of solid and molten rock called the mantle. As they move, the tectonic plates might simply move away from each other, come together in a collision, or slide along the edges, causing earthquakes and volcanoes. It is in these zones movement that the activity of the Ring of Fire occurs. The phenomenon encloses tectonic plates such as the vast Pacific Plate and the smaller Philippine, Juan de Fuca, Cocos, and Nasca plates.

▼ The Pacific Ring of Fire lies over the Pacific plate, and accounts for 70 per cent of the Earth's volcanic activity, and 90 per cent of all our earthquakes have their origin in this area

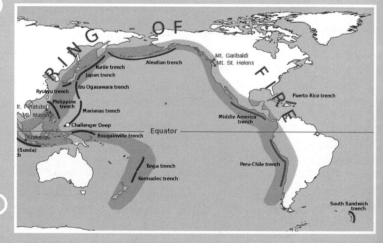

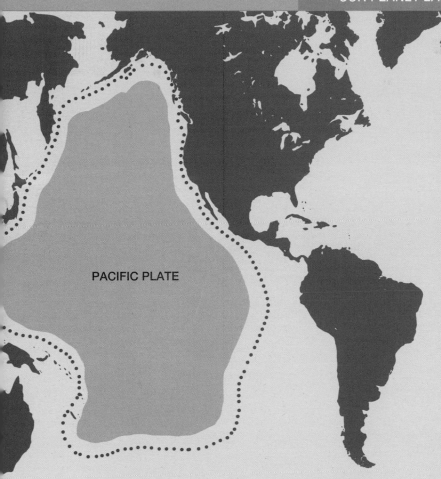

PACIFIC PLATE

Volcanoes

Active volcanoes lie along the western edge of the Ring of Fire. Some areas in the western edge are Russia's Kamchatka Peninsula and Japan's islands. Every 50 years, Mount Ruapehu (9,177 feet) in New Zealand, has a major eruption. But it also has minor eruptions annually. This activity is caused by the movement of the Pacific Plate as it passes beneath the Australian Plate. Mount Fuji in Japan and Popocatepetl in Mexico are some examples of the dangerous active volcanoes in the Ring of Fire.

Isn't It Amazing!

Most of the active volcanoes in the Ring of Ring of Fire are situated underwater. At a depth of 1,100 metres, West Mata is the deepest recorded volcano.

Life at Risk

There are many concerns raised about the string of active volcanoes in the Ring of Fire, especially in the Pacific region. For example, if Mount Rainier erupts, more than two million people living in this region would have to quickly evacuate their homes for safety. It includes heavily populated cities like Seattle in the US. Mount Rainier is snow-capped, which is another concern as activity here could cause an avalanche.

Another example is the Santa Maria volcano in Guatemala. It once erupted in 1902 and caused great destruction. This area is heavily populated, so if it were to erupt, it would put a lot of lives in danger. In fact, more people would be affected than when it last erupted in 1902. So, the people who live in the area of the Ring of Fire are extremely vulnerable to the unpredictable activity that takes place here.

Volcanic eruptions are also common in this region and that can be really dangerous for the residents. Threats are not only from the active volcanoes but the dormant ones as well. For example, Mount St Helens was a dormant volcano before it erupted violently in 1980, causing a lot of damage.

▼ *Santa Maria volcano*

▼ *Earthquakes and volcanic eruptions can cause tsunamis*

Tremors and Terrors

Like volcanic eruptions, earthquakes are also natural disasters. An earthquake is a sudden shaking of the ground due to movements of the large masses of rocks beneath Earth's crust. Earthquakes are constantly happening around the world. However, we do not feel the majority of them because they are too small to be significant. Like volcanic eruptions, earthquakes cause great damage to life and property.

Causes

As we know, Earth's crust is made up of large rock slabs or rock masses called tectonic plates that move slowly but constantly. These tectonic plates collide, diverge or move against the edges. Most of the time, the tectonic plates brush against each other without causing any damage. Over time, this movement causes great pressure to build up.

When the pressure becomes immense, the tectonic plates suddenly shift along a crack in the crust, called a **fault**. This

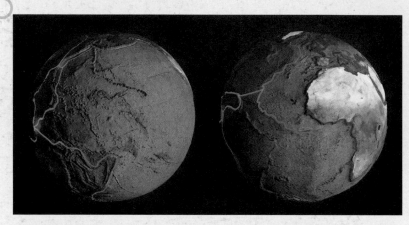

▲ *The orange lines are Earth's fault lines between the tectonic plates*

sudden release of energy causes seismic waves that make the ground shake. Two blocks of rock or two tectonic plates rub against each other, and after a while the rocks break because of the pressure. When these rocks break, an earthquake occurs. Before and after a large earthquake, there are smaller earthquakes: the ones that happen before the main earthquake are called foreshocks, and the ones that happen when the earthquake is over are called aftershocks.

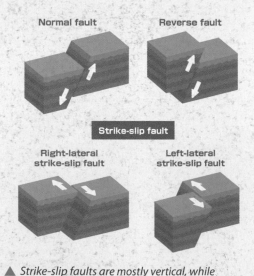

▲ *Strike-slip faults are mostly vertical, while normal and reverse faults are often at an angle to the surface of the Earth*

Types of Faults

Faults are classified into three types—normal, reverse, and strike-slip. Normal and reverse faults are also known as dip-slip faults. In a normal fault, the cracks form as one rock mass slides downwards and moves away from the other rock mass. They occur along divergent plate boundaries. In a reverse fault, the cracks form as one rock mass collides with another rock mass. They occur along convergent plate boundaries but also along areas where the plates are folding up. Here, one rock mass slides beneath another and pushes it upwards. In a strike-slip fault, the cracks form as two rock masses slide along each other's edges.

Where Do Most Earthquakes Occur?

Most earthquakes occur along a fault line or the tectonic plate edges like those in the Pacific Ring of Fire, Alpide Belt, and the mid-Atlantic Belt. An earthquake can strike in any part of Earth, but it occurs mainly in the above-mentioned areas.

Earthquakes often cause roads to collapse and power lines to be disrupted

Along Fault Lines

Faults are basically cracks that occur in the continental or oceanic plates because of their slow and constant movement. The crust is highly unstable near fault lines and disturbances along them might trigger massive earthquakes.

◄ _The fault line is like a fracture on Earth's crust_

Along Plate Edges

Earthquakes are common at points on Earth where the tectonic plates meet. These plates may form the bottom of oceans or the surface of the land and are constantly moving. These movements in Earth's crust result in earthquakes.

The Pacific Ring of Fire

This is an earthquake belt that experiences more than 80 per cent of the largest earthquakes in the world. The young, growing mountains and volcanoes, deep ocean trenches, edges of tectonic plates, and other tectonically active structures make the Pacific Ring of Fire highly prone to earthquakes.

The Alpide Belt

The Alpide Belt extends from the Java and Sumatra islands in Indonesia, across the Himalayas in the Indian subcontinent, all the way through Central Asia into the Mediterranean Sea, and out into the Atlantic Ocean. 17 per cent of the earthquakes of the world take place in this belt. Iran and Turkey lie in this belt and have experienced severe earthquakes.

☀ Isn't It Amazing!

San Francisco is moving toward Los Angeles at the rate of about 2 inches per year. This is about the same speed at which nails grow on your fingers. This is occurring as two sides of the San Andreas fault slowly slip past one another. The cities will meet in several million years. There is a worry that California will fall into the sea—however, it is largely unfounded.

The Mid-Atlantic Belt

The Mid-Atlantic Ridge is a mid-ocean ridge that is located along the Atlantic Ocean's floor. It separates the Eurasian and North American plates in the North Atlantic Ocean and the South American and African continental plates in the South Atlantic Ocean. This region has a high rate of tectonic activity, and is hence deemed to be an earthquake prone area.

▶ _The Mid-Atlantic Ridge_

Studying Earthquakes

Earthquakes are also known as tremors. In ancient times, people had all sorts of ideas about earthquakes. They thought that some large, restless beast lived beneath Earth's surface. People had no idea why and how these tremors occurred. However, the earthquake of 1750 in England and a tsunami in 1755 moved scientists to learn more about these natural phenomena. This event marks the beginning of the modern era of seismology, encouraging numerous studies into the causes, locations, and timing of earthquakes.

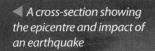

◄ A cross-section showing the epicentre and impact of an earthquake

🌐 Seismic Waves and Seismology

The shifting of rocks during an earthquake causes **vibrations**. These are seismic waves that travel within Earth's surface. They are also caused due to volcanic activity, magma movement, and landslides.

They can be very big or very small. Seismic waves are broadly divided into body waves, i.e., waves that travel within the body of Earth, and surface waves that can only move along the surface of the Earth like ripples on water.

Seismology is the study of earthquakes and seismic waves that move through and around Earth. A seismologist is a scientist who studies earthquakes and seismic waves. They are recorded with something called a seismograph. This instrument detects and measures the movement of the Earth.

◄ A record produced by a seismograph on a display screen or paper is called a seismogram

🏅 Incredible Individuals

Charles Francis Richter (1900–85) and Beno Gutenberg developed the Richter scale to measure the intensity of moderate earthquakes. Charles Richter was born near a town called Hamilton in Ohio, USA. After attending the University of Southern California, he graduated from Stanford University in 1920 and received a doctorate in physics from the California Institute of Technology in 1928. Richter worked at the Seismological Laboratory of the Carnegie Institution of Washington from 1927–36. The Richter scale was published in 1935 and soon became the standard measure of earthquake intensity.

▲ Charles Francis Richter

Hypocentre and Epicentre

The **hypocentre**, or focus, is the point where an earthquake begins. It is always found below the surface of Earth. The place directly above this on the surface is called the **epicentre**. Earthquakes are the strongest at this point on the surface, and the destruction caused here is directly proportional to the size and depth of the rupture of rocks. When talking about the epicentre, news reports refer to the estimated location of this rupturing. It is difficult for the scientists to predict an earthquake. Therefore, seismologists use seismographs to study the epicentre. As they study these epicentres, they are able to tell the exact location of unknown faults and crustal plate boundaries. Though, it is difficult to say where the exact epicentre of the earthquake is.

So, the epicentre and hypocentre both mark the origin of the earthquake. However, the epicentre occurs on Earth's surface while the hypocentre occurs beneath it. With the help of a seismogram, experts can tell how far the earthquake will spread and how strong it is.

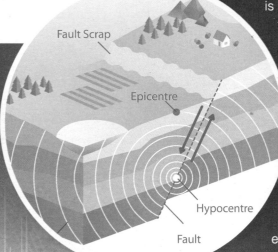

Seismic waves spread out radically with decreasing intensity from both the epicentre and the hypocentre

▶ *The Mercalli scale is a magnitude scale with icons representing the level of threat posed by an earthquake*

The Richter Scale

The strength of an earthquake can be determined either by the destruction it has caused, or by careful calculations made using the readings on a scale called the Richter Scale. This scale is used to measure an earthquake's **magnitude** (size or extent). It was devised in 1935 by seismologists from USA named Charles Francis Richter and Beno Gutenberg.

The Richter scale is a mathematical technique to measure the intensity of an earthquake. Today, this scale has been replaced with those that give more accurate readings. The scale is not a normal number scale but a **logarithmic** scale, meaning an earthquake that shows the measure of two on the Richter scale is 10 times more destructive than an earthquake that gives the measure of one. Earthquakes showing a proportional increase in the magnitude release 32 times more energy. The Richter scale was not a perfect measure as even from its conception, it was used to measure the magnitudes of earthquakes of moderate size. So, this scale measures earthquakes based on the amount of energy released when they occur. The weakest earthquakes are close to zero on the scale and the strongest measure about nine. The Mercalli scale measures the amount of destruction caused by an earthquake on a scale of 1 to 12.

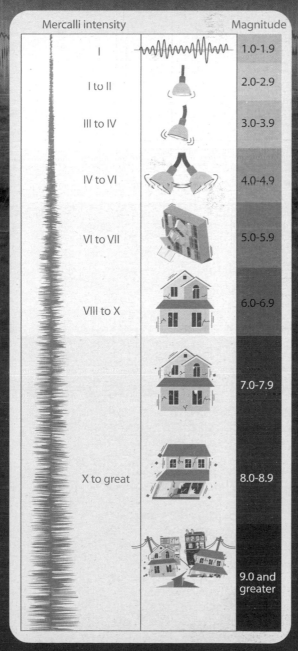

Mercalli intensity		Magnitude
I		1.0-1.9
I to II		2.0-2.9
III to IV		3.0-3.9
IV to VI		4.0-4.9
VI to VII		5.0-5.9
VIII to X		6.0-6.9
		7.0-7.9
X to great		8.0-8.9
		9.0 and greater

The Aftermath

The effects of earthquakes are massive. They destroy life and property, and in the process, affect the mental and physical health of those who have encountered it. Some earthquakes are so devastating that they can erase entire towns and cities from the map. The type of impact mostly depends upon where they are occurring, whether in an urban or a rural one. It also depends on the population of that place, and of course, the ability of the infrastructure to bear the tremors.

Fires

Earthquakes can cause great damage to buildings, bridges, pipelines, railways, embankments, dams, and other structures. Changes at the Earth's surface due to earthquakes include changes in the flow of groundwater, landslides, and mudflows. Fires are also associated with earthquakes because fuel pipelines rupture, and electrical lines are damaged when the ground shakes.

The 1906 San Francisco earthquake is the best example of the destruction an earthquake can cause. It caused large fires in the downtown area of the city. These fires burned for three days and caused some of the greatest property losses ever seen. Fires, as a by-product of earthquakes, also damaged life and property in the Tokyo earthquake of 1923.

▲ San Francisco burning after the 1906 earthquake

Tsunami

Underwater earthquakes can cause gigantic waves to move towards the shore. This is called a tsunami. 'Tsunami' is a Japanese word for 'harbour wave'. During a tsunami, a series of waves in the ocean force the water to first pull back from the shore, and then move towards the shore, sometimes reaching heights of hundred feet as they travel. These waves can travel very fast and by the time they reach the shore, they gain a lot of speed. Tsunamis have the ability to destroy coastal settlements.

Liquefaction

During an earthquake, the ground shakes so much that it can loosen rock and unconsolidated materials to such an extent that they can transform a solid rock into a mass that flows like a liquid. This process is called liquefaction.

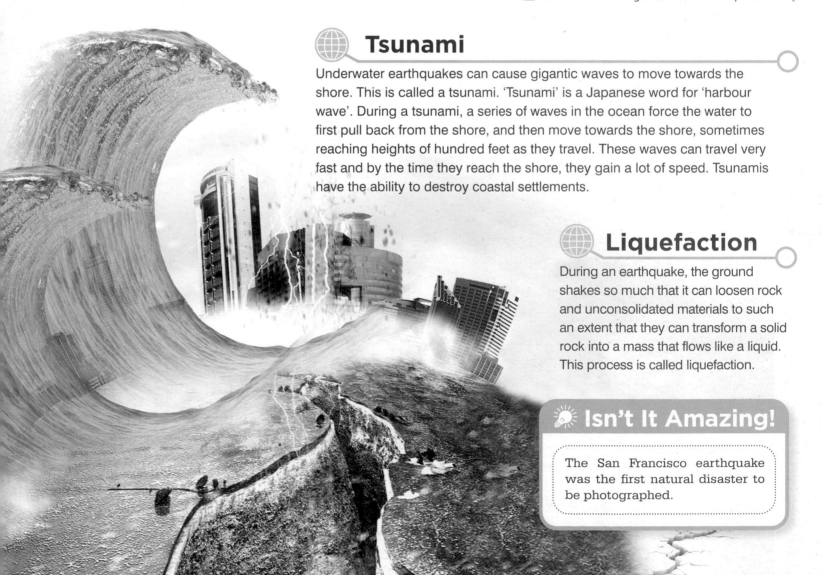

💡 Isn't It Amazing!

The San Francisco earthquake was the first natural disaster to be photographed.

Famous Earthquakes

There have been more than 50,000 earthquakes recorded in history. Among these, some were quite big in magnitude and caused substantial damage to life. But it is difficult to predict how much damage an earthquake can cause. The earthquake that struck the Indian Ocean in 2004 produced tsunamis that almost wiped out India's Nicobar islands. However, the largest earthquake ever measured—the 1960 Chile earthquake—caused a tsunami too, but it caused a lot less damage.

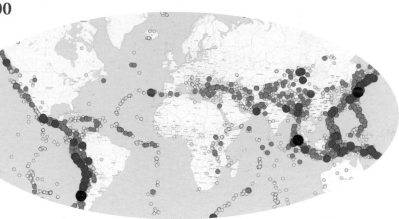

▲ *World map with yellow spots representing earthquake zones*

 ## Aleppo, Syria

Another famous earthquake occurred in Aleppo in Syria on 9 August 1138. The city crumbled, and rocks cascaded into the streets. A citadel collapsed and killed hundreds of residents. This citadel was constructed by European crusaders near Harim. But it was completely levelled by the earthquake. Several towns and forts were reduced to rubble. Approximately 230,000 people were killed by this earthquake. Even Damascus, which was 354 kilometres away, felt the tremors. The Aleppo earthquake was the first of several occurring between 1138 and 1139 that devastated areas in northern Syria and western Turkey.

▼ *An artist's vision of the aftermath of an earthquake in an urban area*

Kanto, Japan

The earthquake that occurred on 1 September 1923, in the Kanto region of Japan also caused damage in places such as Tokyo and Yakohama. Along with severe earthquakes, subsequent firestorms also wrecked the city and burned down around 381,000 houses. Though it is often known as the Great Tokyo Earthquake, Yokohama registered more damage. About 142,800 people were killed in this earthquake.

The Kashmir Earthquake

The earthquake that occurred in Pakistan-occupied Kashmir on 8 October 2005, had a magnitude of 7.6 on the Richter scale. Some parts of India and Afghanistan were also affected. At least 79,000 people died, and more than 32,000 buildings collapsed in Kashmir. This was one of the most destructive earthquakes of contemporary times. The timing of the earthquake added to the death toll as it left hundreds of survivors without shelter from the coming harsh winter.

Earthquakes: A Case Study

A case study shows the analysis of a particular occurrence or event like an earthquake. It is mainly conducted to support research on a subject.

The Great Lisbon Earthquake

1755
1 Nov

On 1 November 1755, an earthquake occurred in Lisbon, Portugal, causing serious damage. The earthquake killed around 60,000 people in Lisbon alone. Violent tremors demolished large public buildings and about 12,000 other structures.

As 1 November is All Saints' Day, a large part of the population was attending mass when the earthquake struck in the morning. The churches, unable to withstand the seismic shock, collapsed, killing or injuring thousands of worshippers.

Research indicates that the faults that occurred on the seafloor along the tectonic plate boundaries of the mid-Atlantic ridge were the main seismic source of the earthquake. Damage was even reported in Algiers, which was 1,100 kilometres away from

▲ *The Carmo Convent church was destroyed after the earthquake*

the epicentre. People were also killed by drowning in floods, and in fires that burned throughout Lisbon. Altogether, the earthquake and all of its disastrous by-products lasted for about six days. This disastrous earthquake was later also depicted in art and literature.

This earthquake caused the birth of seismology. It did not take long after the initial crisis to start the re-construction. The leaders of Lisbon quickly hired architects and engineers to re-build the city. Within a year, the debris created from the earthquake was cleared and the re-construction was in full swing.

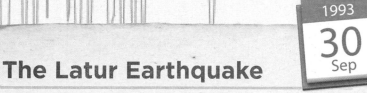

The Latur Earthquake

1993
30
Sep

The Latur earthquake, which occurred in Maharashtra, India, was one of the deadliest earthquakes in recent history. It began at 3:56 am on 30 September 1993. During the earthquake, 52 villages were destroyed, 30,000 people were injured and 10,000 were killed. The epicentre was at a place called Killari. A large crater was formed here that can be seen to this day. The earthquake measured a magnitude of 6.2 on the Richter scale. As the area was densely populated, casualties were high. Since the earthquake's **focus** was 12-kilometres deep, the shock waves caused more damage and destruction.

▲ Relief teams providing disaster relief in the form of food, medicines, and water

Several foreign and local donors reacted immediately to the tragedy by sending relief teams and rescue workers. A team of 50 doctors was pressed into service. Schools nearby were converted into emergency hospitals. Food, water, and other provisions were supplied in the affected areas by volunteers of the Indian Army. Even ordinary citizens volunteered their time through administrative channels or independently. The government and other organisations distributed clothes and household goods.

▼ An earthquake hit Van, Turkey, on 25 October 2011, killing more than 600 people and injuring 4,152

⊛ Incredible Individuals

Lucy Jones better known as 'The Earthquake Lady' is considered to be among the world's most influential seismologist. In 2012, she warned residents of the US about upcoming disasters and tried to battle the apathy and denial of those who did not believe in climate change.

Devastating Waves

Tsunamis are an extremely powerful and destructive natural disaster. These are a series of ocean waves that are caused by underwater earthquakes and volcanoes. When the ocean floor at a plate boundary folds, falls or rises without warning, it displaces the water above it, causing the water to surge forward in giant, continuous waves known as tsunami. These waves can almost beat the speed of jet planes. As they near the shore, the tsunami waves can soar up to a great height, rising to as much as 30 metres approximately.

1755 ▶ 1868

 ## Lisbon

The Lisbon tsunami occurred on 1 November 1755. It followed the Lisbon earthquake and caused great damage to the Lisbon port in Portugal. The violent tremors demolished buildings and killed thousands of people. This earthquake caused tsunami waves of about 20 feet high at Lisbon and 65 feet high at Cadiz, Spain. The waves travelled a distance of 6,100 kilometres to the west in 10 hours, having reached a height of 13 feet above mean sea level.

▲ *Tsunami waves might rise higher than buildings*

 ## Chile

There was an earthquake that occurred in northern Chile, on 13 August 1868, in the offshore area near Arica, Peru. This generated a Pacific-wide tsunami that caused extensive damage to villages and towns along the coast of southern Peru and northern Chile. It killed hundreds of people in the immediate region. There was no definite figure of the death toll and several aftershocks occured in the following days and months.

👥 In Real Life

Despite a delay of many hours between an earthquake and tsunami, most people are taken by surprise by the giant rolling waves as many places do not have proper tsunami warning systems in place.

2004 2011

🌐 Indian Ocean

The tsunami that started in the Indian Ocean in December 2004, was the deadliest one recorded so far. On this day, an undersea earthquake struck the coast of the Indonesian island of Sumatra with a magnitude of 9.1. Over the next seven hours, a tsunami ravaged the coastal areas as far away as eastern Africa. It destroyed islands and coasts of more than 10 countries in South Asia and East Africa. The waves washed away entire villages and killed more than 200,000 people. The death toll was the highest in Indonesia, Sri Lanka, India, Thailand, and the Maldives. Some locations reported that the waves had reached a height of 30 feet or more when they hit the shoreline. This tsunami caused immense economic and environmental damage.

▲ The destruction caused by tsunami waves

🌐 Japan

The tsunami that occurred in Japan on 11 March 2011 was created by an underwater earthquake. This earthquake took place in the Pacific Ocean off the coast of Honshu, one of Japan's main islands. This earthquake triggered a series of large tsunami waves that devastated many coastal areas of Japan, most notably north-eastern Honshu. The tsunami also caused a major nuclear accident at Fukushima Daiichi power station along the Pacific coast, which lead to another set of consequences that are still being dealt with.

▲ A concept image showing how earthquakes start at one point and impact areas many kilometres away

Safety Measures

Volcanic eruptions and earthquakes are natural phenomena that cause extensive damage to life and property. There are some safety measures that can be useful when one is faced with such disasters.

SAFETY FIRST

Safety During Volcanic Eruptions

If a volcano erupts near any settlement, it is advisable to evacuate that place and stay clear of lava, mudflows, flying rocks, and ash. The river areas and low-lying regions should be avoided. People should wear clothes that cover the whole body and cover their faces with masks. Doors and windows should be closed, and any vents in the houses should be blocked to prevent the entry of ash. Authorities around the world take measures like putting up warning boards to caution people about volcanoes. If evacuation is not necessary in some situations, people should stay indoors. They should be careful to keep their windows and doors shut. People should also avoid driving cars and motorbikes, as ash can damage engines and metal parts.

▲ *A mask protects us from inhaling the smoke, ash, and toxic gases released during an eruption*

▼ *The caution board warns of the volcanic fumes ahead in a national park Kona Island, Hawaii*

What to do in case of an: EARTHQUAKE

1 KEEP CALM

2 ELIMINATE FIRE SOURCES

3 STAY AWAY FROM WINDOWS OR OBJECTS THAT MAY FALL

4 DO NOT USE THE ELEVATORS

5 SETTLE INTO SECURITY ZONES

6 LOCATE EVACUATION ZONES

Safety During Earthquakes

Earthquakes can cause death and destruction through secondary effects such as landslides, tsunamis, fires, and fault ruptures. The greatest losses in life and property occur due to the collapse of artificial and subsurface structures caused by the violent tremors of the ground. So, it is important to learn the safety measures and methods to prepare for an earthquake. People should be aware of the actions that they need to take when the tremors begin.

A professional should be consulted to learn how to build homes that would be sturdy enough to withstand earthquakes, especially in earthquake prone areas. Those living in such areas should bolt the bookcases to wall **studs**, install strong latches on cupboards, and strap water heaters to wall studs so that they do not fall off the walls during the tremors, injuring people beneath them. During an earthquake, the use of elevators and electrical gadgets should be avoided entirely. It is advisable to stand where nothing can fall on you. Such people should also stock up on food and water in case of emergencies. Everyone should keep a first-aid box at home. It is advisable to have dust masks, battery-operated radios, and flashlights in accessible places. Everyone should know to turn off the gas and other electrical appliances to avoid fires.

▲ *In case of an earthquake, take shelter under a table or a desk*

When the tremors begin, drop to the floor and take cover under a desk or table. Even if you are standing under a doorframe, hold on and do not leave its cover until the tremors stop entirely. Stay indoors until the tremors stop and you are sure that it is safe to exit. Even after this, stay away from bookcases or furniture that can fall suddenly. If you are outside when an earthquake hits, stay outside. Move away from buildings, trees, utility wires, and telephone poles.

In Real Life

20 per cent of earthquakes that are of a magnitude of 6 or more occur in Japan. As the world's most seismically active country and as part of its preparation, schools in Japan often perform earthquake and tsunami drills. Children enter simulations to understand how tremors feel. All buildings have deep foundations and use custom-designed shock absorbers so they do not fall apart.

WEATHER AND CLIMATE

Nice Weather, Isn't It?

Look out of the window. Is it sunny, windy, cloudy, rainy, or snowy? How would you describe the **weather**? What is the **climate** like where you live? How can you tell the difference between these two words? Weather and climate are the conditions that prevail on Earth. These conditions regulate every aspect of every being's life. But how do these conditions change so frequently?

Earth's **atmosphere** is constantly changing because of reciprocal actions between warm air and cold air, and warm ocean currents and cold ocean currents. It is also affected by storms moving across the continents, mountain barriers forcing the air to rise and fall, etc. When these phenomena occur, there are changes in temperatures, **precipitation**, **humidity**, pressure, winds, and cloudiness. All of these together make up the weather. Hence, weather is the condition of the atmosphere of a particular place at a particular time. While climate is the average pattern of these weather conditions for a particular region, over a long period of time.

▼ *Sensors on weather satellites can take measurements of reflected lights and infrared temperatures, digitze them, and then send them back to Earth, so that meteorologists can better predict the weather*

What Is Weather?

Weather is the day-to-day condition of the atmosphere in a specific place at a specific time. It is nothing but a temporary state of the atmosphere that changes on an hourly or daily basis. It can be expressed in terms such as sunny, rainy, windy, or cloudy. Not all regions experience every type of weather. For example, a region in Africa under the desert climate will never experience snowy weather.

▲ *Weather is affected by the Sun along with the cloud and wind conditions*

What Causes Weather?

On Earth, weather is influenced by the heat of the Sun and the movement of air. There are certain elements that make up the weather of a place at a given point of time. They are temperature, precipitation, atmospheric pressure, wind, humidity, and cloudiness.

Temperature

Do you know what 'temperature' is? It can be defined as the measure of the hotness or coolness of any place. The angle of the Sun determines the increase or decrease in temperature. It can change quite quickly. Temperature influences the volume, pressure, and density of air. When temperature increases, air density decreases but its volume and pressure increase. So, warm and dry air will rise when it is surrounded by cool air because it is less dense than cool air.

Precipitation

Precipitation is the water formed in the atmosphere that falls on Earth's surface as rain, snow, and sleet. It is a result of the **condensation** of water vapour.

Atmospheric Pressure

The air that surrounds Earth has weight. This weight is termed as atmospheric pressure and it pushes downward on anything that is below it. The rise of warm air and fall of cold air cause changes in the atmospheric pressure. Rising air creates low pressure on Earth's surface, whereas sinking air creates high pressure. Therefore, atmospheric pressure is the highest close to waterbodies. For instance, islands and coastal areas are located close to waterbodies like oceans and seas. They frequently experience storms as a result of this, leading to constant and sudden changes in the weather.

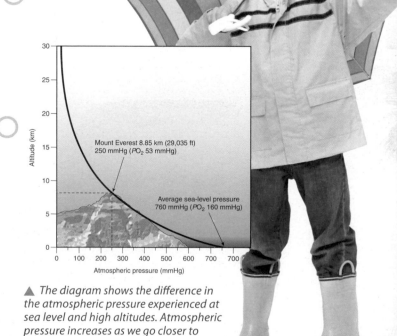

▲ *The diagram shows the difference in the atmospheric pressure experienced at sea level and high altitudes. Atmospheric pressure increases as we go closer to the water*

Cloudiness

Look up at the sky. Is it clear with few clouds, or is there a heavy cloud cover? What colour are the clouds? Cloudiness is the state of clouds in the atmosphere at a given time over a region. There are different types of clouds, and they affect the weather in different ways. For instance, fewer and whiter clouds indicate little or no rainfall. On the other hand, lots of dark, heavy clouds indicate heavy rainfall and even upcoming thunderstorms. Clouds can also stop the amount of sunlight reaching Earth's surface for a certain period of time. This makes the day cooler.

Humidity

Humidity is the amount of water vapour present in the air. It impacts the weather of a region. When the humidity is high, the day becomes hotter, and we begin to perspire. The level of humidity can help predict upcoming storms.

Wind

Wind is moving air formed due to differences in temperature and atmospheric pressure between nearby regions. Generally, winds tend to blow from areas of high pressure (where it is cooler) to areas of low pressure (where it is warmer). You might feel the wind against your face when it is moving. When the speed of the wind increases, the air moves faster, reducing warm air. This lowers the temperature and makes the weather cooler than normal.

⊙ Incredible Individuals

The anemometer was invented by Leon Battista Alberti in 1450. This device was used to measure the speed of the wind. It was a disk that was perpendicular to the direction of the wind.

▲ The rain clouds appear to be grey because of their height and thickness. When the sky looks like this, it means that there might be some rainfall in the future

Atmosphere: The Air Up There

There is an invisible layer surrounding Earth. It is composed of different gases. This layer is called the atmosphere. The word 'atmosphere' originates from the Greek words for vapour, '*atmos*' and sphere, '*sphaira*'.

A Gas Envelope

Earth's atmosphere contains oxygen and nitrogen in large quantities and then carbon dioxide, argon, helium, and neon in smaller quantities. Water vapour and dust are also a part of the atmosphere.

The atmosphere extends from the land, oceans, and snow-covered surface of the Earth right to the outer space. The gases in our planet's atmosphere are required for our survival and growth. Other planets also have atmospheres, but they contain different gases.

 Incredible Individuals

Stratosphere accompanies all electrical storms. It was recognised as a chemical compound by German chemist, Christian Friedrich Schonbein in 1840. He named it 'ozone' due to the German word '*ozon*' which means 'to smell', as it had a pungent smell.

Layers of Atmosphere

The atmosphere is divided into layers just like the interior of Earth. There are five major layers—troposphere, stratosphere, mesosphere, thermosphere, and exosphere. Beyond the exosphere is outer space.

Exosphere
The exosphere is the highest layer of the atmosphere, extending 9,900 kilometres above Earth's surface from the thermosphere. It has the thinnest cover of air, gradually fading into space.

Thermosphere
The thermosphere is the fourth layer of the atmosphere. It extends for 690 kilometres from the mesopause, which is the boundary between the mesosphere and the thermosphere.

Space shuttles orbit in this layer. The temperature can rise to 1500° C here. The main feature of this layer is that it has free ions and electrons that are the result of the **ionisation** of gas particles. Radio waves bounce off the ionosphere, allowing communication between countries.

Mesosphere
The mesosphere is the third layer of the atmosphere. It lies 85 kilometres above Earth's surface. Air becomes thin in this layer as air molecules are further apart. There is a drastic fall in temperature here, as low as -120° C. Meteors burn out when they reach this layer.

Stratosphere
The stratosphere is just above the troposphere, extending from the tropopause to approximately 50 kilometres above Earth's surface.
This layer has small amounts of ozone, a form of oxygen that absorbs the harmful rays of the Sun, preventing them from reaching Earth's surface. The region in the stratosphere where this thin sheet of ozone is found is called the ozone layer. Aeroplanes and jet planes fly in this layer as it is calm and stable.

Troposphere
The troposphere is the first layer of Earth's atmosphere. This is the place where life can exist. It extends from the surface of Earth till the stratosphere. Its upper boundary is called the tropopause. It extends for 10–18 kilometres above Earth's surface. All the different weather changes occur in this layer. It contains almost all the water vapour of the atmosphere. Here, the temperature decreases as we go higher in altitude.

Ozone layer

◀ *The diagram shows the different layers of Earth's atmosphere, indicating the layer in which regular planes and jet planes can reach and also the one where we send our satellites!*

The Current Affair

The term current refers to a body of water or air that moves in a definite direction. Generally, the current moves through a surrounding body of water or air which has less movement. Water is a substance that has the ability to flow and change shape accordingly. However, air is also considered a fluid.

Air Currents

There are water currents present in the oceans, similarly, currents are also present in the atmosphere and are constantly flowing from one place to another. Air currents are formed when winds blow from a high-pressure region to a low-pressure region.

What Causes Air Currents?

The shape of planet Earth is spherical and therefore, the rays of the Sun fall unevenly on its surface, making some places warmer than the others. This heat warms up the air in some places, which then expands and becomes lighter. It rises, creating warm air currents.

Meanwhile, cooler and heavier air thrusts itself downwards to replace the warm air, creating cold air currents in the process. Differences in temperature can also cause air currents as warm air is less dense than cool air, which makes it lighter. Being lighter, warm air moves under the cool air, forming air currents.

Famous Air Currents

Air currents that occur in some places are famous because of their impact on the weather, for example, the Santa Ana winds that occur in Southern California. These are gusty northeast winds that flow during winter, sweeping downwards from the Mojave Desert and the Great Basin towards the Pacific Ocean. The resulting air currents blow from the east to the west. As they approach the ocean, they compress and heat up, leaving the region dry and hot.

▲ *A view of the mountains in the Santa Ana region of California*

Jet Streams

Jet streams are narrow bands of strong winds that occur in the upper levels of the atmosphere. They blow from the west to the east and often follow the boundaries between the hot and cold air. As it happens in the upper level, mountaineers climbing Mount Everest experience this movement of air.

▶ *Sunrays distribute heat unevenly, so the tropics are hot while the polar regions are cold*

What Is Climate?

Climate is the atmospheric condition of a particular place over a long period of time. It is the general pattern of weather that is recorded for 30 years or more. This does not mean that the area will only experience one type of weather. For example, a region that experiences a dry climate for most of the year can sometimes have rainy days, making the weather hot and humid for a short time.

Factors Affecting Climate

Different parts of the Earth experience different climates. Some places are extremely cold, some are very hot, and some experience rainfall throughout the year. The climate of any place is influenced by several factors. These are its **latitude**, **altitude**, distance from the sea, shape of the land or relief, ocean currents, and direction of winds.

Latitude

The climate of any region is determined by its latitude. How far is its distance from the Equator? This question will influence the temperature of any place, thus affecting its climate. The Sun's rays fall directly on the Equator and make the places close to it extremely hot. However, the Sun's rays have to pass through a thicker layer of atmosphere at the poles than the equator, making the climate near the poles cooler.

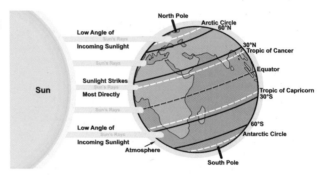

▲ As the Sun's rays fall unevenly on Earth's surface, the climate varies

Altitude

The climate of a place can be affected by its altitude. Mountains receive more rainfall than low-lying areas. As air is forced over the higher ground, it cools. This leads the moist air to condense and fall as precipitation. As we travel to places that have higher altitudes, we experience a fall in the temperature. Therefore, a place at sea level will have higher temperature than a place near tall mountains. Consequently, a place at sea level will experience a warm climate, and places on tall mountains at higher altitudes will experience a cooler climate. This fall in temperature has a cooling effect which causes condensation. It leads to precipitation on the windward side of the mountains, which is the side facing the wind.

▲ Mountains affect the climate of a place

▼ Beaches are the preferred destination in summers because of their warmer climate

Distance from the Sea

During the daytime, the Sun heats up the surface of the land and the ocean. Land warms quicker than the water in the oceans. This means that the air above land heats up quicker than the air above water. Warm air above land rises steadily, leading to low pressure near the surface. Conversely, there is high pressure over the water surface as the air is cooler. This cool air sinks lower and moves from high pressure to low pressure, cooling the land. This is called **sea breeze**.

The opposite of this process occurs at night. The warm air is now above the water. As the Sun goes down, the land loses heat quickly, cooling the air. However, the water in the ocean retains its warm air above it. Therefore, there is low pressure above the ocean and high pressure above the land. The air moves from land to ocean. This is called **land breeze**.

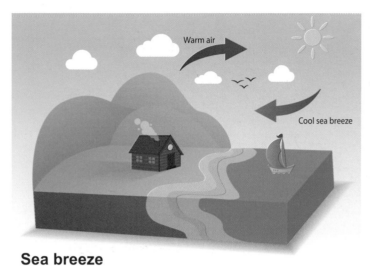

Sea breeze

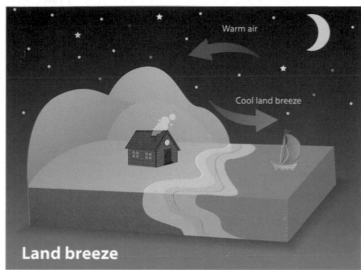

Land breeze

▲ *The sea breeze and the land breeze have a great impact on the climate of a place*

Ocean Currents

If the wind blows in from the ocean, the warm and cold ocean currents can affect the climate of an area along the coast. Warm ocean currents heat the air above the water and carry warm air to the land, increasing the temperature of coastal areas.

▶ *Ocean currents take more energy to change temperatures than land. Land warms and cools faster than water*

Ocean Currents

Warm Water

Cold Water

Direction of Winds

Winds blowing from the equator are warm. This makes the region hotter. Whereas, the cold winds from the polar regions make the adjacent areas cooler. Thus, winds can affect the climate of a place.

Types of Climates

Due to different factors, the world has varied types of climates. Some places are extremely cold, some have a moderate climate and some places are hot throughout the year. The climate across the globe has been divided into five climate groups—tropical, dry, mild, continental, and polar. These climate groups are further divided into climate types.

Polar (Tundra and Ice caps)

The polar region is split into two climate types—tundra and the ice caps. They lie near the Arctic and Antarctic Circles. The average tundra temperature is 10° C. The water is rich in nutrients and supports a wide variety of plants and animals. The ice cap climate is so severe that few organisms are able to survive. The temperature is rarely above freezing point (that is 0° C). Antarctica is covered by an ice cap and is one of the driest deserts on Earth.

▲ *In the Arctic tundra, the average temperature varies from -34 to -6° C and can support animal species*

▼ *This map of the world is colour coded according to its climate type*

Continental (Warm Summer, Cool Summer, Subarctic)

The continental zone is split into warm summer, cool summer, and subarctic or boreal climate types. This zone is the transition region between the mild zone and the polar zone. It has cool winters, long-lasting snow, and short growing seasons—periods conducive to agricultural practices are shorter. The seasonal changes are extreme.

Tornadoes and thunderstorms are quite common in this type of climate. In the winter, this zone can experience snowstorms, strong winds, and very cold temperatures, which can drop below -30° C. A hot summer in the continental climate features an average temperature of at least 22° C in its warmest month. These regimes are mostly in the Northern Hemisphere and the warmest month is usually July or August. The frost free periods last for 4 to 7 months within this climate regime. The continental climate is dominant in Europe, covering northern Ukraine, eastern Belarus, Russia, most of Finland, and northern Sweden. Winters are much colder and longer, with greater snow cover.

▲ *Northern Sweden experiences continental climate*

Dry (Arid and Semi-arid)

The dry zone is split into the arid and semi-arid climate types. Places that fall under the dry zone have low precipitation. Arid regions receive 10–30 centimetres of annual rainfall. Grasslands cover the semi-arid regions and receive sufficient rainfall to support them. There are large variations in daily temperatures. The hottest places on Earth lie in this climate zone. The arid and semi-arid dry climates occur in the regions where the movement of warm, moist air is blocked by mountains. For example, Denver in the USA is situated to the east of the Rocky Mountains, so it experiences this type of dry climate.

▲ *The semi-arid region in north-eastern Brazil is also known as sertão*

☉ Incredible Individuals

How do we know the distribution of the climate types around the world? It is because of a Russian-born, German meteorologist named Wladimir Koppen. He prepared a map of the world demarcating the different climatic regions. He studied atmospheric science, contributing greatly to the subject of climatology and meteorology.

▲ Tropical Brazilian rainforests

🌐 How Climate Affects Us

Climate has a great influence on the development of any region. The crops farmers grow, the clothes people wear and the houses they build for themselves are all influenced by the climate of a place. Food habits depend on the type of crops that are grown in a particular region. People who live in cold climates wear clothes made from wool or fur. However, in places that are warm, people tend to wear light clothes made of cotton.

Mild (Mediterranean, Humid Subtropical)

A place has mild climate based on its latitude. Mild climate is also known as temperate climate. The places in these regions have warm summers. They have mild, short and rainy winters. The characteristics of this climate are clear skies, cool nights and little rainfall. Places like Savannah in Georgia, Shanghai in China and Sydney in Australia experience hot and humid summers. On the other hand, winters are very cold. This is the humid subtropical climate.

The marine west coast climate, named so as it is occurs on the west coast of the various continents, is a mild climate found in cities like Seattle, Washington, in USA, and Wellington in New Zealand. These places experience longer, cooler winters than the Mediterranean climate.

▲ Savannah Park in Georgia, USA

Tropical (Wet, Monsoon, Wet, and Dry)

All places that lie near the Equator have a tropical type of climate. It is characterised by its warm temperature and regular rainfall. The tropical type of climate is further divided into three groups—tropical wet, tropical monsoon, and tropical wet and dry.

Regions with a tropical wet climate are also known as rainforests. The weather in these regions does not change much. Days are hot with warm nights and some rainfall. As the seasons change, the climate experiences small changes as well. Hawaii in USA, Kuala Lumpur in Malaysia, and Belem in Brazil are all examples of areas with tropical wet climate.

The tropical monsoon climate prevails in southern Asia and west Africa. But what is the monsoon? It is a wind system that reverses its direction every six months. These winds flow from sea to land in the summer and from land to sea in the winter. The summer monsoons bring in rain in abundance. India and Bangladesh experience the tropical monsoon climate. The farmers of these countries depend upon the monsoon to water their crops.

The tropical wet and dry climate type is also referred to as the 'savanna' climate. In these regions, people depend on the rains of the wet season. If the rainfall is not sufficient then it can lead to a **drought**. However, these regions also experience heavy rainfall, sometimes leading to floods. Places like Cuba in Havana, Kolkata in India, and parts of Africa experience this climate.

Climatic Zones

Earth is divided into three major climatic zones. They are the tropical or torrid zone, the temperate zone, and the frigid zone. The tropical zone lies between the Tropic of Cancer (23.5°N) and the Tropic of Capricorn (23.5°S). The temperate zone lies between the Tropic of Cancer and the Arctic Circle (66.5°N), and then again between the Tropic of Capricorn and the Antarctic Circle (66.5°S). The frigid zone lies between the Arctic Circle and the North Pole (90°N), and then again between the Antarctic Circle and the South Pole (90°S).

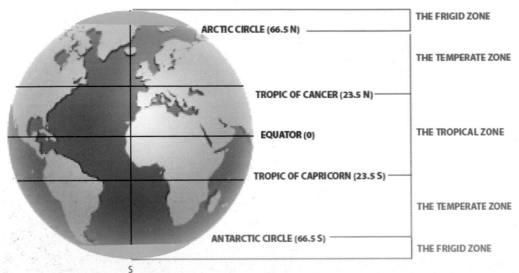

ARCTIC CIRCLE (66.5 N) — THE FRIGID ZONE

THE TEMPERATE ZONE

TROPIC OF CANCER (23.5 N) —

EQUATOR (0) — THE TROPICAL ZONE

TROPIC OF CAPRICORN (23.5 S) —

THE TEMPERATE ZONE

ANTARCTIC CIRCLE (66.5 S) — THE FRIGID ZONE

▲ *The major climatic zones are divided into the North and South Hemispheres by the Equator (0°)*

🌐 The Tropical or Torrid Zone

The tropical zone has the Equator running through the centre. This region includes countries of South America, Africa, Asia, Australia, and parts of North America. The tropics have a warm climate round the year as these areas get the maximum heat from the Sun. The only two types of seasons experienced here are the dry and wet seasons. The amount of rainfall varies from place to place. The Sahara Desert in Africa experiences very little rainfall and is drier than the Amazon Basin of South America, where rainfall is plentiful.

◄ *The Congo Rainforest is a tropical rainforest*

The Temperate Zone

The temperate zone has a broad range of temperatures and well-defined seasons. Weather is quite unpredictable in this zone. Some of the countries of the temperate zone are Canada, USA, India, and Japan. Countries of the Middle East, Northern Africa, and all the countries of Europe also fall under this climatic zone. The climate here varies widely. Some places have an oceanic climate as seen in London, Dublin, Melbourne, and Auckland. Some parts of the temperate zone have a Mediterranean climate. This is described as a dry summer climate. Cities like Madrid, San Francisco, and Adelaide experience this climate. In places like Chicago, Almaty, Moscow, Minsk, and Helsinki, people experience severe winters and hot summers.

◀ The Kew Gardens in London is a botanical garden site hosting a diverse collection of plants that can grow in the temperate zone

The Frigid Zone

The frigid zone includes the polar regions. The climate at both the North Pole and the South Pole is extremely cold and freezing. The countries in the north polar regions are Alaska in the USA, Canada, Greenland, Norway, and Russia. Antarctica is in the southern polar region. This zone has cold temperatures as it lies far away from the Equator. Some areas are permanently covered with ice. The frigid zone receives slanting rays of the Sun as the region lies farthest from the equator.

▼ The Kola Peninsula, Russia, experiences long and harsh winters. Plants like mosses, lichens, and Arctic birch are common in these forests

🔆 Isn't It Amazing!

Can you see the Sun clearly in the sky at midnight? In the Arctic Circle and the Antarctic Circle, the Sun is visible during the midnight hour. If the weather is calm, during some days of the year, the Sun can be visible for all 24 hours of the day. Why does this happen? This is because the axis on which Earth rotates is tilted, so the Sun does not set at high altitudes during the summer season.

Seasons

Seasons are the divisions in a year influenced by the changes in weather and climate. There are four seasons in a year—spring, summer, autumn or fall, and winter. Every season has its own characteristics. Seasons follow each other after a gap of three months. Each season is characterised by its own average temperatures, weather types, and durations of day and night. For instance, in summer the days are longer than the nights, while in winter the days are shorter than the nights.

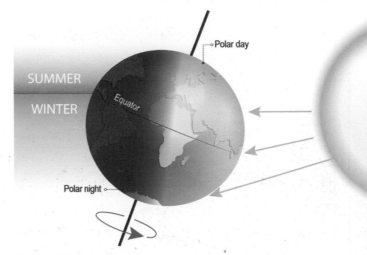

▲ The Equator divides Earth into the Northern Hemisphere and the Southern Hemisphere

Equinox and Solstice

Equinox is that time of the year when day and night are approximately of equal length. It is when the Sun is directly over the Equator. There are two equinoxes each year. They occur around 20–21 March and 22–23 September. The word equinox is derived from two Latin words meaning 'equal' and 'night'. The March equinox is called the vernal equinox and marks the beginning of spring, whereas the autumnal equinox is the beginning of autumn.

Solstice is another phenomenon that also happens twice each year. The name is derived from the Latin words 'sol' that means 'sun' and 'sistere' that means 'to stand still'. It occurs when the path of the Sun is farthest north or south of the Equator. In the Northern Hemisphere, the summer solstice occurs on 20–21 June when the Northern Hemisphere is most tilted towards the Sun, and it marks the beginning of summer. At this time the Sun's rays are directly over the Tropic of Cancer. The winter solstice in the Northern Hemisphere occurs on 21–22 December, when the Sun's rays are directly over the Tropic of Capricorn. It marks the beginning of winter. The situation is reversed in the Southern Hemisphere. The day of the summer solstice in any hemisphere is the longest day of the year and the winter solstice is the shortest day of the year.

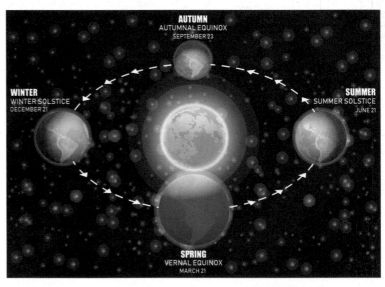

▲ The position of Earth in its orbit during the solstices and equinoxes

◄ Spring is the time for most flowers to blossom

Spring

Spring is the season between winter and summer during which temperatures gradually rise and the climate becomes moderate. In the Northern Hemisphere it extends from the March equinox (20–21 March) to the summer solstice (20–22 June). In the Southern Hemisphere, spring begins from 22–23 September and lasts until 21–22 December. During spring, the changes in temperature occur mostly in the middle and high latitudes. However, near the Equator, temperatures do not vary much. The polar regions have very short spring seasons.

▼ *Summer is the most preferred season for outdoor activities*

Summer

Summer is the season between spring and autumn. This is the warmest season of the year. It extends from the summer solstice to the autumnal equinox in the Northern Hemisphere and from December to March in the Southern Hemisphere. During summer, the days and nights are more or less equal in length.

Autumn or Fall

The autumn season comes in between summer and winter when temperatures begin to drop. This season is also called fall, as trees shed their leaves during this time. The leaves fall to the ground. Autumn extends itself from the autumnal equinox (22–23 September) in the Northern Hemisphere to the winter solstice on 21–22 December. This is the year's shortest day. Whereas in the Southern Hemisphere, it extends in the period between 20–21 March and 20–21 June. In the polar regions, the autumn season is very short.

In Real Life

During autumn, due to less light, there is no photosynthesis and leaves stop producing the green pigment called chlorophyll. As the green colour of the leaves begins to fade, orange and yellow **carotenoids** that are present in the leaf take the chance to shine. Therefore, the colour of leaves appears to be orange.

Winter

Winter is the coldest season of the year. It falls between the seasons of autumn and spring. In the Northern Hemisphere, winter extends from the winter solstice on 21–22 December to the vernal equinox on 20–21 March. In the Southern Hemisphere, the winter season extends from 20–21 June to 22–23 September. The temperatures decrease considerably at this time in the middle and high latitudes of Earth. However, as we have seen for all other seasons, the temperatures in equatorial regions do not change much.

▲ *During the winter season, trees and plants stop growing. Animals and birds migrate to warmer places. Some animals hibernate, which is a long sleep taken by animals to regulate their body temperatures*

Oceans and Continents

Our planet Earth is made up of five major oceans and seven continents. The oceans cover 70 per cent of Earth's surface and govern life on Earth. They play a vital role in influencing the weather and climate on the planet.

What Oceans Do

The water of the oceans absorbs and stores heat. This has a great impact on the weather and climate of the world. Both oceans and land absorb the Sun's heat, but the oceans take more time to release this heat than land. Therefore, coastal regions have a temperate type of climate. Warm ocean water evaporates into the atmosphere, resulting in condensation. Clouds are formed thereafter, resulting in precipitation or rainfall. The vast heat storage capacity of the ocean regulates the climate on Earth.

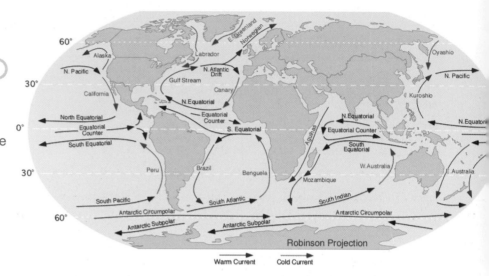

▲ The map shows ocean currents around the world. If there were no ocean currents flowing through the water bodies, then habitation by human beings, animals, and plants would have been restricted to only some parts of Earth

Ocean Currents

Ocean currents also play a key role in determining the climate on Earth. The currents of water in the ocean flow for thousands of kilometres and form a sort of **conveyor belt**. Ocean currents transport warm water from the equator to the poles and cold water from the poles to the tropics. This water can warm or cool the air and, indirectly, the land over which it is blowing, thus exerting an influence on the weather of that place.

Influencing Climate

Oceans influence regional climate along with global climate. There is always a difference of temperature between the land in the middle of a continent and the land surrounding oceans. This steers the development of monsoon. During winter, the cold air over a continent flows towards the ocean. In summer, the hot air over a continent draws moist air inland, bringing in the summer rains.

▲ Large rifts as the one in the picture has appeared on Earth's crust because of the movement of tectonic plates

Tectonic Plates

Tectonic plates, which are huge slabs of rocks beneath Earth's crust, are constantly moving due to the heat and pressure coming from Earth's core. The crust is moving by centimetres every year. This phenomenon has an influence on the world's climate. But how does this affect us?

Well, millions of years ago there was a supercontinent called Pangaea. This broke into pieces and brought about a massive change in distribution of land, ocean and atmospheric circulation patterns. During this process, there were several drastic changes that took place in the climate. Some 35 million years ago, the plate carrying the modern region of India started moving under the Asia plate to create the Himalayan mountains. This has affected global wind patterns. This change in tectonic plate movements drives the monsoon season to this day. In short, the climate system can be called interrelated—as the ocean, atmosphere, and land interact with each other, influencing the climate.

Water Cycle

Three-fourth of our planet's surface is covered with water. This water is constantly circulating in the air and on land. Water on Earth is available in all the three forms, i.e., as solid, liquid, and gas. The water cycle is a natural process by which water is transported from oceans into the atmosphere and then it returns to land. There are three main processes in the water cycle—evaporation, condensation, and precipitation. Clouds are made up of water droplets and crystals of ice. Snowflakes are made up of **ice crystals**. Rain is liquid water. Steam is water vapour. In this way, water exists in all three forms.

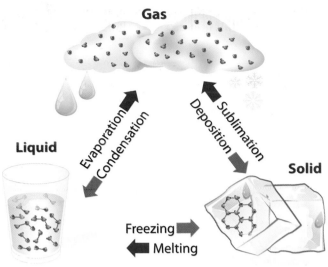

▲ *The transformation of water from one state to another*

Evaporation

Evaporation is the process by which a liquid changes into gas. In the water cycle, water from oceans, seas, rivers, and lakes evaporates due to the Sun's heat. The water rises and forms water vapour. Water vapour is also formed directly from ice and snow in places that experience extremely cold weather with bright sunshine and strong winds. This is termed **sublimation**. **Transpiration** is another process by which water is transformed into vapour. This happens when plants release water onto the leaves, and then this water evaporates into the air as vapour. Some water reaches the land directly and flows across the ground. It gets collected in the waterbodies. This water is referred to as 'surface run-off'.

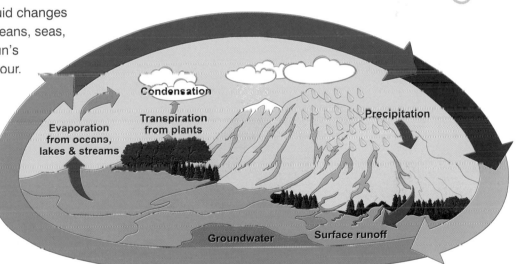

▲ *The continuous movement of water on Earth and its environment is called the water cycle*

Condensation

Condensation is the process where a gas changes into liquid. It happens when water vapour in the air condenses and forms clouds either at higher levels in the atmosphere or even at ground level. This is a vital step in the water cycle.

Precipitation

Precipitation is any liquid or solid form of water that falls on Earth's surface due to condensation. When ample water gathers in a cloud, it becomes heavy. Droplets of water form and fall to the ground. Water that falls during precipitation either becomes a part of a body of water like an ocean or lake, or it seeps into the ground. Precipitation occurs in the form of rain, snow, sleet and hail (depending on the temperature of that place).

👤 In Real Life

During the water cycle, water circulates in all its three forms—solid, liquid, and gas. The solid state of water is ice found in huge glaciers and ice capped mountains. This ice melts and flows as liquid, which is found in different water bodies on Earth. Due to the heat of the Sun, water from these water bodies evaporates into the air as water vapour, which is the gaseous state of water.

Shaping Clouds

Clouds are masses of condensed water vapour floating in the atmosphere. They are formed when warm air cools down and the water vapour condenses into droplets of water. As more and more air cools down, more droplets form and finally become a cloud.

 ## Types of Clouds

Clouds have been classified into three types—cirrus clouds that are thin and feathery, cumulus clouds that look like piled up heaps and puffs, and stratus clouds that are stretched and layered. These clouds are further categorised according to their nature by adding prefixes like 'alto' (height) and 'nimbus' (rain). Clouds are also grouped according to their height—low level clouds (below 7,000 feet), middle level clouds (from around 7,000 to 23,000 feet), high level clouds (from around 16,000 to 43,000 feet), and vertical level clouds (ranging from 1,600 to 43,000 feet).

Low Level Clouds (Stratus, Nimbostratus, Stratocumulus)

Stratus clouds resemble a thick blanket covering the sky. These clouds are grey in colour and can bring rain. Stratus clouds near the ground cause fog. They are capable of considerable precipitation in coastal and hilly areas. They form between 2,000 feet to 4,000 feet. Stratocumulus clouds are seen in puffy layers ranging between 1,000 feet to 4,000 feet and can cause a drizzle. Nimbostratus are quite thick and also bring rain.

Middle Level Clouds (Altostratus, Altocumulus)

Altostratus clouds appear uniformly in the sky and are generally found in layers with ice crystals on the top, ice and snow in the middle and water droplets at the bottom. Altocumulus clouds are middle level clouds that are small, white and puffy.

Nimbus Clouds

These types of clouds are dark and seen during a thunderstorm. Rain or snow fall from them. These bring thunder and lightning along with rainfall. Sometimes, there is a combination of two types of clouds, for example, the cumulonimbus clouds. These are puffy black clouds with rain falling from them. Another example is the stratonimbus cloud, which forms a dark blanket of cloud cover with rainfall.

In Real Life

On 26 July 2005, a sudden **cloudburst** and torrential rainfall devastated Mumbai in India. It brought the city to a standstill for a couple of days as the heavy rainfall resulted in a flood.

Cloudburst

A cloudburst is an extensive amount of sudden rainfall for a brief period of time in a particular place. Cloudbursts are accompanied by thunderstorms. During these rainstorms, the air currents that rush upwards prevent the raindrops from falling. Therefore, large amounts of water get accumulated in the atmosphere. If the currents stop flowing, the accumulated water suddenly falls on a small area with great force. This creates havoc. All these processes happen due to the rapid condensation of the clouds. Cloudbursts happen mainly in mountainous regions as the warm air currents of a thunderstorm tend to move towards the upward slope of a mountain. Cloudbursts cause heavy floods and massive destruction.

High Level Clouds (Cirrus, Cirrostratus, Cirrocumulus)

Cirrus clouds are high level clouds that are thin and feathery. These clouds are usually between 16,000 feet to 43,000 feet beyond the tropics and are considerably higher in the tropics. They appear during good weather. These clouds are thin because they are made of ice crystals instead of water. Clouds like cirrocumulus and cirrostratus are very high clouds. Cirrostratus clouds are flat and signal that it may rain in a couple of days.

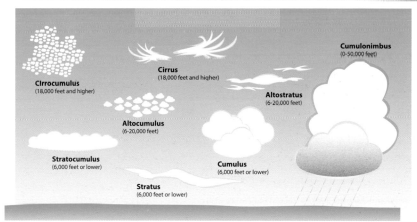

▲ The illustration shows different types of clouds at different altitudes

Vertical Clouds (Cumulus, cumulonimbus)

Cumulus clouds are bloated and scattered clouds floating in the sky. The word 'cumulus' means 'to pile up' in Latin. These clouds are formed when warm air rises with water vapour. They are puffy and are a sign of good weather. On the other hand, when these cumulus clouds grow tall, they turn into cumulonimbus clouds. These clouds stretch from the low to the high level and are responsible for thunderstorms, heavy rains, hail, and even snow.

Precipitating Weather

Precipitation is a product of condensation. It is any type of water in solid or liquid form that falls from the atmosphere on the surface of Earth. Precipitation includes rain, snow, sleet, and hail.

▶ *Types of precipitation*

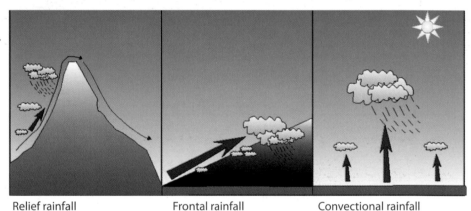

Rain	Freezing Rain	Sleet	Snow
Frozen precipitation Melts and reaches the ground as rain.	Frozen precipitation melts in warm air. Rain falls and freezes on cold surfaces.	Frozen precipitation melts in shallow warm air. Then refreezes into sleet before reaching the surface.	Snow falls through cold air and reaches the surface

 ## Rain

Rain is a type of precipitation where water drops with diameters greater than 0.5 millimetre fall to the ground. Smaller droplets of precipitation are called drizzle. Raindrops are spherical in shape. Rain occurs when warm and moist air cools down, leading to condensation and water droplets. However, there are three different ways the air cools and causes rainfall.

In relief rainfall, warm and wet air is forced to rise over high land. As the air rises, it cools. Then, condensation takes place and clouds are formed. Next, precipitation happens in the form of rain.

In frontal rainfall, the warm air comes in contact with cold air. The warm air then cools, condenses, and forms stratus clouds that get saturated, bringing rain.

In convectional rainfall, the warm air rises up, condenses, and forms cumulus clouds. These cumulus clouds get saturated and bring in heavy showers. That is why the Amazon Rainforest experience heavy rainfall in the afternoons.

In recent times, **acid rain** has become a common occurrence as pollutants such as sulphur and nitrous oxides mix with rain. These are harmful for plants and also pollute water bodies.

Relief rainfall   Frontal rainfall   Convectional rainfall

▲ *Small raindrops travel at 7.2 km/h, while large raindrops can be as fast as 32 km/h!*

 ## Snow

Snow is a kind of precipitation in the form of ice crystals. It occurs when temperatures fall below the freezing point, and water vapour condenses directly into ice. These then absorb more water vapour from the surrounding air, grow into snow crystals or pellets and fall on the ground. Snow can take many shapes, including those of thin needles, flat plates, and traditional snowflakes. Each type is a result of the combination of temperature and humidity in the atmosphere. Snow is actually present in every drop of rainfall. However, it often melts before reaching the ground due to temperature differences. A version of **virga** is produced by snow called fall streaks. These are usually seen with high, wispy cirrus clouds.

▲ *A cover of sleet and snow form on the grass*

Sleet

Sleet is nothing but melted snow that freezes into ice pellets before hitting the ground. It occurs under similar conditions as snow. Sleet is in the form of pellets of ice that form when snow falls into a warm layer and melts into rain. The rain, in turn, falls into a freezing layer of air and gets frozen again. Sometimes the snow does not melt completely and the partially melted snowflakes refreeze into snow pellets.

Freezing rain is a bit different from sleet. It occurs when snow falls into a warm layer and melts, but the freezing layer being thin, the liquid water falls onto surfaces that are below freezing point and solidifies. This is an even coating of ice visible on everything, from streets and trees, to cars and power lines.

Hail

Hail is a form of precipitation that falls on Earth in the solid form. It is made up of irregular lumps of ice. They are pellets of frozen showers of rain from cumulonimbus clouds. Ice crystals form in these clouds and start to fall to the ground, but before they can fall, the winds push them back into the clouds. The ice crystals grow in size and fall to Earth as chunks of ice. These chunks are known as hailstones. Hailstones can even cause damage to cars and glass-roofed structures.

▶ *Hailstones can measure between 5 millimetres–15 centimetres in diameter. They may be round or jagged*

Isn't It Amazing!

Each winter in the USA, at least 1 septillion ice crystals fall from the sky. That is 1,000,000,000,000,000,000, 000,000. (1 followed by 24 zeros!)

In Real Life

There is a myth that it almost rains everyday in the city of London, UK. However, in reality this is not the case. London is considered to be an overcast, damp city and rainfall stays consistent throughout the year. Although according to climate data, the city of London receives on average 583.6 millimetres of rainfall every year but it is not equally distributed among the 365 days.

Fog and Mist

Fog and mist should not be confused. Fog occurs in the form of clouds. Mist is in the form of tiny water droplets that hang in the air. Read on to learn more about these two phenomena in detail.

Fog

Fog is a cloud that touches the ground and may appear on land or sea. Fog can be thin or thick and lowers visibility, it is also denser than mist. It can be so thick that sometimes it becomes quite difficult to even see objects a kilometre away from us. When fog forms at high levels it creates a cloud called stratus.

Fog Formation

Fog is formed when water vapour transforms into tiny liquid water droplets hanging in the air. It can be visible because of the presence of the water droplets, but the formation of fog also depends on the dust particles and amount of pollution in the air. It also occurs when there is a lot of humidity in the air because there is a lot of water in the air already. When fog appears near seas, it is called sea fog. In this case, it is formed as water vapour condenses around bits of salt. Some are called flash fogs because they are formed suddenly and disappear very fast.

▲ Fog is made up of droplets of water. It contains up to 0.5 millilitre of water per cubic metre

Mist

Mist is tiny droplets of water hanging in the air like fog, but it is not as thick. Mist is usually formed when warm air comes in contact with the cold surface. However, it can also form when warm air from land suddenly encounters cooler air over the ocean. Even volcanic activity can create a mist. This happens when hot water vapour is discharged along with gases and lava by the volcano.

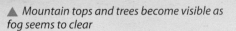

▲ Mountain tops and trees become visible as fog seems to clear

In Real Life

The Meuse Valley near Liege, Belgium was one of the leading steel industry sites with a high concentration of iron mills and smelters. In the year 1930, due to this industrialisation, a thick smog containing various pollutants, including sulphur, covered the densely populated valley for several days. This led to several deaths and thousands got infected with pulmonary diseases. This incident became one of the earliest cases that showed a connection between acute air pollution and severe health issues.

Types of Fog

There are four types of fog—radiation fog, advection fog, valley fog, and freezing fog. Radiation fog forms mainly in the evening when heat absorbed by Earth's surface during the day is radiated into the air. Water droplets are formed when this heat is transferred from the ground into the air. This type of fog is also known as ground fog.

Advection fog forms when warm, moist air passes over a cool surface. The term 'advection' is used in the field of science to name any moving liquid or fluid. When the moist, warm air in the atmosphere makes contact with the cooler surface air, water vapour condenses to create fog. This type of fog is visible in regions where warm tropical air comes in contact with the cold ocean water.

Valley fogs are formed in mountain valleys, in winter. The mountains prevent the dense air from escaping and valley fog develops. The fog gets trapped in the bowl of the valley.

Freezing fogs are formed when the liquid fog droplets freeze as they come in contact with solid surfaces. There are some mountaintops that remain covered by clouds. Fog is visible on these as freezing fog. When the fog lifts, the surroundings like the trees, ground, etc., are shrouded in frost. Antarctica experiences freezing fog due to its cold, damp climate.

▲ *The two images of a fog and mist clearly show the difference in visibility levels*

💡 Isn't It Amazing!

A rainbow is often visible when it rains. However, a rainbow can even appear during a fog. It is called a fog bow.

▶ *You will instantly notice that a fogbow is not as colourful as a rainbow*

 Fog or Mist?

Fog and mist both are formed when water vapour condenses. However, the difference between fog and mist is nominal. Fog is thicker than mist and lasts longer. It is a cloud that reaches ground level, but mist forms wherever water droplets are suspended in the air.

Another difference between them is the level of visibility. Fog reduces visibility to less than 1 kilometre, whereas mist can reduce visibility to between 1–2 kilometres.

Extreme Weather

Extreme weather is a condition of the weather system when some unexpected, unseasonal, and unusual phenomena happen. These occur suddenly and sometimes cannot be predicted. They can cause destruction to life and property. Some prominent and severe weather conditions are storms, hailstorms, avalanches, typhoons, tornadoes, hurricanes, and cyclones.

Storms

Storms are powerful disturbances in Earth's atmosphere. A storm is usually accompanied by strong winds, heavy rainfall, thunder, and lightning. The term 'storm' is generally used to describe everything from torrential downpours to snowstorms and thunderstorms. The most common type is the thunderstorm.

▲ *A lighthouse is splashed by powerful waves of water during a storm. The waves have grown over the height of the lighthouse*

Snowstorms

A snowstorm is heavy snowfall accompanied by very strong winds. Snowstorms are usually caused when moist air rises in a low-pressure area. The low pressure pushes the warm and wet air upwards over a cold air mass. If the air near the surface is not sufficiently cold, then there will be rain instead of snowfall. Sometimes, very strong winds blow leading to blizzards. A blizzard is a severe snowstorm with winds in excess of 56 kilometres per hour.

Thunderstorms

A thunderstorm is a violent disturbance in the weather for a short period. It is always associated with lightning, thunder, gusty winds, and heavy rainfall. A thunderstorm occurs when warm moist air rises to cooler areas in the atmosphere. The moisture in the **updraft** condenses, forms cumulonimbus clouds, and precipitates. Lightning during a thunderstorm is common. High above in the thunder cloud, there are bits of ice that collide with each other while moving. This collision produces electricity and that is what lightning is. Shock waves are produced when lightning heats the air through which it passes. Thunderstorms occur in many parts of the world, but are rare at the poles. They occur in the troposphere and extend up to the tropopause.

▼ *Lightning can travel through buildings, trees, and even people. It can be fatal*

Typhoons and Tornadoes

A typhoon is a tropical storm that occurs in the western North Pacific and Philippines. It occurs mostly in the north-western Pacific Basin. The word comes from the Cantonese word '*tei feng*', which means 'big wind'. In a typhoon, winds blow at over 120 kilometres per hour.

▲ *A typhoon seen from orbit*

 ## Approaching Typhoons

The approach of a typhoon is marked by a serious fall in the atmospheric pressure, rough waves and a storm surge. As a typhoon gets nearer, cumulus clouds appear in the sky and the wind **squalls** intensify. The typhoon reaches a climax with a sweeping wall of dense clouds, raging winds, and torrential rainfall.

 ## One Deadly Typhoon

The deadly Typhoon Mangkhut struck the Philippines and Hong Kong, and moved inland towards China in 2018. It was the most ravaging storm in four decades. It was said to have the strength of five hurricanes. Winds travelled at 175 kilometres per hour in the city. It set a record **storm surge** of up to 3.35 metres. The ocean climbed to its highest level in Hong Kong. Waves offshore rose to 13 metres. The typhoon brought widespread damages to Guam, the Philippines, and South China.

 ## Tornadoes

Tornadoes are dangerous storms that are violent rotations of air which actually extend from a thunderstorm. They are spinning, funnel-shaped clouds with winds that move at speeds of up to 500 kilometres per hour. A tornado can cause great damage to life and property as it touches the ground. Tornadoes are formed when there is a change in the speed of wind and its direction. This creates a horizontal spinning effect within a storm cell. This effect is then tipped vertical by rising air moving up through the thunderclouds. Green clouds signify an approaching tornado.

 ## Deadly Tornadoes

One of the deadliest tornadoes occurred in Bangladesh on 26 April 1989, which killed approximately 1,300 people. Bangladesh is prone to tornadoes and has experienced at least 190 between 1967 and 1996 causing great destruction to life and property. Tornadoes are very common in the USA. It experiences around 1,000 tornadoes a year, more than anywhere on Earth. The country is prone to tornadoes due to the Rocky Mountains and the Gulf of Mexico. These natural features create conditions for thunderstorms, which in turn lead to tornadoes.

An approaching tornado

Hurricanes and Cyclones

Hurricanes and cyclones are storms of similar nature. These storms are named according to the location where they occur. The term 'hurricane' is used in the Atlantic and Northeast Pacific. The same type of storm is called a 'cyclone' when it occurs in the tropical regions.

Hurricanes

Hurricanes are large whirling storms. They have the capacity to produce winds that can travel 119 kilometres per hour faster than a cheetah. These are formed over warm ocean waters. As a hurricane reaches the ground, it pushes a large amount of water towards the shore. Usually, this type of storm is accompanied by a heavy downpour and can cause massive floods. Often, more than one hurricane is happening at one time. Therefore, these hurricanes are given names to track them better.

Parts of a Hurricane

It is quite interesting to know that a hurricane has three parts. The first part is called the eye. This is a hole at the centre of the storm where the winds are light. There are cloudy (and sometimes clear) skies here. The eye wall is another part of the hurricane. This is a ring of thunderstorms. These storms swirl around the eye. In this part, winds are the strongest and rain is the heaviest. The rain bands are another part of the hurricane. These are the bands of clouds and rain that surround the hurricane. They stretch for hundreds of kilometres. These clouds can bring in thunderstorms and even tornadoes.

◄ *The colours denote the wind velocity. The strongest winds are indicated in red, then yellow, and green denotes the weakest wind speeds*

Cyclones

Cyclones are the same as typhoons and hurricanes. When these storms are found in the South Pacific and the Indian Ocean, they are termed tropical cyclones. A cyclone is also a spinning storm that rotates around a low-pressure centre or the eye. This area is calmer than the spinning parts of the storm.

Cyclones are formed when warm, moist air rises over oceans. While rising, it creates a low-pressure zone below itself. The air that is cooler pushes itself into the low-pressure zone, creating wind. The warm air cools down at a height and clouds are formed. Now the storm builds up and winds gets the clouds spinning. When the whirling winds gather at a speed of 120 kilometres per hour, cyclones are formed.

▶ *A cyclone making landfall*

Types of Cyclones

The three types of cyclones are the tropical cyclones, polar cyclones, and mesocyclones.

- **Tropical cyclones:** These are the most common form of cyclones as they occur over tropical ocean regions. As the name suggests, these occur in the South Pacific or Indian Ocean. Tropical cyclones are classified on the basis of the speed of winds. Winds that move at speeds of 120–150 kilometres per hour are the weakest. Winds that move at speeds of 250 kilometres per hour are devastating ones.

- **Polar cyclones:** These occur in the polar regions in places like Greenland, Siberia, and Antarctica. These cyclones are stronger during the winter season. They also occur in areas that are sparsely populated. Therefore, they do not cause too much damage or destruction.

- **Mesocyclones:** These occur when a part of a thunderstorm cloud begins to spin. The word 'meso' means 'middle', so this is the middle-point between one type of storm and the other.

▼ *A cyclone seen on the surface of the globe*

Predicting Weather

Weather forecasting is a field of meteorology in which a person tries to predict the weather. Weather forecasting is a scientific application by which one can predict the atmospheric conditions. The weather forecaster tries to describe what the weather of a place will look like for the next couple of days.

 ## History

From the pre-historic age, human beings were able to detect changes in the weather by observing nature. They were able to spot the signs that predicted forthcoming snow, rain, or wind. This helped them move from place to place in search of food and shelter. In modern times, weather forecasts are made by meteorologists after the collection of information about the atmospheric conditions of a place through **meteorology**.

 ## Meteorology and Meteorologists

Meteorology is the science of the atmosphere. It is derived from the Greek word for meteors meaning 'in the air', and '*logia*' meaning 'to discuss, study, and explain'. People who study meteorology are called meteorologists.

Meteorologists record temperature, humidity, wind speed, air pressure, and other weather patterns. They use this information to understand and predict the weather. They use mathematical models and computers to prepare their weather forecasts. Meteorologists also study the impact of the weather on the environment. They study climate and its patterns. Technology helps them understand long-term changes in the atmosphere.

Many organisations use weather forecasts for their benefit.

 ## Thermometer

A thermometer gives a reading of the current air temperature. This reading gives information about whether the weather is cold or hot. A thermometer contains a thin tube of mercury that expands with heat and determines the temperature of a place. Today, digital thermometers measure the temperature electronically.

It must be noted that the thermometer used to measure body temperature is a different instrument altogether, though both the thermometers work on the same principle.

◀ *The three major temperature scales used in thermometers are Fahrenheit, Celsius, and Kelvin*

 ## Tools Used to Predict Weather

Meteorologists use a variety of tools to predict the weather and climate. Some well-known examples are thermometers, barometers, anemometers, computer models, and weather satellites.

Barometer

A barometer is a device that is used to measure atmospheric pressure or barometric pressure. Like a thermometer, a traditional barometer indicates pressure on a linear scale or on a circular dial. However, these days, digital models also have an electronic display. A rising barometer generally indicates that the weather is clear and a falling one indicates that a storm is approaching.

Anemometer

An anemometer is an instrument that measures wind speed. It is usually made of three or four cups attached to horizontal arms. These arms are attached to a vertical rod. As the wind blows, the cups rotate, making the rod spin. This rotation helps calculate the speed of the wind. Another type of anemometer is the windmill, which counts the revolutions made by windmill-style blades. The rod of windmill anemometers rotates horizontally. Because wind speeds are not consistent, they are usually averaged over a short period of time.

▲ The barometer was invented in 1643 by an Italian mathematician Evangelista Torricelli

Computer Models

Meteorologists these days use sophisticated computer models to predict weather several days in advance. The model is a programme that predicts the intensity of air pressure and how high and low pressure zones will change over a given period of time. There are many models for meteorologists to calculate weather conditions.

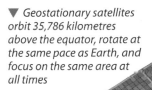

▼ Geostationary satellites orbit 35,786 kilometres above the equator, rotate at the same pace as Earth, and focus on the same area at all times

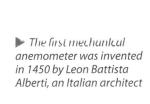

▶ The first mechanical anemometer was invented in 1450 by Leon Battista Alberti, an Italian architect

Weather Satellites

There are two types of satellites that monitor the weather conditions on Earth—geostationary satellites and polar orbiting satellites. A geostationary satellite watches the weather over a particular region and provides continuous coverage of storms. This helps the meteorologist follow the same storm for a couple of days. The polar-orbiting satellite covers the whole Earth in about 12 hours. It takes images of many different regions to assist in better weather prediction.

⊛ Incredible Individuals

Daniel Gabriel Fahrenheit is famous for his invention of the mercury thermometer in 1714 that is widely used for measuring temperature. He also invented the alcohol thermometer in 1709. The Fahrenheit temperature scale, named after him, is still in use in the USA.

Changing Climate

Global warming today is a serious issue that needs to be addressed properly. Increased levels of greenhouse gases in the environment, mostly from human activities—such as the burning of fossil fuels, deforestation, and farming—cause climate change. While the Earth's climate is also influenced and changed through natural causes such as volcanic eruptions, ocean currents, the Earth's orbital changes, and solar variations, but human-led factors are speeding up several processes to the point of no return.

 ## Natural Causes

Global warming is caused by the **greenhouse effect**. The atmosphere acts as a greenhouse and traps some of the heat of the Sun. Gases like carbon dioxide, water vapour, and methane behave as if there is a thin sheet of glass surrounding the planet. The Sun's rays pass through this layer of greenhouse gases and warm up the Earth. In turn, Earth lets off heat that radiates into space. Some of this radiation does not pass through the atmosphere but is reflected back to the Earth. The greenhouse gases in the atmosphere trap the heat and keep the planet hotter than it would otherwise be. This is called the natural greenhouse effect. Without this natural phenomenon, Earth would be much colder than it should be in order to support life.

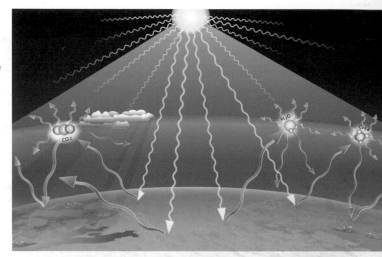

▲ *The greenhouse effect is good to a certain extent, but too much emission of these gases is harmful to life*

Volcanic eruptions are a natural factor that affect the climate. The gases, lava, and dust particles emitted during an eruption can influence the climate. The particles spewed from volcanoes can cool the planet by shading it from incoming solar radiation. This cooling effect sometimes lasts for months or even years. It can change the climate of that particular region. Volcanic eruptions are also a cause for global warming as gases like carbon dioxide, methane, sulphur dioxide, and more can contribute to the greenhouse effect. A massive eruption can emit excess amounts of these greenhouse gases into the atmosphere, causing global warming.

Human Activities

Industrialisation, burning of fossil fuels, and excessive use of vehicles has enhanced the greenhouse effect, which is a major cause of global warming. A large amount of carbon dioxide is emitted from factories, vehicles, and other human activities. Along with these, over the years, deforestation or the felling of trees has been another major cause of concern. Forests cover approximately 31 per cent of Earth's surface, and every year we cut down close to 18.7 million trees. Deforestation endangers wildlife and also increases the amounts of carbon dioxide in the atmosphere. Deforestation further contributes to greenhouse gas emissions through burning of forest biomass and decomposition of remaining plant material and soil carbon. Greater quantities of the Sun's heat are now being trapped by the atmosphere, and this is making the planet warmer. In other words, the burning of fossil fuels, which at present provides 80 per cent of energy, is adding to global warming. This problem is only getting worse, and in the process Earth's temperature is also increasing, making life difficult on this planet.

▲ *Factories emit harmful gases that contribute to the greenhouse effect*

Climate Change

Climate is the pattern of weather in a place over a period of 30 years or more. Change has been constant, and Earth has naturally gone through massive climate changes. In the past it has been very cold at times, like during the Ice Ages, and at other times extremely hot. However, these changes were uniform, making the whole planet either hotter or colder.

Today, climate change is a different issue altogether. Scientists believe that the changes taking place are because of global warming. Changes have now become erratic and unpredictable, making some places hotter, some cooler, some drier, etc. For example, deforestation in the Amazon Rainforest has considerably reduced rainfall, causing drastic climate change in the region that has also impacted the plants and animals there. Similarly, in the polar regions, glaciers are melting due to climate change, and consequently sea levels are rising, leading to frequent floods and excessive erosion.

We should make every effort to stop the climate from changing so drastically. The best way to do so is to plant trees, try to conserve energy and water, and use electricity carefully. While each individual should take necessary steps to adopt sustainable habits, as a society we should seriously consider a shift to alternative sources of energy, and move towards more sustainable living—both personally and commercially.

In Real Life

There is more carbon dioxide in the atmosphere presently than in the last 800,000 years.

Word Check

MOUNTAINS, FORESTS, & OTHER ECOSYSTEMS

Abiotic: It refers to non-living factors that affect the environment, like wind and heat.

Asthenosphere: It is the layer of Earth that lies below the lithosphere and comprises the mantle.

Biome: It is a naturally occurring community of flora and fauna occupying a habitat.

Biotic: It refers to living things.

Boreal: It is a forest in the north or northern regions of the world.

Canyons: They are deep gorges, typically with a river flowing through them, as found in North America.

Caprock: It is the layer of hard, impervious rock that seals a deposit of coal, gas or oil.

Compression: It is the action of squeezing or condensing by causing an increase in pressure.

Coniferous: Trees that have needle- or scale-like leaves, and reproduce by forming a cone to contain seeds. Coniferous trees are evergreen, but not all evergreens have cones.

Continental crust: It is the thick, older part of Earth's crust that formed landmasses.

Deciduous: A deciduous forest has trees with broad leaves and loses them in the autumn of each year.

Dune: It is a mound or ridge of sand or other loose sediment formed by the wind, especially on the sea coast or in a desert.

Ecosystem: It is a region wherein biotic and abiotic components depend on each other to support life.

Erosion: It is a gradual destruction of things. In the context of landforms, it is the gradual weathering away of rocks by the forceful movement of wind and water.

Foliage: It is a collective term, referring to all leaves of the trees in an area of the forest.

Geology: It is the scientific study of rocks and the Earth's crust.

Graben: It is an elongated block of Earth's crust which lies between two faults. The graben is pushed downwards in comparison to the horst forming a rift valley.

Horst: It is the elevated and elongated part of Earth's crust that lies between two faults.

Landform: It is a physical feature on Earth's surface that is formed by natural processes. Mountains, hills and plateaus are some examples of landforms.

Leeward: It is the drier side or the side of a mountain where the trade winds pass after they hit a mountain.

Lithosphere: It is the layer of Earth that comprises the upper mantle and crust.

Meander: It means to move slowly in no particular direction or with no clear purpose.

Muskegs: Swamps or bogs in North America

Oases: They are fertile spots in a desert, where water is found.

Orogeny: It is a process by which a section of Earth's crust is deformed or folded by horizontal/lateral compression, in order to form a mountain range.

Permafrost: It is any ground that remains completely frozen for at least two years. These permanently frozen grounds are most common in regions with high mountains, near the North and South Poles.

Pollination: To transfer pollen from one flower to another so that new seeds can be produced

Reflectivity: The reflective quality of a surface.

Sap: It is the liquid in the vascular system of a plant.

Sediment: A thick substance that settles at the bottom of any liquid.

Subduction: It refers to the downward and sideways movement of Earth's crust into the mantle, beneath another plate.

Summit: It is the peak of a mountain.

Timber: Wood that is used for buildings

Windward: It is the side of a

mountain that faces the wind.

Natural Wonders

Archipelago: It is a sea with many islands.

Atoll: A coral island with a reef that surrounds a lagoon.

Avalanches: They refer to masses of ice and rocks falling rapidly down a mountainside.

Buttes: A small, solitary hill or mountain with steep slopes, as opposed to a mesa.

Canyon: It is a deep gorge, typically with a river flowing through it.

Carbonate: It is dissolved carbon dioxide.

Cataracts: A segment of river where the water abruptly drops in a precipitous drop.

Cavern: It is a chamber in a cave.

Chasm: It is a deep fissure.

Delta: A triangle-shaped area of low, flat ground where a river splits and branches out into numerous tributaries before entering the sea

Electrons: It is a stable subatomic particle with a charge of negative electricity.

Endemic: Restricted to a particular region.

Frostbite: It is a kind of injury to the body tissues caused by exposure to extreme cold. It usually affects the nose, fingers and toes leading to gangrene.

Glaciations: The process of being covered by ice sheets or glaciers.

Gorges: It is a narrow valley between hills or mountains that have steep rocky walls and a stream running through it.

Grottoes: It is a small cave, especially an artificial cave.

Herbaceous: Related to herbs.

Ions: They are atoms or molecules that have either gained or lost one or more than one electrons.

Islets: They are small islands.

Karst: It is an area of land made of rocks such as limestone that is worn away by water to make caves.

Magnetic shield: It reduces the magnetic field in a space by blocking the field with barriers made of magnetic materials.

Molluscs: These are invertebrate animals like snails, slugs, mussels and octopuses, which have soft bodies.

Precipices: It is a steep cliff or rock face.

Ravines: It is a deep narrow gorge with steep sides.

Translucent: It refers to materials that are not entirely transparent and allow some light to pass through.

Uranium dating: A method of dating archaeological or geological specimens according to their decay activity of the uranium in a given sample.

Oceans & Waterbodies

Aquaculture: The rearing and cultivation of aquatic animals and plants for food.

Archaea: They are microorganisms which are similar to bacteria but are radically different in molecular organisation.

Bacteria: They are a member of a large group of unicellular microorganisms which have cell walls.

Brink: The extreme edge of land before a steep slope or a body or water.

Canyon: It is a deep gorge that a river flows through.

Comet: It is a celestial object consisting of a nucleus of ice and dust that travels near the Sun and develops a tail of gas and dust particles pointing away from the Sun.

Crest line: An elongated crest or a linear series of crests.

Delta: It is a triangular tract of sediment deposited at the mouth of a river, typically where it diverges into several outlets.

Density: It is the solidity of a substance.

Estuary: It is the mouth of the river where the tide and stream meet.

Inferno: It is a large fire that is dangerously out of control.

Isthmus: It is a narrow strip of land which has the sea on either side.

Lagoon: It is a strip of salt water that is separated from a sea by coral reefs or sandbanks.

Microscopic: It describes an organism or substance that is too small to see with the naked eye. It can only be viewed through a microscope.

Overfishing: It is when fishermen fish too quickly and too much from one water source, at a rate at which the fish cannot be naturally replaced.

Refrigerants: They are working fluids used in the refrigeration cycle of appliances, where they transition from liquid to gas and back.

Salinity: It is the quantity of salt that is dissolved in the water.

Sodium chloride: It is the chemical name of common salt.

Tidal bore: It is a giant wave which moves forward from the sea onto the rivers along with an unusual tide.

Tributary: It is the smaller branch of a river flowing into a sea.

Twilight: The time after the sun has set and before it gets completely dark.

Rocks & Minerals

Abrasion: It is a process by which a rock is scraped up or worn down.

Atoms: They are the smallest units of a chemical element.

Clastic: It describes rocks that are composed of broken pieces of older rocks.

Compaction: It is the exertion of force on something so that it becomes denser.

Compound: It is a thing that is composed of two or more separate elements.

Crystalline: It means to have the form of crystals.

Crystallisation: It refers to lava or molten magma cooling down and hardening into rocks with crystal structures in the process.

Extrusive: It refers to rocks that have formed on Earth's surface from the lava or volcanic matter that burst out from underneath its crust.

Inorganic: It is the matter that is not composed of animals or plants.

Insulator: A substance that does not allow the easy passage of heat, electricity, or sound.

Intrusive: It refers to the rocks that have formed beneath Earth's crust.

Lustre: It is the appearance of a mineral's surface, which depends on its reflecting qualities.

Malleable: It refers to materials that can be hammered into shape without breaking them.

Microscopic: It is used to describe something that is so tiny that it is only visible through a microscope.

Molecules: They are a group of atoms bonded together, representing the smallest fundamental unit of a chemical compound that can take part in a chemical reaction.

Obtrusion: Something that extends or protrudes outwards.

Opaque: A substance that cannot be seen through.

Ores: They are naturally occurring solid materials from which a metal or mineral can be extracted.

Phaneritic: It is a descriptive word for rocks that cool slowly and have a texture such that the grains are visible and there is significant crystal growth.

Pigments: They are the natural colouring matter of plant or animal tissue.

Salts: Another word for a mineral or a saline mixture, for example, Epsom salts.

Stalactites: A natural, thin icicle-like structure hanging from the roof of a cave made from the calcium salts deposited by dripping water.

Texture: It is the feeling, appearance and consistency of the surface of any substance.

Topography: It refers to the study of how natural structures are arranged in a certain part of land.

Vesicular: It refers to rocks that contain holes made by gas escaping from cooling lava.

Volcanoes & Earthquakes

Ash plume: It is a column of hot magma rising in the mantle, which can cause volcanic activity.

Cataclysmic: It refers to events that result in a great deal of devastation or a sudden, violent change.

Cinder: It is a piece of burnt coal that has stopped giving off flames but is still inflammable.

Crater: It is a large bowl-shaped cavity on top of a volcano that is created by a volcanic explosion.

Debris: They are the scattered pieces of rubbish created after a natural disaster. They are made up of destroyed structures.

Dormant: Volcanoes that have been dormant for a long time may erupt at some point in the future; reactivating.

Epicentre: It is the point above the hypocentre where the earthquake is the strongest.

Fault: It refers to a crack formed in the crust by the movement of tectonic plates, creating immense pressure on the crust.

Fissure: It is a split or crack in the ground that forms a long, narrow opening.

Hypocentre: It is the point where an earthquake begins inside the Earth's crust, and is also called the focus.

Intrusion: It is the process of forcing a body of igneous rock between or through existing formations, without reaching the surface.

Lava: It is the hot molten or semi-fluid flow of rocks that is pushed out of a volcano during an eruption.

Logarithm: It answers the question, how many of this number do we multiply to get another number, for example, how many 2s must we multiply to get 8? The answer is 3.

Magma: It is the hot fluid or semi-fluid material below or

within Earth's crust.

Magnitude: It is a number that explains the intensity of an earthquake.

Pyroclastic flows: It is a current of volcanic matter and hot gases that quickly gushes out from a volcano at speeds of 100–700 kmph.

Ridge: It is a long, narrow elevation on the ocean floor.

Spatter: It refers to small drops of liquid on a surface.

Stratosphere: It is the layer of gases surrounding Earth at a height of between 15–50 kilometres that is not affected by the weather, and in which the temperature increases with height.

Studs: They are upright timbers in the wall of a building to which plasterboards are nailed.

Subduction: It is a situation when one tectonic plate in Earth's crust is forced under another.

Supervolcano: A big volcano that has a magnitude of 8.

Tectonic plates: They are giant slabs of solid rocks that cover Earth's crust. They can vary greatly in size. They are constantly, but slowly, moving.

Topography: It is the physical appearance of a land's natural features, especially the shape of its surface.

Vesicular: It is a rock that has many cavities both inside and on its surface.

Vibrations: It means shaking or tremors.

Viscosity: In any substance with fluid properties, it is the property of resistance to flow.

Volcanologists: They are also called vulcanologists, and refer to those who study all volcanic activity like the processes involved in the formation and eruption of volcanoes.

Weather and Climate

Acid rain: Gases emitted from power stations, factories and cars, for example, nitrogen oxides and sulphur dioxide react with the tiny droplets of water in clouds to form sulphuric and nitric acids. The rain from these clouds is known as "acid rain" which is harmful for the environment.

Altitude: It is the height of a place in relation to the sea level

Atmosphere: It is the cover of gases surrounding a planet like Earth or Mars.

Carotenoids: They are fat-soluble pigments; mainly red, yellow, or orange. They serve two roles in plants and algae—(i) They absorb light energy for use in photosynthesis. (ii) They protect chlorophyll from photo damage.

Cloudburst: It is a sudden and violent rainfall.

Condensation: It is the water which collects as droplets on a cold surface when humid air comes into contact with it.

Continental climate: It is a type of climate that has severe winters and hot summers.

Conveyor belt: It is a

continuous moving band of rubber or metal used for transporting objects from one place to another.

Drought: It is a scarcity of water caused by a long period of little to no rainfall, which can result in famine, epidemics, loss of vegetation, soil erosion etc.

Equinox: It is the day of the year when the Sun's rays fall directly on the Equator and there is an equal amount of daylight and darkness on Earth.

Greenhouse effect: The greenhouse effect is a natural mechanism that causes the surface of the Earth to remain warm. When sunlight strikes the Earth's atmosphere, some of it is reflected back in to space, while the remainder is absorbed and re-radiated by greenhouse gases.

Humidity: It is the amount of water vapour present in the air or in any gas.

Ice crystals: Precipitation that consists of slow falling crystals of ice.

Ionisation: Ionisation is a physical process by which an atom or molecule gets converted into an ion by adding or removing charged particles such as electrons or other ions.

Jet streams: Jet streams are air currents in the atmosphere formed where large temperature differences exist. They move eastward at altitudes of about 8 to 15 kilometres.

Landfall: It is the event of a storm moving over land after being over water. More broadly, and in relation to human travel, it refers to 'the first land that is reached or seen at the end of a journey across the sea or through the air, or the fact of arriving there'.

Land breeze: It is the wind moving from a landmass to the water.

Latitude: It is the angular distance of a place, lying north or south of Earth's Equator, usually expressed in degrees (°) and minutes ('), for example, the Tropic of Cancer lies 23° 26' 21'' N.

Meteorology: It is the branch of science that studies the atmosphere; it is very useful in predicting the weather.

Mist: Mist is a phenomenon caused by small droplets of water suspended in air.

Nimbus: It is a large, grey raincloud.

Precipitation: It is a form of water that falls from the atmosphere. It can be rain, snow, sleet, ice pellets, dew, frost, and hail. These are formed by condensation from water vapour and fall under gravity.

Sea breeze: It is the wind moving from water to a landmass.

Solstice: The time or date (twice each year) at which the sun reaches its maximum or minimum declination, marked by the longest and shortest days (about 21 June and 22 December).

Stratus: It is a horizontal grey cloud that precipitates rainfall or snow.

Squalls: A sudden strong wind which has a brief duration and is often accompanied by violent rain or snow storm.

Sublimation: It is a process where a solid turns into gas without being converted into the liquid form.

Transpiration: It is the exhalation of water vapour through leaves.

Updraft: It refers to the upward movement of air.

Virga: Streaks of water drops or ice particles that fall out of a cloud and evaporate before reaching the ground.

Weather: It is the condition of the atmosphere in a place during a short period of time.

a: above, b: below/ bottom, c: centre, f: far, l: left, r: right, t: top, bg: background

Cover

Shutterstock: Front: Troutnut; Dennis W Donohue; vladsilver; Vaclav Sebek; Sergey Uryadnikov; robert_s; Sarunyu_foto; Sunti; Anan Kaewkhammul; Eric Isselee; Johan Swanepoel; Radek Borovka; Albachiaraa; **Back:** V_E; Smit; Romolo Tavani; Bonita R. Cheshier; sumire8; Tatyana Mi; lusia83; Kletr; wacomka; Sararwut Jaimassiri; Rattachon Angmanee; Incredible Arctic; vladsilver

Wikimedia Commons: Front: File:File-Black and grey wolf (female from Druid pack,"Half Black") walking in road near Lamar River bridge / By Jim_peaco/ wikimedia commons; https://commons.wikimedia.org/wiki/File:File-Black_and_grey_wolf_(female_from_Druid_pack,%22Half_Black%22)_walking_in_road_near_Lamar_River_bridge;-Jim_Peaco;-December_31,_2003_(963894d1-f1af-40c7-9b8c-241479893d2f).jpg

MOUNTAINS, FORESTS, & OTHER ECOSYSTEMS

Shutterstock: 3b/everst; 4tr/Drp8; 4 & 5 bottom/Altitude Visual; 5tr/melissamn; 5br/feygraphy; 6cl/MBL1; 6bl/Romolo Tavani; 6 & 7tc/Brian B Fox; 7tr/Olga Danylenko; 7cl/Galyna Andrushko; 7bl/Jose F. Donneys; 9b/Patrick Poendl; 9cl/Edler von Rabenstein; 9tr/Jim Sanderson, CC BY-SA 3.0 <https://creativecommons.org/licenses/by-sa/3.0>, via Wikimedia Commons; 9tr/rocharibeiro; 9b/Patrick Poendl; 10tr/Sean Pavone; 11tr/AnilD; 11b/meganopierson; 11br/Jiaye Liu; 12tr/mountainpix; 12cl/Creative Jen Designs; 12 & 13b/; 13tr/Radek Borovka; 13bl/Daniel Prudek; 13bc/Lucky-photographer; 13br/Dmitry Rukhlenko; 14cr/IKO-studio; 14bl/eastfootage; 14 & 15 b/hrui; 15tr/Calin Stan; 15br/Nick Pecker; 15br/Nahlik; 16tr/Madmuazel Bonanza; 16bl/Designua; 17tr/Petr Klabal; 17tr1/Martin Mecnarowski; 17cr/Simia Attentive; 17br/finchfocus; 18bl/Evgeny Haritonov; 18 & 19c/Checubus; 19cr/Erdal Akan; 19br/RunArt; 20background/Eakkarut Choeichin; 20cr/aapsky; 21tr/dugdax; 22 & 23c/TTphoto; 22cr/Serjio74; 23cr/Ana Gram; 23bl/Vaclav Sebek; 23br/Chase Dekker; 24t/Ronsmith; 25cl/JaySi; 25b/06photo; 25b/Susan Schmitz; 26cr/HelloRF Zcool; 26b/LutsenkoLarissa; 27br/David Steele; 29b/Troutnut; 29br/Randy Rimland; 29br/Sergey Uryadnikov; 30tl/Kletr; 30b/Andriy Solovyov; 31bl/Alexandros Michailidis; 31br/Chinnapong

Wikimedia Commons: 8bl/File:Rain shadow effect.jpg/Meg Stewart, CC BY-SA 2.0 <https://creativecommons.org/licenses/by-sa/2.0>, via Wikimedia Commons/wikimedia commons; 10bl/File:Puy de Dôme - 136.jpg/© William Crochot / Wikimedia Commons/wikimedia commons; 21br/Amur Tiger Panthera tigris altaica Cub Walking 1500px.jpg/ Photo by and (C)2007 Derek Ramsey (Ram-Man). Curves adjustment by Lycaon on 08:30, July 20, 2007., GFDL 1.2 <http://www.gnu.org/licenses/old-licenses/fdl-1.2.html>, via Wikimedia Commons/wikimedia commons; 22tr/File:Distribution Taiga.png//wikimedia commons; 24br/File:Waterfall amid Tussock Grass (5751001669).jpg/Liam Quinn from Canada, CC BY-SA 2.0 <https://creativecommons.org/licenses/by-sa/2.0>, via Wikimedia Commons/wikimedia commons; 25bl/File:Controlled burn in grassland (5474620598).jpg/U. S. Fish and Wildlife Service - Northeast Region, Public domain, via Wikimedia Commons/wikimedia commons; 27t/File:Deserts.png/Emilfaro at English Wikipedia, Public domain, via Wikimedia Commons/wikimedia commons; 28tr/File:Guatiza - Jardín de Cactus - Lanzarote - J30.jpg/Luis Miguel Bugallo Sánchez (Lmbuga), CC BY-SA 3.0 <https://creativecommons.org/licenses/by-sa/3.0>, via Wikimedia Commons/wikimedia commons; 28cl/File:Camelface.jpg/Henryhbk, Public domain, via Wikimedia Commons/wikimedia commons; 28b/File:Joshua Trees on a rare, rainy day in Joshua Tree National Park.jpg/RonFost, CC BY-SA 4.0 <https://creativecommons.org/licenses/by-sa/4.0>, via Wikimedia Commons/wikimedia commons; 29tr/800px-Map-Tundra.png/Katpatuka (talk · contribs), FAL, via Wikimedia Commons/wikimedia commons; 31tc/Sunderlal Bahuguna at New Tehri cropped.jpg/रघुवीर सिंह, CC BY-SA 4.0 <https://creativecommons.org/licenses/by-sa/4.0>, via Wikimedia Commons/wikimedia commons

Natural Wonders

Shutterstock: 3b/Lorcel; 4bl/OLOS; 4cr/Serjio74; 4 & 5 b/Amanda Mohler; 5cr/Jane Rix; 6tr/Edward Haylan; 6cl/Vojce; 6bc/Rich Carey; 6b/Vlad61; 6br/Rich Carey; 7tr/Rainer Lesniewski; 8tr/Avigator Fortuner; 8cl/Kateryna Kon; 8 & 9c/Songdech Kothmongkol; 8 & 9c/reisegraf.ch; 8br/Evan Austen; 9cl/Anan Kaewkhammul; 9bl/Steve Collender; 9tl/Ondrej Prosicky; 9br/Mark Green; 10bl/saiko3p; 11tr/Markus Kassel; 11b/Roney Lucio; 12 & 13 b/Daniel Prudek; 14bl/muratart; 15t/Pi-Lens; 15cr/Mo_Chen; 15cr/Simon's passion 4 Travel; 16 & 17c/Zarbail Zarbailov; 17tr/pokku; 18tr/Peter Hermes Furian; 18bl/Felix Lipov; 19tr/Benjamao Pooh; 10b/Matt Elliott; 20tl/Peter Hermes Furian; 20 & 21c/Smolina Marianna; 21tr/Nick Fox; 21tl/Alexander Chizhenok; 22cr/AndreAnita; 22br/trubavin; 23cr/Independent birds; 23b/Ruslan Gubaidullin; 24cl/Breck P. Kent; 25br/Evgeny Haritonov; 26tr/Peter Hermes Furian; 26b/Jess Kraft; 27cr/FOTOGRIN; 27br/Watch The World; 29tr/Pete Niesen; 29b/Globe Guide Media Inc; 30tr/Robert Biedermann; 30bl/Happy Auer; 30 & 31c/Jimmy Tran; 31tr/Eagerrr; 31c/Mike Workman

Wikimedia Commons: 5tr/John_Wesley_Powell.jpg/Painter: Edmund Clarence Messer (1842 - 1919), Public domain, via Wikimedia Commons/wikimedia commons; 13tr/Yuichiro_Miura,_August_1966,_Tasman_Glacier,_Mt._Cook/Archives New Zealand, CC BY 2.0 <https://creativecommons.org/licenses/by/2.0>, via Wikimedia Commons/wikimedia commons; 13br/Alpine Chough by Jim Higham.jpg/Jim Higham from UK, CC BY 2.0 <https://creativecommons.org/licenses/by/2.0>, via Wikimedia Commons/wikimedia commons; 16tr/File:JordanRiver en.svg/Own work, Public domain, via Wikimedia Commons/wikimedia commons; 22tr/File:সুন্দরবনের মানচিত্র.svg/Nirvik12, Public domain, via Wikimedia Commons/wikimedia commons; 24 & 25c/Cristales_cueva_de_Naica/Alexander Van Driessche, CC BY 3.0 <https://creativecommons.org/licenses/by/3.0>, via Wikimedia Commons/wikimedia commons; 25tr/File:Édouard Alfred MARTEL.jpg/LA SOCIÉTÉ DE GÉOGRAPHIE, Public domain, via Wikimedia Commons/wikimedia commons; 28tr/File:Belize Districts.png/Elelicht, CC BY-SA 3.0 <https://creativecommons.org/licenses/by-sa/3.0>, via Wikimedia Commons/wikimedia commons

Oceans & Waterbodies

Shutterstock: 3b/Lorcel; 4bl/OLOS; 4cr/Serjio74; 4 & 5 b/Amanda Mohler; 5cr/Jane Rix; 6tr/Edward Haylan; 6cl/Vojce; 6bc/Rich Carey; 6b/Vlad61; 6br/Rich Carey; 7tr/Rainer Lesniewski; 8tr/Avigator Fortuner; 8cl/Kateryna Kon; 8 & 9c/Songdech Kothmongkol; 8 & 9c/reisegraf.ch; 8br/Evan Austen; 9cl/Anan Kaewkhammul; 9bl/Steve Collender; 9tl/Ondrej Prosicky; 9br/Mark Green; 10bl/saiko3p; 11tr/Markus Kassel; 11b/Roney Lucio; 12 & 13 b/Daniel Prudek; 14bl/muratart; 15t/Pi-Lens; 15cr/Mo_Chen; 15cr/Simon's passion 4 Travel; 16 & 17c/Zarbail Zarbailov; 17tr/pokku; 18tr/Peter Hermes Furian; 18bl/Felix Lipov; 19tr/Benjamas Pech; 19b/Matt Elliott; 20tl/Peter Hermes Furian; 20 & 21c/Smolina Marianna; 21tr/Nick Fox; 21tl/Alexander Chizhenok; 22cr/AndreAnita; 22br/trubavin; 23cr/Independent birds; 23b/Ruslan Gubaidullin; 24cl/Breck P. Kent; 25br/Evgeny Haritonov; 26tr/Peter Hermes Furian; 26b/Jess Kraft; 27cr/FOTOGRIN; 27br/Watch The World; 29tr/Pete Niesen; 29b/Globe Guide Media Inc; 30tr/Robert Biedermann; 30bl/Happy Auer; 30 & 31c/Jimmy Tran; 31tr/Eagerrr; 31c/Mike Workman

Wikimedia Commons: 5tr/John_Wesley_Powell.jpg/Painter: Edmund Clarence Messer (1842 - 1919), Public domain, via Wikimedia Commons/wikimedia commons; 13tr/Yuichiro_Miura,_August_1966,_Tasman_Glacier,_Mt._Cook/Archives New Zealand, CC BY 2.0 <https://creativecommons.org/licenses/by/2.0>, via Wikimedia Commons/wikimedia commons; 13br/Alpine Chough by Jim Higham.jpg/Jim Higham from UK, CC BY 2.0 <https://creativecommons.org/licenses/by/2.0>, via Wikimedia Commons/wikimedia commons; 16tr/File:JordanRiver en.svg/Own work, Public domain, via Wikimedia Commons/wikimedia commons; 22tr/File:সুন্দরবনের মানচিত্র.svg/Nirvik12, Public domain, via Wikimedia Commons/wikimedia commons; 24 & 25c/Cristales_cueva_de_Naica/Alexander Van Driessche, CC BY 3.0 <https://creativecommons.org/licenses/by/3.0>, via Wikimedia Commons/wikimedia commons; 25tr/File:Édouard Alfred MARTEL.jpg/LA SOCIÉTÉ DE GÉOGRAPHIE, Public domain, via Wikimedia Commons/wikimedia commons; 28tr/File:Belize Districts.png/Elelicht, CC BY-SA 3.0 <https://creativecommons.org/licenses/by-sa/3.0>, via Wikimedia Commons/wikimedia commons

Rock & Minerals

Volcanoes & Earthquakes

Weather and Climate